Customer Experience Strategy

The Complete Guide
From Innovation to Execution

By Lior Arussy

Published by **4i,** *a Strativity Group Media Company*
365 West Passaic St. Suite 255
Rochelle Park, NJ 07662
Tel (201) 843-1315

ISBN 978-0-9826648-0-3

Printed in the United States of America

www.CEStrategyTheBook.com

Dedication

Dedicated to The Thousands of people who were willing to listen to me and take actions. Your Actions provided me with strength to continue.

With Gratitude

This book was born out of many trials and errors, mistakes, successes, failures and ideas. To be able to fail and to create success you need courageous people who will allow you to do so. My gratitude is to all our courageous clients who were determined to become customer centric and were willing to endure the trials and tribulations on the way to the promised land. Working with you enriched this book in countless ways. I hope that the experience and wisdom we gathered together will spread the light to the many that will follow on the customer experience journey.

To the many people who inspired me with their writing and actions. Thank you for shedding new lights and showing me new possibilities. You inspired my thinking and ability to help others. Thanks for the ideas.

The Strativity Team and especially, Rachel Yurowitz, Michael Blackmire, David Spindel, Steve Cohn, Michael Starr, Diane Binn and Robin O'Neill thank you for all your support contribution and exceptional work. Together we deliver exceptional experiences to our clients every day.

To my editors who labored over this manuscript. Thank you for hundreds of hours of trying to get into my brain and make sense of the ideas. I am definitely more understood when you are explaining it.

To my children Dalya, Cheli, Liad, Netanel and Ronya thank you for understanding when abba is not around. I was going to help others. To my loving wife of 20 years Drora my deepest gratitude for enduring my passion. I know how much you sacrificed. I am grateful for all of it. Thank you G-d.

Contents

Customer Experience Strategy:

Introduction

So, another book about customer experience. Is that what the world needs right now? I tried to answer this very question as I considered venturing on another journey of writing a book. I needed to convince myself that the journey would be worth it.

Customer experience and customer experience management (CEM) has been on the corporate agenda for several years now, and interest in the topic seems to be gaining momentum. Reams of paper are devoted to books and articles published on the topic. So why this book?

In helping organizations design and implement customer experience strategies, my colleagues at Strativity Group and I have been in the trenches many times. There, we learned how to convert blue-sky concepts into real-life results. We struggled to transform rather stubborn product-centric organizations into customer-loving companies. And we succeeded. During the process, I discovered something rather simple. All the customer experience experts are publishing literature that tells *why* you should improve your customer experience but not *how*.

I ultimately decided to venture into writing *Customer Experience Strategy* to deliver a practical roadmap with four primary characteristics:

1. **Strategic, not incremental.** Many of the approaches proposed in existing literature describe incremental efforts, such as measuring customer experience or training employees. They don't detail a total strategic approach to customer experience. This book helps you build a complete strategic framework.

2. **Prescriptive, not descriptive.** Many experts dedicate their efforts to describing the financial and statistical rationale for customer experience investment. Others enjoy telling the classic stories of

Ritz-Carlton or Disney experiences that inspired them. Yet, the market needs a blueprint for performance, not more inspiration. It's time to stop the description and provide prescription.

3. **Operational, not anecdotal.** The market is full of esoteric, anecdotal examples of how to improve customer experience. *If you only measure Net Promoter Score, all your problems will go away. Design your retail store in brand-new colors and customers will love you.* These are good ideas, but they aren't operational guidelines. It's time to turn customer experience into operational performance.

4. **Organization-wide, not isolated.** Many of the published success stories describe projects conducted in isolation. Website redesigns and call center improvements are important. But each is but a single touch point. A well-designed website can't compensate for other touch points that disappoint the customer. It's time to stop settling for single touch point work and time to measure and manage the complete journey. It's time to think total organization.

The compelling case for customer experience has been made eloquently by many experts and research projects. Our studies support similar findings. A differentiated, emotionally-engaging customer experience will deliver more profitable business in the form of lower complaints, higher satisfaction, lower cost of sales, and greater referral rates. Critical goals, but how do you achieve them? The existing customer experience literature doesn't answer the pragmatic questions:

- Where do you get started?
- How do you build the business case?
- How do you innovate and design experiences?
- How do you obtain senior leadership commitment?
- How do you build organization-wide collaboration and break the silos?
- How do you engage employees?
- How do you measure the initiative's success?
- How do you build a program that will last?

We at Strativity struggled with these very questions as we designed customer experience programs for our clients. After years of working in the trenches, answering those questions and many others, we developed a complete strategic framework to achieve customer experience success. We began teaching this framework in our public CEM Certification course, attended by practitioners from all over the world. Following this success, we decided to bring this true and tested strategic framework to you in this book.

In writing *Customer Experience Strategy*, I worked to combine a complete strategic and executional blueprint with an easily accessed reference book. My goal is to allow you to find practical guidance and new ideas to enhance your customer experience journey, no matter your entry point into the strategy. Are you struggling with leadership's sponsorship? There's is a chapter for that. Missing the business case? There's a chapter for that. Looking for guidance on how to innovate? There's a chapter for that. Just getting started in exploring this customer-centric endeavor? There's an entire blueprint, from start to launch and beyond, for that very purpose. No matter your current stage in the customer experience journey, this book is designed to help you achieve the next level.

It's time to stop focusing on others' customer experience stories and create your own success story. It's time to stop staring at such legends as Starbucks, Nordstrom, Virgin, Southwest Airlines, Whole Foods and Four Seasons and start creating your own legendary customer experience. It's time to execute.

It will be my privilege, through the journey that is this book, to be part of your travels, and watch you create your own legend.

—*Lior Arussy*

CHAPTER 1

Customer Experience –
The Myths, the Facts and the Profits

Lavishing customers with delightful, memorable experiences seems like such a nice, cheery thing to do. And indeed it is. Who doesn't want an environment with more cheerful smiles? But customer experience, despite the misconceptions and prejudices of many behind closed marketing doors and in aerie executive suites, is hardly the business of just being nice. It is the business of being in business. Customer Experience Management (CEM) is a business strategy leveraging customer-centric innovation and problem-solving that absolutely provokes smiles, certainly, but the biggest smiles come when companies examine bottom-line profits.

Simply said: *Customer experience is profitable.*

To illustrate that point, consider this fact proven again and again by our consulting clients: You can meet and beat your financial targets even in tumultuous financial times with existing customers. Without adding a single new customer, you can reach bottom-line goals by capturing the absolute value of consumers already within your system.

Retention is one factor. For example, utilizing an economics-of-relationship model, we were able to demonstrate to a credit card company that it was leaving a maximum of $3 million a day on the table from customers choosing competitors' cards. Greater customer value is another factor. Delivery of an excellent customer experience allows companies to avoid such tactics as discounting to remain competitive. Delivering strong customer experiences allows you to charge more—premium prices for premium services. Then, consider what happens to your financial targets when word of a brand's unique, delightful excellence reaches potential new customers.

The benefits you can expect from customer experience initiatives are many and varied. Each business must find its own motivation and justification based on its business model and the type of relationship it has with customers. With that fact in mind, here is a general list of the advantages that a customer experience program can bring to you.

- Increase in customer wallet share
- Decrease in customer attrition rate
- Increase in annual customer value—cross-sells and up-sells
- Increase in lifetime customer value
- Increase in customer referrals
- Decrease in customer complaints
- Increase in customer ideas and insight
- Increase in customer and prospect purchase consideration
- Decrease cost of customer acquisitions
- Increase in overall customer base
- Improvement of corporate brand and image
- Increase in the number of customer "thank-you" letters

Our Strativity Group 2009 *Customer Experience Consumer Study* of 1,994 consumers in the U.S. and Canada shows that customers continue to reward exceptional customer experience—even in tough economic times. Premium price, longer relationships and willingness to purchase more are among the ways customers reciprocate for exceptional experience—which, in fact, they increasingly demand. This demand comes with the promise of more-profitable business. Responding to this demand, however, is not optional. Customers participating in the study indicated that they penalize companies that fail to deliver the desired experiences, either by demanding discounted prices, or by terminating their relationship altogether.

To determine the impact of delivering exceptional customer experiences, we asked consumers to rate the company with which they most recently conducted business using Fred Reichheld's Net Promoter Score (NPS) system of rating the likelihood that they would recommend a company to a friend or colleague. The question was used both because of its popularity and because it distinguishes between loyal customers (promoters), indifferent customers (neutrals) and disloyal customers (detractors). When Strativity Group then asked the consumers about their purchasing behavior, the results were rather surprising, especially considering the tough economic times.

- **Share of wallet.** More than 70% of consumers surveyed indicated a willingness to increase their spending by 10% or more with businesses that exceed their expectations.

- **Premium pricing.** 40% of loyal customers said that they are willing to pay a premium of 10% or more to continue purchasing from companies delivering great experiences, in contrast with 9% of dissatisfied customers. And 52% of dissatisfied customers expect discounts of 5% or more to continue doing business with a company while no loyal customers expect discounts.

- **Customer retention.** Loyal customers are almost three times as likely than dissatisfied customers to expect to continue doing business with companies for another ten years or more. Dissatisfied customers are ten times more likely than their loyal counterparts to expect to attrite in the next year.

Customers are probably more attuned to their customer experience today than ever before. They know it's tough for companies out there (it's tough on them, as well). Understanding that, they pay close attention to their relationships with vendors. They examine which vendors play for long-term zrelationships and which vendors rush to the quick cost reduction. The behavior and treatment they encounter at any time, tough economy or not, will most likely leave a long-term signature on your relationship with your customers. They won't quickly forget how you behaved at the moment of truth.

The credit card example I gave above validates customers' claims that they're willing to spend more for a better customer experience. We can see further validation in the results of our *2009 Customer Experience Management (CEM) Benchmark Study*; each year, Strativity benchmarks the state of customer experience by interviewing 869 executives around the world. The study indicates that, in contrast with their counterparts that invest less than 2% of their revenues in customer experience, companies that invest 10% or more of their revenue in that area:

- Have significantly lower customer attrition rates.

- Enjoy referral rates that are twice as high.

- Are twice as likely to have customer satisfaction scores of 81% or more.

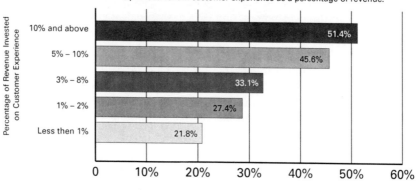

Percentage of companies with a referral rate of 10% or more broken down by investment in customer experience as a percentage of revenue.

Percentage of Companies with Referral Rates of 10% or More

Similarly, companies that have increased their investment in customer experience over the past three years report higher satisfaction and lower attrition rates than those that have decreased their investments during the same period. Specifically, companies that have increased investment:

- Report satisfaction scores that are 60% higher.
- Are 30% more likely to have attrition rates of 5% or less.

In short, these companies enjoy the benefit of running a more-profitable business. They reduce their cost of service by enjoying higher satisfaction rates and fewer complaints. They enjoy a greater percentage of repeat business, which lowers sales costs. They also benefit from the lower cost of new sales, as a greater portion of their business comes from referrals.

Most important of all, CEM is one of your most powerful tools in battling commoditization of products and services. In today's environment, with fierce competition, infinitely faster communication, and rising customer expectations, customer experience provides critical differentiation.

Customer Experience Strategy is a roadmap to beating commoditization, modernizing your customer relationships, and achieving greater profitability. But before we begin the journey, let's learn more about what customer experience *is* (a profitable business practice) by establishing what it is *not* (bigger smiles and nothing more).

Customer Experience: The Myths

At the outset of one of our client engagements, the CEO who had just hired Strativity Group took me into his office. "Lior," he said proudly as he picked up a massive binder from his desk and plopped it down before me, "we've already done most of the work for you. We've done a bunch of research, evaluated the possible customer experience strategies, and constructed a launch plan. Look it over and let me know if there's anything we missed."

As I paged through the tome's pie charts and formulas and lengthy bullet points, I politely noted aloud that customer experience management strategies must begin at the ground level, far before the stage that would produce such a document. The design, I explained, must incorporate initial goal-setting, customer research, evaluation of corporate infrastructures, audits of current customer experience practices, and much more. Eventually, I convinced this CEO that his team's customer experience work was based on several of the many myths surrounding customer experience and its management, and how it's developed.

The myths I saw in that document included some of the classics.
Here are just a few:

- *Employee roles and freedom to make decisions were largely unchanged.* You cannot accomplish customer experience without deep employee involvement.

- *Organizational structures and departmental roles and communications were also largely unchanged.* You cannot accomplish customer experience without undertaking significant change and without governing it with powerful change management.

- *Design and execution of the customer experience strategy was focused in a center-of-organizational tier.* You cannot accomplish customer experience without upper management championing the program.

- *The strategy was applied only to customers.* You cannot accomplish customer experience without creating experiences for other stakeholders, including your employees and your B2B suppliers. Customer experience is everywhere.

- *The plan sought only to create a unique experience within the company's industry.* You cannot accomplish customer experience without taking into account the whole of customers' exposure to excellence, including companies outside your industry.

- *The goal of the new strategy was to consistently meet expectations.* You cannot accomplish customer experience unless you consistently *beat* expectations. You must surprise, and you must delight.

- *The plan involved T-shirts.* And slogans. And posters and mugs, all touting the new attitude that the customer is number one. You cannot accomplish customer experience with doodads and attitude alone— you must operationalize this new and critically important strategy. I've never seen a company that has achieved significant transformation with T-shirts and posters alone. Granted, every company I work with utilizes such promotional touches, yet customer experience practitioners must remember that these are but small tools used in the overall endeavor.

As you can see from some of the evidence above, marketing can do wonders creating exciting brand perception in the outside world. The key question is whether you can turn the perception inside and make your entire organization operate by the rules that the branding has established.

Customer experience strategy, therefore, must be deeply engrained and effectively executed throughout the entire company. It's not a superficial show, an attitudinal goal, a poster slogan. Customer experience is not just a matter of being nice, nor is it altruism. It's not just cleaning up the customer-relationship house and making improvements. And most certainly it's not just a good idea that will generate some vague karmic pay-off somewhere down the line. Customer experience is a business practice definable in financial terms that stakeholders from the CEO, and the CFO on down will understand. Customer experience is a strategy to maximize revenues and value, and you must be very disciplined in your approach to this strategy. Such discipline leads to specific financial payoff. As I once termed it for a curious and very successful CEO, customer experience is "greed through love."

In the case of our CEO, and his earnestly developed plan, we were dealing with a highly successful company, one that had been growing 3% each year, despite being in a very mature market. But after we dispensed with the myths and misconceptions his customer experience team labored under and instituted a disciplined companywide approach to customer experience management, the company experienced 40% growth the next year.

The Inherent Conflict Syndrome

Achieving such results entailed considerable work, and considerable reconsideration of how to increase customer value to the company. On the day that the CEO handed me his strategy tome, I walked him through our procedures, which, in part, includes a two-pronged approach: 1) Putting our staff out in the field, posing as customers and evaluating the side of the customer experience that cloistered marketers rarely see. 2) Sitting with the employees during their day-to-day work, experiencing and evaluating the procedures and the atmosphere that those who create customer experience deal with each day. In fact, I personally conducted a "side-by-side" exercise where I listened to incoming calls at the client's 500-seat call center. I was paired with Amy, and I began listening in, taking notes, and generally observing. About an hour into the exercise, Amy turned off her phone, removed her headset, wrote something on a sheet of paper, and left the room. She took more notes when she returned. About an hour later, she jotted more notes and left the room. I noticed that other associates were doing the same. When she returned, I asked her what she was doing.

"That's my washroom time." She explained that she and all the other associates were required to note times related to bathroom absences—clocking into the washroom, you might say. Later, the department head told me that, armed with such information, he could produce reports based on any criteria I wanted to help bring greater efficiency to the call center—time of year, day of week, individual (a chart he showed me indicated that Samantha averaged 22 minutes a day and Henry, the slacker, averaged 45). Apparently if you took more time than what was benchmarked, you had some explaining to do—like what you had for dinner the night before. When the CEO asked me how to more efficiently gather this information, he didn't immediately spark to my suggestion involving infrared sensors on both the associates' chairs and the toilet seats in tandem with timers and RFID chips imbedded under the associates' fingernails. Five minutes later—finally—he asked if I was kidding.

This anecdote represents the heart of the problem that companies face when working to institute customer experience management—that what's good for the company is good for the customer. Such an attitude builds disconnects—in this case, between an efficiency model and the customer experience model—that simply cause trouble and that must be eliminated.

- Such disconnects relate closely to what we call "The Inherent Conflict Syndrome," in which two conflicting gravitational forces are at work: an organization's quest to reduce costs, and the quest to increase customer satisfaction.

- When you slash costs, streamline services, inflate margins, who pays for the reductions? The customer, of course. Companies often assume that they can reduce value yet maintain prices—and it's a dangerous assumption, indeed. Most companies that cut costs fail to measure the direct impact of such reductions on customer spending.

- These companies operate only within their own ecosystem, without ever visiting that other world, the customer's ecosystem—or without ever acknowledging that such an ecosystem exists in the first place. Picture a customer who's contacting the call center that employs

Amy. When that customer woke up that morning, she was concerned about her health, her happiness—dreams, status, family, peace of mind, religion, fears, aspirations, security . . . and not a single concern in her ecosystem exists in a company's ecosystem. A company's ecosystem is crowded with manufacturing, supply chains, purchasing, advertising, taxes, outsourcing, currency fluctuations, real estate, hiring, and dozens of other details that your customer could not care less about—in particular, how much time Amy spends in the washroom.

- Not only do these two ecosystems not overlap, but also they don't in any way connect in the first place. Inhabitants of one ecosystem pop over to the other for a short visit and quickly return home. And companies believe they can alter their ecosystem without affecting the customers' ecosystem, even though the relationship of these two worlds is something of a mathematical equation—change one side of the "equals" sign, and the other side must change, too. To think otherwise is to invoke Inherent Conflict.

- Think of the Inherent Conflict Syndrome in terms of customers being from Venus, while companies are from Mars, recalling the classic book about male-female relationships. The Martians are spinning about in their own ecosystem, staring at their numbers and pressing for quick deals with the Venusians to land their quarterly bonuses. The Venusians are backing off, wondering where the relationships and the "Customers Are Number-One" proclamations in the advertisements have gone. The Venusians understand that relationships take time, and, besides, they have their own eco concerns to deal with. One of those concerns is getting greater value from their purchases, and over on the other side, the Martians aren't listening to that concern.

- This separation of company and customer ecosystems is aggravated by companies that extend myopic product-centricity to inwardly-focused organization-centricity. Organization-centric companies focus on the divisions within themselves—the silos and touch points isolated from each other even while they share a common outreach to the customer. Such companies are prone to carving up each customer, as it were, and territorially assigning various portions of customer service to the silos on the org chart. We call this poor parceled consumer "The Organization-Centric Customer."

- I liken this practice to taking a pair of scissors to a customer portrait and cutting it into separate squares. When the customer calls in with a problem, the rep answering the phone at the organization-centric company says, "That, sir, is a right-nostril question. You've reached the left-nostril department, where we're committed to excellence in the service of left nostrils. You'll have to take your right nostril down the hall. I'll give you the phone number that you can call after I hang up." In such fragmented organization-centric companies, customer shipping needs are isolated from customer service needs, the marketing approach to the customer never touches the R&D approach, and finance finds itself invoicing customers who never received their product in the first place. And so on.

- The customer-centric organization revolves around a single full, connected customer view—and does so even if components of the organization are outsourced. Turning certain functions over to third parties doesn't require nor does it justify withholding a full view of the customer with the outsourced vendor. If customer care associates can't see, for instance, accounting's view of the customer, they can't solve the problem.

Organization-centricity leads to another debilitating misconception—that customer experience is a corporate add-on, an addition to the to-do list, something that one of those other departments can worry about. Yes, customer experience impacts every corporate agenda, but it is in fact integral to those agendas—not an adjunct and not a subsidiary. When you propose the customer experience strategy, it is imperative that you present it as an integral part of the overall corporate agenda. Make absolutely clear that customer experience supports the existing objectives each function/ touch point is trying to achieve. Customer experience does not displace or alter those objectives, nor does it bury them with just one more thing to do. When individuals, departments, executives or even the entire organization perceives such initiatives as just another responsibility thrown on top of what they're already chartered to do, resentment and lack of cooperation result. Only when viewed as complementing and accelerating existing agendas in the organization will customer experience receive a fair chance of success.

One Company, One Experience

As examples, let's examine the objectives of different functions and how the customer experience strategy would support them—and not run counter to them:

- **Marketing.** *Goal:* Increasing brand relevance. *Customer experience support:* Creating experiences that fulfill the brand promise and increase the overall brand strength. Customer experience also allows marketing to achieve another prized objective: making the brand authentic through the performance of the employees.

- **Lead generation.** *Goal:* Identifying and qualifying prospects and ushering them into the pipeline. *Customer experience support:* Providing guidance and mechanisms for engaging prospects in ways that add targeted value and solutions more naturally. By doing so, lead generation becomes less costly while generating more genuine interest.

- **Service.** *Goal:* Reducing costs and increasing efficiency and satisfaction when customers call with problems, questions or comments. *Customer experience support:* Providing the means for relevant, first-time resolution that cuts time to resolution, reduces the number of people handling each customer engagement, and improves employee morale.

- **Compliance and legal.** *Goal:* Obtaining customer and organization compliance. *Customer experience support:* Designing a legal experience that will not intimidate customers but rather make them want to cooperate, making compliance far easier to achieve.

- **Collection and finance.** *Goal:* Receiving timely payment. *Customer experience support:* Treating customers—even the late-payers—with compassion and dignity so that they are more apt to choose to pay and pay quickly the company that demonstrates a human side. Customer experience can speed payment, and help increase collection and overall cooperation.

- **Human resources.** *Goal:* Obtaining the best people and retaining them in the organization. *Customer experience support:* Creating an environment of pride. Employees are proud to work for companies that treat customers with exceptional experiences. They share their pride with their friends and create a buzz. Research shows that those companies that place customer experience at the core of their business enjoy significantly higher level of employee loyalty and longevity of employment.

- **Innovation and R&D.** *Goal:* The tough job of coming up with the next big thing. *Customer experience support:* Leveraging the perspective, energy and input of loyal customers. If you count only on your ideas, you will leverage a limited opportunity pool. Customer experience engages customers so that they're willing to share ideas, dreams, hopes and aspirations. By courting and utilizing your customers' experiences and insights, you're more likely to develop relevant innovation that customers will pay for.

The assumption that customer experience joins a long list of competing corporate agendas such as leadership, innovation, employee engagement, achieving strategic targets, and so on is false. All these initiatives are ultimately in place to support a simple goal—create and retain customers. That simple goal not only aligns with customer experience, it comprises the whole of customer experience. Creating and retaining profitable and engaged customers is achieved by delivering differentiated customer experiences. Innovation, leadership, employee engagement—these are all tools to support the one simple goal. Therefore, customer experience doesn't compete with the other initiatives. Instead, it is in and of itself the overarching objective all initiatives are serving.

Finally, the broadening series of gaps between customer and organization is further widened when product-centric and organization-centric company executives think, "Things have turned out quite nicely so far—why should we change?"—representing an inertia that takes numerous and often even more constricting forms. For instance, many of your colleagues are likely thinking, "Our organization is a mature company in a mature market. We have no opportunity for innovation or for this customer experience notion." I personally don't believe in mature markets or tired industries. I believe in tired executives. I believe in people and organizations too tired to innovate and take customer service to levels of everyday excellence.

The classic example of the myth of maturity is Starbucks. How mature is the coffee shop industry? Such shops have been around since about ten minutes after the discovery of coffee. Yet, Starbucks invigorated the industry with innovation, customer experience and excellence—and very little marketing. They built a chain of 10,000 retail stores selling a commodity before issuing a single advertisement. Starbucks invented nothing—not coffee, not cappuccino, not latte. With smart execution of customer experience, Starbucks lives among the Venusians, operating within the customer ecosystem, and not a self-contained coffee-retail ecosystem.

Ten thousand locations without a single advertisement—such is the power of experience.

Reality Check: The Executive View

To more fully see the seriousness of such myths, misconceptions and disconnects in the everyday business world, let's turn to the viewpoint expressed by executives themselves in our *Customer Experience Management Benchmark Study*. The study shows that over 80% of respondents say that customer experience is more important it was three years ago. Everyone now is in a race to love the customer more, and create more compelling experiences. But do their actions match their declared interests? Are they saying, "Yes, more important" in between selecting T-shirts for the next company meeting, or are they preparing for foundational transformation?

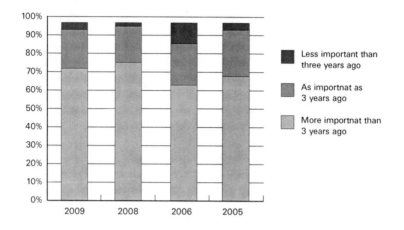

Customer experience management is soaring high on the priority list because experience allows organizations to fight the number-one enemy of ROI—discounting, which flourishes in tough economic times as executives default to the easy economic excuses to slash costs and reduce value to customers to the bare minimum. Because they're standing on a shaky economic stage, executives intoning "Customer care is about price and only price" sounds pretty convincing. As the enemy of ROI flourishes, customer experience leading to premium pricing becomes increasingly important.

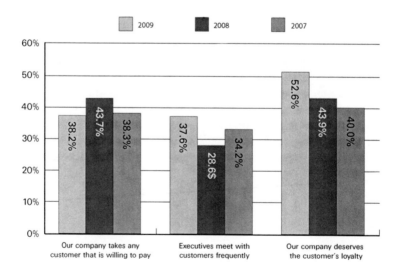

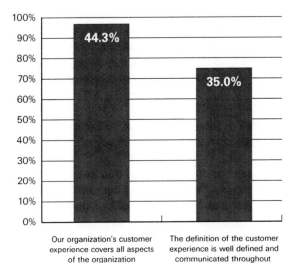

When we look at execution of customer experience, however, we see the vastness of the say-do gap so typical of surveys. For example, only 35% say that they have defined who their customers are or who they want their customers to be, and have communicated that definition throughout the organization. That means that 65% have no idea who their ideal customers are, no idea what customers expect and need, and no idea of what they expect of customers. And only 44.3% say that their organization's customer experience covers all aspects of the organization.

Only 37.6% of executives say they meet with their customers frequently. More than 62% say they don't engage with customers? How can you know about your customer if you're not talking with them? What are these executives doing instead? The cynical side of me wants to say that they're golfing because that's what they do best. And if they don't understand the power of meeting the customers, that may indeed be true.

And when we asked executives if they believe that their companies deserve their customers' loyalty, a shockingly high 47.4% said "No." Almost half were admitting that when they review the total value proposition their company offers, they don't deserve customer loyalty. This represents a crisis. If your executives don't believe customers deserve loyalty, then how can the rest of the organization act in ways that generate greater loyalty? This is more than an admission of failure—it is a self-fulfilling prophesy. By the way, *Business Week* once asked us how we got executives to tell us this information. We told them we're from New Jersey and we sent Tony, our VP of Customer Truth."

A significant number of executives said that their company takes any customer that's willing to pay—38.2%. This figure is down from the 43.7% who said this the previous year, and, though the decrease is heartening, the number is still troublingly high. Organizations that take any customer who is willing to pay end up neglecting their best customers and spending too much time with customers who don't deserve attention, time and resources.

Now, let's take a look at the survey results below, where I suspect you'll find some resonances with your own situation.

While 52.3% of executives surveyed state that investments in customer experience have remained flat or declined over the past three years, 47.7% report that their companies have increased investments in customer experience over the past three years by 10% or more. In fact, 16.5% reported increasing investments by 20% or more during this time period. These actions indicate a clear commitment among leading companies to retain customer loyalty and not to succumb to a traditional price strategy.

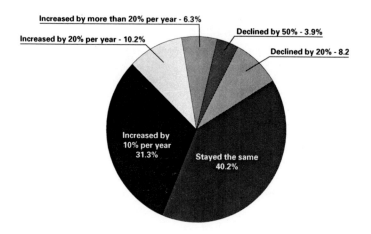

The companies that increased investment represent a new and critically important trend. Instead of succumbing to the traditional boom-and-bust cycle in customer relationships, they elected to go for a long-term customer relationship. Traditionally, during good times, companies increase their investments in customer strategies and indicate interest in building sustainable delightful customer experiences. However, as soon as the road gets rough—market share slips, competition gets aggressive, economic factors bode ill—the customer sees a different approach. Services and quality are cut to the bone and customers are left feeling deceived and betrayed when vendors turn their backs to them. When conditions improve, companies again court their customers with increased investments to regain the customers' love and wallet. Because this boom/bust cycle has characterized customer relationships for many years, customers have developed immunity to this cycle and become cynical when companies court them anew. As a result, investments in customer relationship and loyalty programs become increasingly expensive as customers demand more proof of a company's sincerity and true interest.

The study results demonstrate that select companies indentified the cost and revenue losses associated with this boom-and-bust customer relationship cycle and have decided to change the rules. Not only do they maintain their ongoing investment, but they have actually increased it. This select group of smart companies has realized that the best opportunity for them to shine and demonstrate their sincere interest in customers is when everyone else is decreasing their attention to and investment in customers. By increasing their investment in customer strategies, these companies pass a very important customer-relationship test. They demonstrate that, even in tough times, they're here to stay, creating a clear awareness of their commitment to customers at a time when their competitors remain silent.

The Journey Ahead

Another significant myth reflected in that large study the CEO plopped in front of me is that creating customer experience is a one-off. You flip the switch and customer experience illuminates all, and then you go off and do something else for a while. In reality, customer experience is a journey whose destination is the horizon that you never reach. Thus, the purpose of this book is to dispense with the misconceptions about the posters and the bigger smiles and the greeters at the front door and give you the vehicle and the fuel to embark on that journey and travel it successfully.

Let's begin with an overview of that journey, an aerial reconnaissance of the road ahead that we'll travel cobblestone by cobblestone in the pages that follow.

Customer Experience Management: The Overall View

We create experience by first removing such customer dissatisfiers as quality and procedural issues, and then move beyond the parity established by dissatisfaction removal to create differentiation. A differentiated brand is directly linked to a competitively differentiated and, therefore, profitable customer experience.

We then design the customer experience in four key areas: promise, delivery, communication and growth. The design will consider and affect all touch points within the company. As you would expect, some touch points are more important to customers than others, but I submit that you'll be surprised to discover that some touch points are critically important in the context of customer experience management. For instance, do you consider an invoice a customer experience in and of itself? After all, there's not much smiling involved when invoices are delivered. Yet, you'll see that such elements of consumer engagement are very important indeed.

Once the designed strategy has been launched—with a great deal of structured change management providing the foundation for those T-shirts and mugs—a system of customer experience governance must monitor and reinvigorate the strategy as we follow through on our endeavor over time.

Finally, throughout the process, we will examine ways to assure that the customer experience strategy is supported, enabled and executed through the entire organization. This involves such considerations as hiring the right people, compensating them appropriately, training for experience, and providing insights into the critical role each employee—from the top floor to the basement of your organization—plays in overall customer experience.

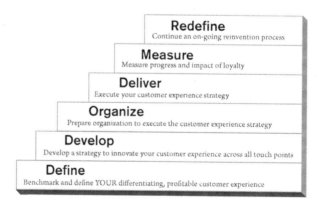

Redefine
Continue an on-going reinvention process

Measure
Measure progress and impact of loyalty

Deliver
Execute your customer experience strategy

Organize
Prepare organization to execute the customer experience strategy

Develop
Develop a strategy to innovate your customer experience across all touch points

Define
Benchmark and define YOUR differentiating, profitable customer experience

As you embark on the customer-experience journey, you will follow these milestones:

Define: Benchmark and define *your* differentiating, profitable customer experience. Taking the first step, you must ask the hardest question of them all: Do you have a customer experience that will draw customers to you naturally? The key word in that question is *naturally*—not because of persuasive salespeople, not because of discounts, not because of snappy advertising—but *naturally.* You want the customers to love you, to buy more from you, to be, all said, more loyal to you. But are you really that great? Is what you sell so appealing that customers would be willing to pay more to transact with you? The questions isn't, "How do you make your customer service people nicer folks?" It's, "What are the customer's total problems that you can solve with excellence and—yes—*greatness* that they'll pay premium prices for?" Brand development must be considered in the context of an organization's value to its customers. If you aren't that great, the cost of sales keeps rising.

Here, too, we will examine the economics of customer experience management in detail, including a method for analyzing how much revenue you stand to lose if you *don't* institute customer experience. We call this the "Return on Nothing" analysis. Together, we'll establish the burning platform— why you must engage in this strategy and why you must do it now. *"Define" is discussed in detail beginning on page 63, in Chapter 4, "Innovation of Customer Experience."*

Develop: Cultivate a strategy to innovate your customer experience across all touch points. What details will your customer experience feature? Knowing this allows you to live by your experience, not just promise it. The strategy must exist as a method of operational behavior, and not just as a slogan. *"Develop" is discussed in detail beginning on page 83 in relation to overall innovation in Chapter 4 and as a continuing strategy in the chapters that follow (in particular, Chapter 13, "Leadership and Change Management").*

Organize: Prepare your organization to execute the customer experience strategy. Do you have the organization—inhouse or outsourced—that can deliver on what the strategy promises? This involves preparing and executing a performance platform that allows employees to perform at their best. Key to this discussion will be, "What's holding your employees back from delivering excellence?" *"Organize" is discussed in detail beginning on page 145 in Chapter 8, "Employee Experience," through Chapter 10, "Performance Platform: The Tools to Deliver."*

Deliver: Execute your customer experience strategy. How do you perform at the moment of truth? Do you succeed? If you fail, why? And what will you do differently? Complaint resolution will be a big component of this discussion. *"Deliver" is discussed in detail beginning on page 219 in Chapter 11, "Deliver the Experience."*

Measure: Measure the progress and the impact of the customer experience strategy on loyalty. What are the right metrics not only for your organization as a whole, but also for departments and individuals? How do you determine which metrics to pay attention to? You'll examine which metrics to ignore, and which to highlight, both internally and externally. *"Measure" is discussed in detail beginning on page 247 in chapter 12, "Measure What Matters."*

Redefine: Continue an on-going reinvention process. How do you put continuing experience governance in place and make it effective? Changes in technology and in taste dictate a constantly evolving set of experiences to delight customers. *"Redefine" is discussed in detail beginning on page 295 in chapter 14, "Reinvent the Experience: A Governance Model."*

Customer Experience: Profit and Opportunity

Is the investment in customer experience worth it? Will it deliver a long-term benefit and payoff? Let me frame my answer—which you've already surmised, certainly—by way of another example: A credit card company once correlated customer willingness to recommend with customer spend. Their analysis calculated a differential of $200 million in spend—that's *per month*—between those who were fully and emotionally engaged and those who weren't. Multiply that by 12 months: 2.4 billion dollars worth of customer satisfaction—in rough economic times.

Companies come to us seeking guidance with customer experience motivated by numerous differing issues—market share, wallet share, customer satisfaction, customer attrition, and so on. But the need for customer experience is ultimately driven by one factor: Commoditization. This is the overarching business problem that the differentiation of customer experience can resolve. Companies are increasingly finding themselves at the heart of commoditization, and at that heart, also find themselves at a juncture. When customers perceive that they're purchasing commodities, price is the only differentiator that matters to them. Commoditized companies must compete on price, which erodes margins and sends profitability spiraling downward.

When customers begin demanding discounts, they're telling you that they don't see the connection between your product or service and the price you charge. They don't understand your value.

You have four choices when trying to escape the heart of commoditization:
- Add pre-sales value.
- Innovate products or services.
- Add post-sales value.
- Default to the last resort.

The fourth choice—the last and least desirable choice, and therefore the last resort—is to provide discounts. When you discount, you might think you're pleasing your customers, but ultimately you're in danger of upsetting them. This week, they see, you're charging $40 for a product. Last week it was $50. Last week you were, in their eyes, ripping them off for $10. Such moves actually destroy customer trust.

Another critical driver of customer experience is profitable growth. No investment that doesn't return growth is worth considering. Investment without solid return does little more than increase the cost of sales. You must demonstrate to yourself and to your executives that customer experience will maximize revenues and allow the company to meet and beat its numbers. You'll find that executives tend to perceive sales alone as the means to meet numbers, so if you hope to move some budget dollars from sales and into service departments, you must demonstrate ROI impact. If you can't demonstrate that to yourself, then don't even pursue customer experience initiatives further. However, I'm confident that you *will* effectively demonstrate profitable growth—and, in fact, that you can demonstrate profit erosion by *not* pursuing customer experience, as I present in detail in Chapter 3, "Economics of Customer Experience."

Summing Up: The Reward Ahead

Establishing the direct financial impact of customer experience can be, I grant you, a challenge for some companies, but consider this example. One of our clients is a utility—the only one in the market, making it a monopoly. The utility already has 100% market share. How can customer experience possibly help raise profits and margins for this organization? *Ease in gaining higher rate hikes.* Any hikes the company seeks are subject to governmental approval after public hearings. Satisfied customers speaking at the hearings enable the company to gain faster approval of hikes, and greater increases in doing so.

In tough economic and competitive times, it's easy to fall into the traditional behavior traps. But experience has demonstrated that short-term cost-cutting efforts often come with a hefty survival cost in the long run. Customer loyalty, as select companies have now discovered, isn't subject to the boom-and-bust cycle. Relationships need long-term investment. Best-in-class companies are learning from recent history and refuse to repeat the tempting mistakes of the past. They're charting a new course of doing business with customers, and refusing to abandon their customers at the time when their customers need them the most. These companies are reaping the financial benefits of this new strategy.

You can as well. Join us in charting *your* customer experience course.

CHAPTER 2

The Customer Experience Framework

Customer experience doesn't just happen. It isn't two people being nice to each other while one pays for a purchase at the point of sale. Customer experience is a discipline and, as such, requires structure, governance and careful management.

By the same token, customer experience doesn't happen only here or there. It occurs everywhere. Experience isn't delivered in a few select channels, nor is it always delivered face-to-face. Customer experience comprises the entire customer journey, from first visit to a website to the last invoice. Customer experience is a manifestation of organizational culture and, as such, requires nurturing, monitoring and formal company commitment.

As a discipline, CEM must be built upon an overall framework, creatively designed and carefully constructed. Without such discipline, your company will have difficulty becoming what we term a "WOW brand," and will instead remain mired along with the other companies that do no better than simply reach parity—and we term those companies "NOW brands."

WOW brands are those few, select organizations that truly live up to their brand promises and deliver exceptional customer experiences—wow experiences. To do so, WOW brands plan for the long haul, focusing on creating sustainable and credible value for customers. They align their organizations (from R&D to finance to customer service) to meet heightened customer expectations and to establish long-term, intimate customer relationships. WOW brands recognize that the key to establishing these relationships is not the promise, but the actual delivery.

NOW brands, on the other hand, rush to over-promise without establishing the infrastructure to deliver on those promises. Once when I was traveling in Europe, I spotted a bank's ad campaign reading "14,000 Branches—Each one a banking pit stop at your service" alongside a picture of a Formula 1 car. This is not only a rush to over-promise, but a rush at the speed of

Formula racing. An average pit stop at Formula 1 is six seconds. Can the bank's service staff solve my problems at this speed? At a pit stop there is no manager—just the mechanics and their tasks. Should I expect a similar performance at the branch?

NOW brands focus on short-term gains and expect immediate rewards for very little investment. They plan for returns within the next 90 days (the typical horizon of today's senior management). These organizations use branding exercises as a quick fix, attempting to avoid the investments needed to create differentiated customer experiences that will command their asking price. NOW brands hope that such quick fixes will solve their inherent problem: They're simply not that great.

Most companies fail to live up to their brand promises because they fail to define and understand how to own, create and deliver wow experiences. In other words, they fail to operationalize their brand promises.

NOW brands unwilling or unable to live up to their brand promises should never make these promises to begin with. No one, least of all customers, appreciates disappointment. Disappointment carries consequences—more often than not, painful financial consequences. Companies that deliver experiences that fail to meet and exceed the expectations created by their brand promise are forced to lower prices to compensate customers who believed the promises made by marketers fixated on such issues as brand recollection and conversion rates, and not promise fulfillment.

WOW brand organizations challenge their branding people to turn the process upside down and begin by guaranteeing organizational delivery capabilities and alignment through a brand performance platform first. Even if they aspire to create a new experience for customers, their design will start with capabilities in mind and will not remain in the domain of the aspiration. It's time to rethink brand strategy in the context of actual brand delivery through customer experiences. Are you willing and able to deliver the promised brand in the form of a wow customer experience?

What WOW brands successfully develop, and what's missing in NOW brands, is a customer experience framework—a brand performance platform that aligns the organization and enables employees to deliver branded customer experiences by:

- Understanding the brand and its impact on the customer
- Ensuring that the whole organization understands the performance required to fulfill the brand
- Recognizing their mission and role in living up to the brand promise
- Empowering their employees with the tools, information and authority to fulfill the brand promise

- Measuring every department against the delivery of the brand promise
- Aligning employee understanding of their role in the brand performance through customer experience delivery
- Motivating their employees to execute the brand promise
- Removing all obstacles to living by the brand promise and values to free employees to perform

Introducing the CCO

All the elements I've mentioned above—commitment, investment, a view of the long term and, most important, operationalizing the effort—are the building blocks of the customer experience framework. As well, a critical component of the framework is ownership—of the experience and of the framework itself. An emerging role, Chief Customer Officer, attempts to address the ownership challenge by taking a holistic view of all customer touch point interactions and ensuring a consistent quality of experience. In some organizations, we've seen the CCO role enacted as merely an advisory function, while at others, the CCO is an operational position. No matter what the title is—Chief Customer Officer, Chief Marketing Officer or Vice President of Customer Experience—companies must create a role that owns the complete value chain from brand promise to customer experience fulfillment and, in doing so, owns the brand performance platform.

At the same time, branding professionals must assume the responsibility for developing of a brand performance platform and ensuring the organization's ability to deliver. Some might claim that these responsibilities are outside the scope of the branding profession. But it's time to rethink branding in the context of *organizational* execution and the ability of the organization to deliver on whatever promise is being made. Through our experience of assisting clients to become more customer-centric, we have witnessed how this core competency of branding professionals causes repeated mistakes that lead to missing the branding effort targets. Thus the importance of the customer experience framework.

In this chapter, I present a structural overview of the framework, and in succeeding chapters I introduce step-by-step how to build upon that framework with creativity, metrics, diligence and passion.

First, let's establish the foundation of the framework with two integral definitions:

Customer experience is the total value proposition provided to a customer, including the actual product, and all interactions with the customer—pre-sale, at point of sale, and post-sale. This value includes experience attributes such as on-time delivery and the quality of products, as well as the experience attitudes, such as the emotional engagement created during interaction with the customers. Customers want a personal company. They want to be treated as people, not account numbers or the sum total of their purchases. And they seek this treatment at all times. You're in the business of the complete value proposition. You can start down the road to customer experience by revamping or fixing one touch-point, one channel, one product line, but you can't stop there. You must complete the excursion.

Customer Experience Management is the science and art of creating, innovating, monitoring and managing that overall framework. CEM oversees all interactions with customers across all touch points in order to maximize the value provided to customers. Mastering the science guides us in meeting customer expectations and fixing broken promises to reach parity. Mastering the art guides us in exceeding those expectations. The science is the attribute. The art is the attitude—and an art indeed it is.

In building a culture of experience and excellence, you must be both analytical and creative. What's more, the whole of customer experience management must come from you and not from the customers. Customers can tell you what's wrong, but they can't innovate for you. When Sony was developing the Walkman—the iPod of its day in terms of both sales and brand visibility—customer focus groups rejected the concept. The customers themselves were anchored in the NOW, but Sony proceeded to develop the WOW. Customers can't tell you what will surprise them because, if they did, delivery wouldn't be a surprise. If it's not surprising, it's not differentiating. And customers aren't coming up with the next WOW idea. That's your job.

By the same token, customer data is extremely valuable, but data doesn't lead to innovation. It provides *clues,* but it will not give you *answers*. Let us, then, begin setting the framework that will give you both clues and answers.

The Experience Ecosystem

In Chapter 1, I spoke of company ecosystems and customer ecosystems. To begin to draw those systems together into the experience framework, you must map the complete *experience* ecosystem in which your organization exists. The illustration on page 30 shows the touch points over which you have control as the ovals below the line. You design and direct such elements as brochures, and your web site, sales, and so on.

The components include *all* touch points, not only customer-facing touch points. In one company, I stepped into the legal department and asked the department head about their role in customer experience. She said, "No no—we don't do customer experience here. We're the legal department." When I asked about the department's role in the company, she explained, "We're here to protect the company."

"Oh," I said. "Protect it from whom? Who's the enemy?"

"From customers, of course."

Yet, the legal department does deliver customer experience, but almost always in the negative. Few people understand, for instance, the terms and conditions of their credit card agreements, or even try to read them, given the density of the language. Legal has written them, it seems, to make the customers feel stupid. Legal and finance must understand how to design documents that respect customers, because such understanding and such execution present an opportunity. Imagine terms and conditions written in real English that customers can understand. *This is you, this is us.* No scary words, no eye-chart-sized fonts that no one wants to attempt to penetrate.

Let's take collection as another example. One of my key questions for those running the collection department is, "Do you want this customer to stay or go away? Because the way you speak to them, they'll never return. Do you want to keep the customer?"

I generally get a response on the order of "Keeping the customer isn't my number. My number is to get the money."

So if getting the money is the number, then keeping the customer, or at least keeping the customer on your side, is also the number for collection in a customer-centric organization. Picture a customer in financial trouble. He owes money to ten different companies, and can pay back only two. Who do you think he's going to pay? The one who treats him with the most respect. Such thinking lays the foundation for building a business case for redesigning the collection experience. After all, you want to be the one customers pay first.

All such touch points impact the customer experience.

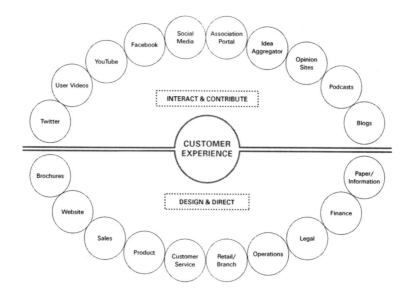

The ovals above the line in our illustration represent touch points outside the company's boundaries—including such social-media vehicles as Twitter, YouTube and Facebook. These touch points shape the value proposition through customers' opinions and sharing their experiences. Companies can't design and direct these touch points, yet they must be monitored—and companies must learn to interact and contribute to these vehicles. You can contribute, but you can't control.

This is the branding manager's biggest nightmare. ***What are people going to say about us out there in the social media?*** I'll discuss the importance of understanding the customer experience that you can't control in Chapter 5, "Customer Experience in the Virtual World," but for the moment, you must understand that your experience exists in this complete ecosystem.

For a peek into the next generation of innovation, consider the companies that have established a new corporate position: Director of Cyber Service. This executive fields a team that signs up for and participates in every social medium. The moment the company's name is mentioned a team member responds. If the comment is positive, the associate responds with humble appreciation and perhaps offers a helpful comment or two. If the comment is negative, the associate addresses the issue directly and honestly, without making excuses. Omni Hotels employs a social media coordinator empowered to take such actions as directing a property to buy a round of drinks for a customer who uses Twitter to invite friends to join him for a drink at an Omni lounge. Such companies seek out customers and potential customers who are interacting at touch points beyond the companies' control, and to respond to them with a philosophy of listening and contribution.

Just as with links in a chain, you are as good as the weakest touch point in your ecosystem, whether internal or—increasingly in electronic times—external. Map all the touch points that exist in your company's ecosystem, making certain that none escape your attention. As you develop the strategy for customer experience and innovation, you'll evaluate and scrutinize every touch point. Part of the evaluation, for instance, will come in determining which touch points are most important to your customers, so you don't waste investment raising the bar at touch points that don't create differentiation. This evaluation will also show that the noisiest channel is not necessarily the most important channel.

In this journey, you must visit all the stops along the way, but some you can consider briefly and move on.

The Experience Value Evolution Chain

Just as in biological ecosystems, customer experience undergoes natural evolution within its own business ecosystem. You must understand this evolution and manage it in this context.

In the illustration on page 30, you'll see the how customer experience evolves within both the touch points we can design and direct, and the touch points that that we can only interact with and contribute to. Those latter touch points—the "Interact and Contribute" touch points—represent external influence on the experience every step of the way. External touch points shape the experience as you deliver it. I've covered some of those external touch points that exist specifically in your ecosystem, particularly the social media influencers that help shape consumer perception of your brand. Other influencers and comparison points are consumers' previous experience with you and with other brands, competitors' promises, and competitive offers.

The four stages of experience value evolution are:

1. The promise of Experience Value. You must understand and, ideally, influence what happens at the promise stage, which sets the stage for the entire relationship—especially in the context of sales. Involve yourself early in establishing the expectations you're delivering against and in establishing the expectations you seek to surpass with delightful experiences. To take the attitude of "I don't want to deal with sales" is absolutely dangerous. You can't exceed expectations if sales overpromises and sets those expectations too high. If the promises are beyond the company's capabilities, you can't even meet expectations. Under-promising and over-delivering is the more effective method of creating close and committed relationships.

2. The delivery of Experience Value. This stage concerns every aspect of delivering the promise—service, products, information, etc. All the details are involved in delivering experience value, from the operation to the website to delivery of invoices.

3. The communication of Experience Value. This is a new phase most companies are not aware of, yet they must be. This is the stage where the problems start. Most companies fail to incorporate mechanisms that demonstrate and display the value they provide through products and services— not how much they cost, but how much value they deliver. If you have any dream of up-sells, cross-sells and long-time retention, you must redesign your communications model. Don't assume that customers will figure out your true value on their own. Value visualization enables customers to calculate in financial terms the value your company delivers.

Create a proactive value-visualization model to assure that customer see, understand and appreciate the value you provide, whether through score-carding, statement summaries, or other means that we'll discuss in greater detail in Chapter 12, "Measure What Matters." In the meantime, understand that if customers can't visualize value, you'll be unable to move to the fourth stage:

4. The growth of Experience Value. This is the ultimate stage of the progression, bringing customer retention, repeat business, and increased profit per transaction. As we all know, retaining and growing business from existing customers is far more cost-effective than acquiring new customers. And if you deliver experience and delight on each of the previous steps, you'll see Experience Value growth from highly satisfied customers who remain with you, and perhaps become evangelists, generating new customers.

Moving the customer along this evolution is critical to the company's ultimate financial success. And move you must. Experiences are not static. They are dynamic. They can range from, in the customer's evaluation, a "Wow!" to a "Never again!" The problem is that companies are often focusing on "OK," the uneventful, with no memorability. Is it any wonder that the customer shrugs?

By way of example, consider the most common word used in call centers today: *average*. Picture this scenario, which is, unfortunately, fairly average in itself: One day, an average employee comes to the call center to take calls from average customers who are handled within average handling time, executing an average wrap-up time. You look at average transactions and see average spend. And when the CEO asks you how things are going, you can rightfully say, "Oh, it's pretty average." At home that night, your spouse asks you how you did that day. You proudly reply, "I was average."

If you do have average customers, by all means, treat them in an average way. But when you deliver averagely OK experiences, you're opening the door and ushering your customers on their way to the competition. Statistics concur. A Forrester study shows that only 17% of satisfied customers will not shop around.

Apply this thinking to personal life. You love the person you've been married to for 10 years. But every Friday night, you go to the same Italian restaurant, you order the same pasta and the same glass of wine. You go home and think, "That was good. This is average—this is what we like." Eventually, someone's going to get bored.

Your customers are no less emotional human beings in a business environment. If all they get is forgettable OK experiences, loyalty will lapse. Let me be very clear: You are not in the business of just delivering services or fixing complaints, because your enemy is larger than the customer problems you solve. Your biggest enemy is boredom. Meeting expectations is boring. Customers are comparing you to more exciting companies, looking for the new standards—delight, differentiation, surprise, and interest. Every time they open a mailer or call the contact center or visit the website, they're opening themselves up to the opportunity to enjoy the new standards, and they expect them. Those who experience average all the time will go elsewhere for a little excitement.

The resistance to average is fueled by an element within the category of external influencers—a massive factor shaping customer expectations in general, in turn shaping those expectations of your value delivery. Customers now demand more from you than simply exceeding the competition in part because the competition is very much like us. More important, the new benchmark for customer experience is set by all the companies customers deal with. Customers are now exposing you to a different context of competition. By measuring yourself only against your direct competition, you restrict your thinking and lower your standards. You may be a retailer or a mobile phone company or a car-rental agency, but the customer who's been to Disney World wonders why your customer service reps don't treat them with similar magic.

And, in fact, one of our clients in the aerospace business wanted to conduct a competitive analysis. We measured this client not against other aerospace businesses, but instead against Disney, Ritz-Carlton, Virgin Atlantic Airways, Starbucks, and Zara. Such is the new world of our customers—businesses once compared themselves to competition only within their individual industries, but no more, particularly in terms of customer service and customer experience.

That's a critical change you must embrace. Not only must you stop operating solely within your own organizational ecosystem, but you also must extend beyond the ecosystem of your industry and into the customer's ecosystem, redefined in the context of the new world of the customer. It's no longer about being best in class, but being the best in the customer's world. If you aim to be a customer experience company, you must compare yourself against the top brands out there.

This is the approach taken by American Express, which doesn't settle for being ranked at the top of the financial services industry in terms of customer satisfaction. It achieves this height by comparing itself with customer-service giants inside and outside the financial industry. When setting your own standards, establish what it will take for your company to become your customer's number-one vendor, period.

This broader view has forced a shift from focusing on products to concentrating on the customer's experience at every organizational touch point, just as the top WOW experience brands do. And it calls for concentrating on solving the complete problem of the customer and weaving emotional engagement into the total experience, as you'll see as the chapters that follow develop the innovation of customer experience.

External influencers also, of course, include the customers' world in general—how their expectations and presumptions are affected by trends, culture, economic conditions and societal changes, as well as the customers' individual histories and experiences.

As an exercise, list your customers' expectations. What do they want from you? What have they asked of you?

Next, evaluate each of the expectations. Are they right or wrong?—and I'll give you the quick answer before you even start. The expectations you have listed are neither right nor wrong. They just are. For better or worse, customers come in with certain expectations based on previous interactions with you or others. They don't start from square one. In particular, consider how the marketing world is changing as younger demographics gain purchase power. The younger the customer, the faster they want response and satisfaction. "I am in control"—this is the customer's belief.

If customers' expectations are too high, you sometimes must re-set their expectations by telling them why you need to do so. But never forget that in the customers' minds, "It's all about me." No matter the situation, the customer is the most important person in the conversation.

You also re-set customer expectations in every engagement—for better or worse. Once you meet or exceed customers' expectations, they expect that you will do it again. And again. Therefore, expanding the context in which you regard customer experience requires adopting the tactics, strategies and strengths of the top experience performers, including instituting faster innovation, more customization and options, personal experiences, the human touch, emotional connection, and the strong element of pleasant surprise and outright delight—in other words, the things they weren't expecting.

The Experience Performance Model

By now you know that when we discuss customer experience, we're not referring to high-level ideas and unfounded corporate commitments. Customer experience is a day-to-day performance through thousands if not millions of interactions. To best understand how to unleash this performance, you must understand the experience performance model. This model identifies the levers that will make the customer experience a reality.

Key to the experience performance model is chemistry—reaction and interaction—between the stakeholders involved in living customer experience. The chemical reaction occurs at the moment of truth, when customer experience is delivered. And because of the nature of this chemistry, no one stakeholder can be regarded, measured or evaluated in isolation.

The experience performance model includes three key stakeholders and their contribution to the overall performance:

The organization hires employees and engages with customers. This organization is represented by the brand promise and its communication. The brand promise is the set of expectations created in the mind of both customers and employees. Organizational communications to transmit and reinforce these expectations only contribute to the strength of the brand promise.

The employees are chartered with making the experience a reality. They do so by designing products and services, by delivering them, and by engaging with customers throughout the duration of the relationships. These employees bring to the relationships their perceptions of the quality of their performance, as well as pre-conceived notions regarding the customers.

The customers, the people who consume and pay for your product and services, bring with them dreams, hopes, aspirations, and problems requiring solutions. They also bring a set of expectations dictated by the brand promise communicated by the organization.

The working experience of Strativity Group demonstrates that to unlock the power of experience performance, you must measure and manage the *relationship* between each pair of stakeholders. This is the point of chemistry, the moment of truth. Instead of relying on traditional measurements of experience performance, the relationship between the organization and its employees determines the quality of their work. The relationship between customers and employees determines the quality of the delivered experience. The relationship between the brand promise and the customers' needs determines overall satisfaction.

Only when measuring the experience performance through the lenses of these relationships—the chemistry that results when two stakeholders interact—can you find the true key to experience performance. Employees can be excellent individuals on their own, but when they interact with customers equipped only with the employees' preconceived notions about customers, they might deliver an unsatisfactory experience. Customers can be high-potential individuals, but when encountering a deceptive or unfounded brand promise, they'll revert to a price strategy and shop with competitors.

Traditional measurements of stakeholders in isolation, such as customer expectations or employee satisfaction or brand equity, don't provide the necessary insight to adapt and drive real change in the experience performance. Traditional single-stakeholder metrics may measure the brand as a standalone, but fail to measure how the brand fulfills customer expectations. It is this failure that marks the difference between using generic metrics and metrics customized to your specific experiences. Generic measures undermine differentiation.

As we establish the customer experience framework in the chapters that follow, we'll discuss specific ways to evaluate the relationships of each pair of stakeholders in your company—company/employee, employee/customer, and customer/company. We'll then show how to identify significant gaps and bridge those gaps at points where customer experience innovation and intervention will bring you the most financial return.

Customer Experience Management and Branding Alignment

I am always amazed that most CMOs I meet don't seem to be concerned with how customer experience management aligns with their branding efforts—if they pay any attention to CEM in the first place. Yet, understanding how CEM relates to branding is critical to overall corporate understanding of a holistic approach to customers.

The CMOs I meet still think their brand is abstract—that it is message, image, a look, a feel. But branding is not communication; branding is performance. Failure of CEM is failure of brand. These marketers must own more than brand promise—they must own brand performance, and instead of delegating CEM to lower-level associates with little operational budget, the CMOs must wake up and fully embrace the discipline that is customer experience.

As I've discussed, because customers are operating against a background of the promises you and your brand make, you face a problem when customer experience efforts fail to align with those from marketing, branding and advertising. The branding makes a big, bright promise to customers, and now you must operationalize the promise. You must make it real.

Customer experience management is a means for such operationalizing. You execute the brand promise through this discipline. If you manage to establish this strong linkage, you not only have created a more efficient platform for delighting customers, but also have placed yourself in a position to benefit from the more-aggressive budgets assigned to branding and marketing.

Designing and innovating customer experience—as explored in the pages that follow—involves building a disciplined structure to assess your brand, your customers' needs and expectations, and the specific execution of experience and delight. This framework can be built from top to bottom, defining the ultimate experience and then flowing that definition into the corporation as a whole, and then down through the customer touch points. It can be built from bottom to top, isolating certain products, customer touch points, or customer groups, and then extended up through the organization and into the brand itself. We'll explore the advantages of each approach later.

For the moment, though, thinking of top-to-bottom orientation, the customer experience framework follows this general flow-through:

At the top is the experience promise. Examine your brand. Define it in terms of the ultimate promise to the customer. What experiences do you promise the customer? How would you like to define the core experience? (In the section that follows, I will lead you through an exercise that will help you answer these questions.)

This flows into the customer pledge. How does the brand interpret the customer promise?

In turn, the customer pledge must be fulfilled through experience delivery, in the various delivery dimensions across the organization: products, people, processes and paper (that is, information).

Each of these delivery dimensions differ through experience delivery touch points through the customer lifecycle, from customer acquisition to account management to, in the worst case, departure.

And all this is based on a solid platform of organizational readiness, in which experience has been defined, and elements such as compensation, measurements, incentives and customized training are carefully designed and enacted. Organizational readiness begins with educating employees. Those in production, finance, legal, and so on must understand what they must do differently to execute the brand. You must proceed step-by-step and understand how different touch points are operating within the organization, identify gaps between current performance and preferred performance, and remove obstacles that block employees from peak performance.

CRM and Customer Experience

I'm often asked about the relationship of CEM and CRM—Customer Experience Management and Customer Relationship Management. Let's start with the basics:

What does it mean when you ask customers to be loyal? You want them to pick you over the competition, and you want them to buy more, but under what condition? The hidden request when you ask for loyalty is that the customers stay with you, but not at the cheapest price. Customer loyalty is contingent upon the fact that you do *not ask* the cheapest price. Otherwise, you're not achieving loyalty—you're just winning the battle of price comparison. In asking customers to bypass price to stay with you, you're asking them to be emotional, to bypass rational considerations. And they're asking for emotional value in return. If you must offer the cheapest price to maintain loyalty, you're not going to succeed.

Terms like *customer loyalty* and *customer relationships* are real-life emotional terms, and the great news is that 95% of customer decisions are emotional. When buying a digital camera, for instance, few people actually sit down and make a matrix and a chart with features, benefits, prices, details, and so on. More than likely, they go into the store with a price range in mind, pick up a camera, play with it and several others, and then make a decision emotionally. There are thousands of digital cameras, and customer choice of a camera isn't so much a matter of choosing a camera but building a relationship with it—or with its vendor.

What is loyalty, then? Ultimately, loyalty encompasses strong relationships. You are building experiences and relationships every day. The relationship begins with people. The customer-facing folks create *experience,* which we define as a pleasantly surprising interaction. Delightful experiences over time, and in every interaction, build a *relationship,* and a strong relationship builds *loyalty.*

Are you building experiences that will last? Or are they just for now? Are you creating great experiences that create great relationships to last a long time? Or mediocre experiences that create relationships that aren't built to last? In every design, in everything you do, ask the question, "Is it built to last?" Relationships are about delightful experiences every time. The more, the better. The weaker, the worse.

So in moving from CRM to CEM, you're migrating to the foundation of customer relationships—the only place where you can influence relationship-building. You can't instigate customer relationships. That's the customer's choice. You can, however, control delivering the experiences that provide the reasons to build relationships. Every email that you send, every in-store display that you create, every front-line interaction that you participate in—all are experiential building blocks that can lead to loyalty.

Understanding this also helps organizations understand that CEM is not an add-on to other company initiatives, such as leadership training, innovation and R&D, employee- retention efforts, and, yes CRM. As I noted before, the ultimate goal of each of these initiatives is to please the customer, and therefore customer experience becomes the umbrella for all of them, and not an adjunct or even a competitor.

CRM and CEM, then, reach to the heart of the customer relationship, and both bring you back to the clear-eyed, difficult question: Do you have the experiences and the quality to bring customers to you naturally? Are you good enough? Will you invest in customer experience, or spend it less efficiently on sales-promise efforts and discounts?

CRM is an outcome of CEM. CRM answers the question of how to increase revenues from customers through better collection and use of customer information, while CEM answers the question of how to create customer loyalty through better value propositions. To realize the benefits of CEM, companies need complementary CRM information. When fully aligned, CRM creates the building blocks on which to build profitable CEM. I recognize that many may not agree with me about how I characterize this relationship between CRM and CEM, yet I've found that such distinctions are the clearest way to explain the role of both, and to demonstrate how they co-exist. In Chapter 10, "Performance Platform: The Tools to Deliver," I will further demonstrate how customer experience management depends on high-quality customer information, which is made available from the realm of customer relationship management. A robust database of customer information that you can slice and analyze and mine in order to create offers and segmentation is a strong tool, but if your product doesn't make sense to the customer, and doesn't fulfill needs, no offer you create to sell that offer will matter.

An industry at the forefront of CRM, armed with transactional information, distinct segmentation and targeted offers is the airline industry, which also finds itself at the forefront of bankruptcy filings. Why? Flying used to be fun. With few exceptions, it's fun no longer. Service cuts and extra fees and employees with artificial smiles . . . the core experience is often dreadful. And that's after years of CRM focus. As Gartner analyst Michael Maoz once said: "CRM has been kicked and tossed and beaten; customer experience seems to have better resonance."

Are your CRM efforts in the same boat (since you don't want to take a plane)? Are your products and experiences great? Do they resonate? If not, how do you make them so?

To help answer these questions, consider this exercise, to be conducted with the principals of your organization:

List all your products and services. Map them according to how they contribute to customer experience differentiation. Classify each product and service into one of four categories:

- **Existence Attributes** are those products and services at the core of your business. If you're Nike, for instance, shoes are your existence attributes. As well, company touch points such as sales, accounting and so on—so basic to operating a business—are also existence attributes. These attributes won't make customers want to share their great memories with others or pay a premium price for your products, but instead are what you need to be in business in the first place, like payroll or IT.

- **Undifferentiated Attributes** are variations and qualities that your competitors can match. Nike's undifferentiated attributes are different types of shoes—for training versus for running, for instance—as well as shoes in different colors and sizes. These attributes are common to all shoe manufacturers.

- **Differentiated Attributes** are those that can command premium pricing. At one point, "air" technology in the soles of Nike's athletic shoes, then unmatched by competitors, was a differentiated attributes. Extras and add-ons offered free don't qualify for this category, as they're simply part of the cost of doing business.

- **Excellence Attributes** are those features and products that not only command premium prices, but also inspire customer evangelism. We'll talk in detail later about another Nike example that inspires such evangelism—customers' ability to customize their shoes. To qualify for this category, products and services must demonstrate reduced marketing costs as your customer base recommends them by word-of-mouth.

The first two types of attributes fall below the parity line. They satisfy basic needs and remove dissatisfiers. Customers expect them because they believe it's necessary or they've seen them at a competitor.

The third and fourth types of attributes rise above the parity line, and are functions of creating excellence. A product or service can't cross the parity line unless it's demonstrably able to command premium pricing.

Classifying your products and services is a demanding exercise—and here's what it seeks to accomplish: The exercise is giving you your sales pitch. Everything you've listed below the parity line is expected, and therefore won't work as sales points. Customers will give you credit only for those elements above the parity line. They will pay you premium prices for the unexpected, and that's what you sell.

Ninety-five percent of what many organizations do today can be summed up by the phrase, "Just making it work." Below the parity line is boring. It isn't enough. Yes, you have to get the basics right, but you can't stop there.

What's more, the exercise will illustrate the difficulty companies have in fully defining and recognizing what products and services exist above and below the parity line. Many companies will proudly point to a service as a differentiator worth a premium price, but when they analyze the service carefully, they might realize that the differentiation is only temporary until a competitor copies it, or that it's a nice-to-have and not a must-have differentiator that customers will pay more for.

We're not in the business of having fun with customers. We're all in the business of making money. Anything you can't charge for is worthless. Not understanding what customers will pay extra for, and how much extra, compromises customer experience. And if the customers can't articulate the value of extra effort and premium service, they won't give you the credit, and they won't be willing to pay extra, and you will have accomplished is working harder.

When you simply meet expectations, you begin to suffer in establishing loyalty, customer experience and satisfaction. To put it bluntly, we live in a world of exceptional value or bust. Exceptional is the new standard; exceptional is what customers demand. The following chapters discuss how to create exceptional, but to build a foundation for that instruction, you must recognize that often when your customers are price-sensitive, they're seeking differentiation of pricing because you're giving them no other differentiation. You must therefore commit to building a WOW brand.

The Critical Need for WOW Over NOW

Picture this scene: Unveiling the new customer experience initiative is held center stage in a glamorous, famous theater. The CEO's music-filled multi-media presentation is truly a production for all to behold. Highlighting the pomp and the dramatic speeches, the lights fall on the backdrop depicting the new logo, which incorporates elements from its predecessor but is now replete with a modern font and a rejuvenated color scheme that reflects hope for a bright future. Everyone gleefully embraces the inspiring slogan that accompanies the logo. Once all the grand words are spoken and the self-congratulations are passed about, attending employees enjoy appetiz-ers with food-coloring to match the logo's new color scheme, and then carry off gift bags filled with the customary slogan-adorned T-shirt, the logo-shaped mouse pad, and the "Customer Is Number-One" mug. The event is a stunning success.

Now what?

The vast majority of employees will perceive this exercise as little more than cosmetics. They'll view the new directive as an experiment concocted in the marketing and brand laboratories and doomed to exist only there. In their minds, the brand is owned not by the entire organization but by the heads of marketing communications and market research. The thinking is that since only these two individuals and their surrogates are responsible for producing new marketing materials, all other employees can return to work and continue business as usual. And put the mug beside all the others.

The irony of this situation is that from a customer's viewpoint, the new di-rective and messages represent a new reality—or at least a second chance. While they might have "seen and heard it all before," they'll still align their expectations with the new promise. If employees aren't willing to change or raise their performance to meet customers' heightened expectations, the new brand will damage the corporate image by leading customers to believe that nothing has changed and it really is still business as usual.

Experience demonstrates that the vast majority of brand-development programs do little to change organizational behavior. Even so, companies launching new brands are more than willing to declare victory when their logos appear in full-page ads in major publications such as *The Wall Street Journal*, *The New York Times* and *USA Today*. They fail to recognize that there's more to revitalizing or changing a brand and its customer experience than launch parties and marketing campaigns.

Imagine a hotel chain launching a multi-million-dollar advertising campaign touting a new five-star hotel in San Francisco. The ad exudes prestige and exclusivity with a careful choice of wording, striking images, and a shiny gold logo. The hotel promises customers unparalleled service, highlighting an extremely attentive staff, a superior spa, and amenities that only a cherished few can afford. Now imagine arriving customers who find that this five-star hotel is little more than a renovated youth hostel that might, on the best of days, be worthy of a three-star rating. The "spa" is in reality a swimming pool with a couple of coin-operated massage chairs on the side. The "attentive" staff barely speaks English when they speak at all. The other "amenities" are nowhere to be found.

Launching this type of a multi-million dollar advertising campaign to promote an inferior experience would rarely, if ever happen. Such an act would be deemed wasteful and downright stupid, because it would lead to a flood of customer complaints, demands for full refunds, and probably some lawsuits for good measure.

What's the big deal? Why does it matter? It matters because a brand represents a promise and expectation made by an organization to its customers. It reflects an organization's competitive identity and should communicate to customers why they should frequent the establishment, pay premium prices and evangelize to their friends and family. WOW brands recognize that a brand represents a value proposition promise, and that their customer experience (regardless of where it is delivered) represents the fulfillment of that promise.

In WOW brand organizations, all employees are responsible for fulfilling the brand promise, irrespective of the department they work in—product design, process improvement, marketing or customer service. The quality of employee performance across all organizational touch points is the ultimate reflection of brand quality.

As critical as the consistency of the brand logo and messaging across all organizational touch points may be, it's even more critical that the brand performance—in other words, the quality of the customer experience—be equally consistent across the organization. When organizational functions aren't aligned around the fulfillment of the brand promise, value becomes commoditized, and customers are left confused, angry, and prepared to take their business elsewhere.

Summing Up: The Road to WOW

WOW brands are no longer optional—they're mandatory. Customers are increasingly seeking experiences that meet or exceed their expectations. Only by exceeding these expectations can organizations differentiate themselves from their competitors, command customer trust, and obtain their loyalty. In a world of sound bites and cost-efficiency measures, companies that can deliver experiences that meet or exceed their brand generated expectations will stand out and be rewarded.

Through creative design, appealing pictures and catchy slogans, companies can easily make grand pronouncements—so easily, that brand and marketing professionals can fall into the traditional branding trap of making them without securing full organizational commitment and, therefore, the ability to fulfill these promises.

To change this branding paradigm, you must ensure that all employees know precisely what they're expected to do to execute the brand promise prior to developing and launching the brand. The presence of senior corporate officers, the press and select customers at a launch party is not a successful recipe for creating wow experiences. Success can be achieved only by following a disciplined approach and building a solid customer experience framework to ensure that the brand promise is incorporated into the customer experience at every organizational touch point. Only by ensuring that the organization is willing and able deliver a wow experience can branding and marketing professionals embark on the road to developing and launching a truly successful WOW brand.

Now, let's begin the travels down that road.

CHAPTER 3

Economics of Customer Experience

Sometimes I think I'm in the business of reliving Bad Business flashbacks. Here's one such flashback, a sour memory that I'm sure I share with many of you. Shortly after you've made a compelling case for introducing a vigorous customer experience program to your brand, the corporate planning committee nods agreement. The CEO says, "Excellent presentation. Full speed ahead." But when you ask about the budget level you have to work with, the CEO stares at you blankly. "What budget?"

Worse yet, the CEO says, "Excellent presentation, but drop anchor. We're making our numbers. Why do we need this additional expense?"

Welcome to my flashback.

Too many top executives don't understand that customer experience is a financial strategy. They see it as an add-on and don't understand the damage of doing nothing. This is not their fault. It is yours. You haven't spoken the corporate language. Customer experience executives speak in terms of *satisfaction* and *loyalty*. They often believe that a customer-centric strategy is "common sense." While many of us might agree with this assessment, the fact remains that customer experience strategies are *not* common sense. If they were, most companies would be implementing them rather than hemorrhaging customers.

In contrast to the customer experience language of *satisfaction* and *loyalty*, investment decisions are made based on the financial language of *revenue, return on investment,* and *profit and loss*. Companies select investments based on the returns they expect to receive on those investments. Companies that successfully transform their experience do so because they have learned to translate the "soft" language of customer experience into the "hard" language of finance.

Our firm is often called on to save a failed customer experience initiative at the last minute. As we quickly discover, many of these failed initiatives share the absence of a sound business case with predefined objectives and time frames. This is the very reason why so many senior executives fail to take customer experience initiatives and strategies seriously.

On the pages that follow, I outline Strativity Group's Economics of Customer Experience framework and methodology for translating customer experience into the language of finance so customer experience initiatives can compete successfully against more familiar investment opportunities like re-engineering efforts and direct marketing campaigns that executives more intuitively frame in the context of profit and loss. The Economics of Customer Experience ultimately establishes "The Number." This is the figure or the figures that catch attention, motivate action, and establish urgency. The Number is a goal and it is a warning bell. It demonstrates possibility for growth, and potential for stagnation if action isn't taken.

By arming themselves with the financial truth about the economic power generated by loyal and devoted customers, customer experience executives gain a critical seat at the table when investment decisions are made because they will be able to demonstrate how specific investments, resources and prioritization in customer experience will lead to higher spending, reduced attrition, increased customer referrals and greater interest in other products and services. Follow these guidelines for building the financial case for customer experience.

Learn the Hidden Meanings of Financial Language

What are top executives and heads of organizational silos really saying when they toss off the frequently heard excuses for not implementing customer experience or for approving implementation without financial support?:

- "We can't afford the investment"
- "We're still making our numbers"
- "We are doing it already"
- "It's too expensive"
- "Customers are just fine without it"
- "We're on par with the competition"
- "Can you guarantee the return on investment?"

All of these statements are corporate idiom expressing one of two beliefs: "I doubt the case for customer impact," and, worse yet, "I doubt the financial case." I called my first book *Passionate and Profitable* to answer those CEOs who say that creating customer passion through customer experience is expensive. Passion is not expensive. Passion is the path to making money, especially if you know how to create passion.

Begin the fight against foot-dragging phraseology with philosophical retorts, perhaps less tart than what I've listed here, to get the execs thinking.

- "We can't afford the investment." *How do we know? What numbers specifically tell us that?*
- "We're still making our numbers." *So, does the potential of making better numbers frighten you?*
- "We are doing it already." *Point to an example and its measured results.*
- "It's too expensive." *Show me the spreadsheet that confirms this.*
- "Customers are just fine without it." *Did customers tell you this? Which ones? Our best customers? Or the customers who left us last week?*
- "We're on par with the competition." *So, why should our customers stay, and why should their customers come to us? Parity does not a strategy make.*
- "Can you guarantee the return on investment?" *No, but I can predict specific ROI levels that are statistically likely, using these figures . . .*

And when executives don't drag their feet, when they say "Full speed ahead, budget not included," it's either because they don't understand the magnitude of the strategy and what it entails or because they believe that they can implement the strategy without additional investment or reallocation of existing organizational resources.

The Efficient Relationship Paradox

Often where customer relationships are concerned, many companies focus on quarterly results and spend less money investing in long-term relationships. We label this behavior "The Efficient Relationship Paradox." Companies minimize investments in customer relationships on the one hand, while trying to collect more money from them with the other. Not exactly a formula for success.

For executives who decide to take the road less traveled, the road requiring serious strategic focus on customers, what's the answer to overcoming the self-deceptive perception? Like any other initiative undertaken in a business looking to make a profit, money talks. Our experience demonstrates that many executives are convinced that investing in customer relationships is a cost item in their budget and is not a way to make a profit. They measure this type of investment against their current margins and see how margins would shrink even further. They've all heard the cliché about the lower cost of maintaining existing customers vs. the higher cost of acquiring a new one, but they just don't buy it. Money is talking to them. And leading them astray.

In general, numbers are equally adept at misleading as they are at illuminating. Often, organizations are susceptible to allowing numbers to soothe them by looking at them incorrectly, or by looking at the wrong numbers in the first place. Let's take an example at a hypothetical case at a company we'll call CoreCorp.

Of CoreCorp's one million customers, each delivering $100 of revenue annually, 40% believe their most recent experience with the company was good or excellent. The other 60% feel the experience was merely a shrug-worthy OK, or was unsatisfactory. Based on averages we've collected in the market, 10% of the dissatisfieds won't place any particular importance on their non-excellent experience, 88% will be unhappy but won't complain, and 2%—12,000 of the original customer base, will speak up. Of those who do, 35% get their problems solved satisfactorily, 35% take their complaints to the web, and 30%—3,600—eventually defect.

The temptation is to look at those numbers and say, "Only 12,000 out of a million have complained? That's only 1.2%. And 3,600 out of a million defect? Meantime, 35% of those complaints are resolved? Those numbers aren't bad."

No, they're not bad. They're frightening, when translated into financial language. The 3,600 customers take more than a third of a million dollars with them. And that's considering only the defectors that self-identify by complaining. Are the quiet dissatisfieds defecting at an equal rate?

Then, consider the 35% of the vocal customers taking their complaints to the web. Our research shows that each customer reaches 500 people, meaning that those 4,200 vocal customers wield the power to scare away 2,100,000 existing and potential customers, with potential losses amounting to $63 million for a hundred-million-dollar company. Even if a company loses only 5% of these existing and potential customers, this translates into a loss of $3.15 million. Now we're talking financials.

If you told your CEO that someone is stealing a million dollars from the company every day, and has been for the previous 63 days, what do you think he will do? He's not going to say, "Let's take care of that when I get back from vacation." No, he will act immediately, because he understands the dollar. Your goal is to show the dollars that are being "stolen" from the company because of inaction.

You treat the product side as a science, and the relationship side as an art. You know the cost of a making and selling a product, the cost of defects, and the profit from selling what you make. But you likely do not know the cost of building and maintaining a customer relationship, the cost of complaints and dissatisfaction, and the profit that results from continued, satisfied customer engagement.

Every conversation around customer strategy must focus on identifying the number that creates the sense of urgency to move ahead. Without The Number, you will get neither the attention nor the resources you need. But when you can come to the CEO and say, for instance, "We're capturing only 25% of our customers' available budget for electronics because they're buying from the competition that's treating them better—and, by the way, that's a loss of $152 million," now you have a story to tell. And, an ear that will listen.

From Satisfaction and Loyalty to Revenues and Costs

Reporting dissatisfaction alone, even with hard numbers, can be ineffective in inspiring action and commitment. A CEO might shrug at a 5% drop in customer satisfaction scores and say, "So? We don't have to report that to Wall Street." Your job is to convince upper management that dissatisfaction, fueled by lack of differentiating customer experience, is not simply a matter of leaving money on the table. Many of the causes of dissatisfaction also increase company costs. For example:

- Customers hate calling more than once to resolve an issue. Companies hate follow-up calls, which increase hard costs.

- Customers get angry when they receive defective goods. Processing returns and shipping replacement items can be expensive.

- Customers don't like to wait to get issues resolved. Long cycle times increase costs.

Do you see the currency being exchanged here? Increasing customer experience reduces company costs. It is a direct and natural correlation. Given such a natural relationship between loyalty and financial return, then, translating from the language of customer experience into the language of finance is eminently doable. We have found that the language of finance most effectively communicates the value of customer experience when it focusing on:

- The 5 P's of Revenue
- Customer-centric Cost Units

The 5 P's of Revenue

It's time to retire a traditional marketing bromide. Product-centric companies still labor under the yoke of the old 4 P's: *Product, Price, Promotion* and *Placement.* At one time, each could be manipulated and leveraged to create brand differentiation, but that ability has been drained away from us. *Products* are commoditized. *Price* is eroded by consumer access to price-comparison tools available on the web. *Promotions* drive company activity instead of consumer activity, forcing them to offer discounts and regularly timed sales to meet the customer expectations the companies themselves established. And *Placement* has become a moot point in the physical world in the day of internet shopping and next-day shipment.

A different set of P's is in order, one that views the income statement through a customer-centric lens. From that perspective, the revenue side of the statement is relatively simple to decipher. Revenue is driven by:
- The number of customers who purchase your product or service, which is determined by:
  o The number of customers you have at the beginning of a time period
  o The number of new customers you gain
  o The number of existing customers who leave
- The amount customers spend on your product or service, which is governed by three factors:
  o The total budget customers spend on a type of product or service
  o The portion of that budget that customers spend on your products or services
  o The price customers are willing to pay for your product or service

Each of these factors is influenced by the experience you deliver to your customers. And each of these factors is captured by the 5 P's:
- **Preference of Company or Product.** Preference captures the number of new customers who purchase your products or services in a given year. To prevent double counting, Preference excludes new customers who are referred by existing customers.

- **Promotion of Company or Product.** Promotion captures the number of new customers who purchase your products or services based on referrals of existing customers. Referred customers often behave differently than other new customers. They often spend more and attrite less, which makes them more profitable, especially since the acquisition cost is lower. Further, they have already established a relationship with you by proxy—the trust they place in the people making the referrals. Because of these factors, the value of referred customers should be quantified separately

- **Permanence of Overall Relationship.** Permanence quantifies how long customers continue to purchase your products and services. As customers stay with a vendor longer, the relationship becomes deeper, stronger and more meaningful. These relationships yield more profitable business, referrals and insight.

- **Portion of Overall Customer Budget.** Portion combines two factors that drive how much a customer spends on your products or services: their total budget for a category of spending and the portion of that budget that the customer chooses to spend with your company. Loyal customers tend to spend a higher percentage of their budget with one company than other customers do.

- **Premium Price.** Premium Price quantifies the willingness of customers to pay a higher price for your products and services than for your competitors. Loyal customers tend to be less price-sensitive than other customers because they focus more on the value they receive than on the price they pay.

Each of the 5 P's is driven by actual customer behavior, and not by customer intentions. They transact with you or they don't; they speak well of you or they're quiet, or worse; they continue their relationship with you or they leave; they buy your products and services or those of your competitors; they pay your price or they seek discounts.

Calculating the Customer Experience Revenue Opportunity

Changes in a company's revenue are based upon the 5 P's. When evaluating the revenue impact of a customer experience initiative, team with finance to quantify the initiative's impact on one or more of the 5 P's.

From there, the formula is simple:

Revenue Opportunity = Preference + Promotion + Permanence + Portion + Premium Price

Although a given initiative may impact all five of these factors, simplify your analysis by focusing on the one or two P's with the greatest impact on the initiative.

Let's now look at how each of the 5 P's is calculated.

Growth vs. Risk

When calculating the 5 P's, first consider whether the investment being considered will save current business at risk due to a sub-par customer experience (Business at Risk) or whether it's designed to capture new business by offering a new and differentiated experience (Business at Growth). The distinction between the two is important. In every organization, some existing business is at risk because of customer dissatisfaction. The risk is that their customers will attrite, spend less or criticize the organization to other customers or prospects—or act in a combination of all three.

Business at Risk comprises the elements of the 5 P's that calculate the existing business an organization will likely lose unless the organization invests to improve the experience for its existing and dissatisfied customers. Business at Risk will be of greatest interest to executives responsible for customer retention. By calculating and explaining the financial opportunity to reduce attrition and spending reductions, customer experience professionals can partner with customer retention executives to generate support for their initiatives.

Business at Growth, on the other hand, measures the opportunity to capture new business by transforming an organization's customer experience. Business at Growth involves adding new customers, securing referrals, and motivating existing customers to spend a larger portion of their budget with the organization. Business at Growth will be of greatest interest to those responsible for customer acquisition, because it will quantify the opportunity to increase acquisition through the customer experience initiatives.

The strategic and financial benefits of constantly delighting customers should drive an increased sense of urgency around designing and implementing a customer strategy. The 5 P's are driven by customer actions, not intentions, and should be the catalyst to obtain leadership's attention, support and resources. The combination of all 5 P's represents a true picture of the benefits and consequences of implementing or not implementing a customer experience strategy.

First, let's examine the impact of doing nothing within the customer experience arena.

The Return on Nothing Loyalty Model

"Business as usual" is not a sign of stability, but instead a symbol of stagnation leading to deterioration. Here's where our friend RON steps in to help you facilitate your company's commitment to Customer experience management.

The Return on Nothing (RON) Loyalty Model assesses the full costs of not implementing customer experience strategies or initiatives. The model helps you develop the understanding you need to prioritize initiatives according to their relative costs and benefits and allocate resources according to each initiative's financial impact on your organization. It is a critical element in developing The Number, the overall motivational dollar figure that will open eyes and spur action.

First, understand that the RON model doesn't measure customer perceptions and intentions or focus on such common customer metrics as customer satisfaction, willingness to purchase, or willingness to recommend. As established earlier, these metrics have no measurable impact on an organization's top or bottom line. RON does measure such customer activity as purchases, referrals, and how long customers stay with the company (relationship longevity), and in doing so provides managers and executives with a tool to make the financial case for prioritizing a customer experience strategy.

In the context of customer experience strategies, the RON Loyalty Model illustrates the business impact of failing to implement customer experience strategies through such economics-of-relationship metrics relationship longevity and portion of budget. RON incorporates both what refer to as Business at Risk and Business at Growth. The inability to deploy customer experience strategies in a timely manner may impact the organization through Business at Risk or Business at Growth.

The sum total of Business at Risk and Business at Growth represents Return on Nothing—the amount of revenue that a company stands to lose by not providing customers with superior experiences. The RON Loyalty Model allows organizations to recognize the scope for potential revenue loss if they continue doing "business as usual" and fail to provide customers with experiences that excite and delight. Given how it affects an organization's top and bottom line, the full impact of RON can be enormous.

The RON Formula: Measuring the Potential Opportunity of Customer Loyalty

When measuring the financial consequences of "business as usual" or providing poor customer experiences, focus on those elements of the model most relevant to your situation. For example, if you don't have a referral program, calculating the number of referrals (and their associated value) is, of course, impossible. In this respect, the model is intended to provide organizations with an individualized framework for determining the scope of business that they would have otherwise generated, had they provided their customers with superior-quality experiences.

- **Preference** = Number of New Customers x Annual Customer Value X Change in Average Number of New Customers

- **Portion of Budget** = Number of Existing Customers x Entire Budget X Change in Portion of Budget Captured

- **Premium Pricing** = Number of Existing Customers x Average Annual Customer Value X Average Percent Change in Unit Price

- **Promotion** = Number of Referrals x Average Annual Referral Value X Average Percentage Change in Number of Referrals

- **Permanence** = Number of Customers x Average Annual Customer Value X (Current Customer Attrition Rate – Future Customer Attrition Rate)

Key Economics-of-Relationship Factors

The RON model allows you to apply the science of customer experience that top management seeks. Based on customer actions rather than on customer intent, the RON model is driven by economics-of-relationship factors, such as repeat purchases or referrals, that illustrate the success of any customer experience strategy or initiative. To employ the RON Loyalty Model, you must do some homework and identify the following financial drivers.

New customers: The average number of new customers per year

Annual customer value: The average value generated by a customer in a given year

Total annual customer budget: The total amount of money customers spend on a specific category (such as office products, entertainment, technology)

Current annual customer budget: The portion of a customer's total budget currently allocated to a specific category

Customer discount rate: The discounts you anticipate giving to customers each year (and over the lifetime of their relationships)

Customer referral rate: The number of customer-generated referrals per year (or the average number of referrals per customer)

Customer relationship longevity: The average length (number of years) of a customer relationship.

Average net price of goods and services: The price of all goods and services paid by customers.

Work with the owners of these numbers, particularly the finance department, to secure the figures you will use. This collaboration also assures that the finance department will later confirm that the numbers are credible.

In addition to the economics of relationship metrics, you must make certain assumptions to determine RON's impact. If company-specific historical data (for example, price erosion over a certain time period) is available, all the better. But you can also base assumptions on available industry standards (for example, customer attrition rates). These numbers can be found in industry studies, such as those conducted by Forrester Research.

Employing the RON Loyalty Model

Establish economic assumptions for each of the 5-P relationship factors. When doing so, consider running multiple scenarios, each with different assumptions (conservative to aggressive), to illustrate the impact of RON to different target executives.

Here's an example of RON at work: ABC Image In Color Corporation is a regional distributor of printers and toner to small and medium-sized businesses in the Kansas City area. The company services 2,000 customers who, on average, remain with the company for five years. By using the RON Loyalty Model, ABC Image In Color Corporation was able to calculate the potential cost of not implementing a customer experience strategy.

Additional facts:
- 200 new customers per year
- Cost of a printer: $400; cost per toner: $150
- On average, customers purchase 1.5 printers and 24 toner cartridges per year
- 50 customer referrals per year
- The average annual value of a customer relationship (including referrals) is $4,200
- The average customer spends a total of $5,440 on printers and toners.

Assumptions for losses on doing nothing:
- **Preference:** 15% decrease in the average number of new customers
- **Portion of Budget:** 5% decrease in customers' portion of budget for printers and cartridges spend with ABC Image in Color
- **Premium Pricing:** 5% decline in product prices
- **Promotion:** 20% decline in number of referrals
- **Permanence:** One-year decline in average customer lifetime relationship

Potential Return on Nothing:
- **Preference:** 200 * $4,200 * -15% = -$126,000

    o ABC Image In Color Corporation stands to lose $126,000 each year from a 15% decline in new customer preference.
- **Portion of Budget:** 2,000 * $5,440 * -5% = -$544,000

    o ABC Image In Color Corporation expects to lose $544,000 in revenue each year as its share of the customers' budget declines.
- **Premium Pricing:** 2,000 * $4,200 * -5% = $420,000

    o ABC Image In Color Corporation stands to lose $420,000 from a decline in its premium pricing each year.
- **Promotion:** 50 * $4,200 * -20% = $42,000

    o ABC Image In Color Corporation stands to lose $42,000 from a decline in referral or promotion revenue each year.
- **Permanence:** 2,000 * $4,200 * (20%-25%)= $420,000

    o ABC Image In Color Corporation stands to lose $420,000 from customers leaving after four years (rather than five years).

Total Losses:

ABC Image In Color Corporation faces losses totaling $1,552,000 from not providing superior experiences to its customers. This breaks down into $126,000 (Preference), $544,000 (Portion of Budget), $420,000 (Premium Pricing), $42,000 (Promotion) and $420,000 (Permanence). This translates into a 18.5% decline in annual revenue

Note that the proposed model doesn't incorporate any changes to consumer spending and product pricing as a result of the economy, general market trends or competitive dynamics. Each organization must to determine the impact of extraneous factors and apply them as they see fit. Additionally, the model is constructed so that individuals can extract those relevant components that will best illustrate the impact of customer experience transformation on their respective organizations.

Developing Financial-Decision Platforms

Once the cost of inaction is determined—and upper management sees the value in initiating and financing action—the methodology supplied by the 5 P's and the RON Loyalty Model now gives you a platform for determining which actions to take.

The English spoken in Bermuda has distinct differences from the English spoken in Scotland. Similarly, the language of numbers and metrics has different, sometimes indecipherable differences from silo to silo within an organization. Such differences aggravate the challenge facing customer experience practitioners as they work to create a shared sense of urgency across the organization, with the ultimate goal of motivating everyone to collaborate in creating a customer-centric culture. Unfortunately, this shared sense can't be developed when individuals within the organization can't translate how an improvement in customer satisfaction or loyalty scores will help them achieve *their* goals and earn *their* incentives. As an example, Zen Airlines has $1M to invest in new initiatives this year. The commitee that governs investment optimization for the airline is evaluating three potential investments:

- A direct-marketing investment that will increase the average response rate by 50 basis points, from .5% to 1%

- A call center initiative that will increase first-contact resolution from 85% to 90% while increasing average handling time by 1 second

- A customer experience initiative that will boost customer loyalty from 40% to 45%

Which investment should the committee select?

The language of finance enables direct marketers accustomed the language of response rates to speak with contact center executives who have been trained to speak the language of service levels and handling times. A distribution center head who speaks the language of cycle times and inventory turnover can communicate with a branding executive who speaks the language of brand equity. By translating each of the individual roles into a common language that focuses on profit and loss, investment and oppor- tunity, company executives can evaluate investment opportunities that, at first glance, have no common bond whatsoever to select the ones that will yield the greatest return to the stakeholders.

Just like all other executives, customer experience professionals must be able to communicate the value they bring to their organizations using the language of finance if they want their initiatives to have a chance of secur- ing the limited investment dollars that are necessary to transform their company's customer experience. Only by translating satisfaction and loyalty metrics into revenue increases and costs savings can customer experience professionals quantify the value they'll generate for the company through their proposed initiatives.

Customer-Centric Cost Units

To derive the greatest effectiveness out of the Economics of Customer Experience methodology, you must further understand and establish costs related specific to customers. Because so many companies believe that customer experience is "common sense" or "nice to have" in addition to their product-centric core, they are painfully unaware of the costs of product-centricity. Strativity Group's *Customer Experience Management Benchmark Study* reveals not only that most corporate executives continue to lack a basic understanding of the actual cost of their current customer experience, but also that even fewer now have this understanding than before:

- 89.3% don't know the cost of a customer complaint
  (up from 84.3% in 2008)

- 91.7% don't know the cost of total service issue resolution
  (up from 88.8%)

- 83.6% don't know their company's average annual customer value
  (up from 79.6%)

- 86.0% don't know the cost of a new customer (up from 84.9%)

Moreover, the costs associated with customer strategy investments are often unknown because they're spread across different departments. As such, organizations frequently make decisions outside the requisite context of the complete customer experience journey. Budget allocation results from political struggles and survival of the loudest, rather than from data-driven, customer-requirement decisions.

This ignorance of a company's customer-related costs is disconcerting but unsurprising since most companies calculate cost units at a functional level rather than a customer level. Take, for example, a metric that many contact centers use to manage their cost structure. This metric, the cost per call, treats each individual call as an isolated event. It factors in the time it takes an agent to handle the call and the per-minute cost of handling a call, based on salary, telecommunications costs, and overhead. To minimize the cost per call, a company can push agents to spend less time on the phone or simply pay them less. This makes sense when one is managing to a cost unit based on an individual call.

But this metric doesn't capture the true cost of servicing customers. A customer who is rushed off the phone or who is serviced by a low-paid (and likely less skilled) agent may find the issue unresolved, necessitating a second call, and additional cost to the company. This second call may not affect the cost-per-call metric in the least. Two calls took three minutes each. Per-call time is three minutes. But per-resolution time is six minutes.

Further, cost per call doesn't factor in the initial reason for the call, which often lies outside the call center. Reducing the cost per call doesn't eliminate the call forced by the corporate web site's lack of key functionality or by a confusing offer or an improperly filled order. As such, a company can employ a very efficient contact center while wasting an incredible amount of money taking calls that could be avoided through better company performance and better customer experiences.

In one of our client studies, the client reported that their cost per call was $3.15. When we probed about how calls were resolved, we learned about typical concessions made to satisfy customers. Factoring in those concessions, the per-call cost jumped to $410.

Or what does a new customer truly cost? For an example, returning to our friends at CoreCorp, let's say that this company employs a four-person sales team at a cost of $1 million per year. This sales team has a travel and entertainment budget of $200,000. Often, the sales team brings in senior executives to meet with prospective clients. The cost to bring these executives in, both in terms of travel costs and time that could be spent focusing on other initiatives, is $75,000 per year. Finally, it costs $100,000 each year to support this team when preparing proposals. The total cost of sales is therefore $1.375 million. Each team member brings in two or three new clients each month, or about 100 new clients from the team each year. As a result, new client acquisition costs CoreCorp $13,750 each. Given this high cost of acquisition, it's critical that this company creates an experience that recaptures the cost of acquisition by reducing attrition.

Companies can understand the cost benefits of a better customer experience only if they move from the functional cost unit of cost per isolated engagement (such as cost per call) to customer-centric cost units, such as cost per customer inquiry. The cost to service a customer inquiry factors in all aspects of the interaction with the customer, including: the cost of attempting to self-service via the web or Interactive Voice Response (IVR) and the total cost of all calls made by the customer to resolve the inquiry.

The key cost units from a customer's perspective are:
Cost per generated lead: These are the organization's marketing costs.
Cost per new customer: When factoring in the cost of sales, organizations must remember to factor in all costs related to sales, not simply the cost of the sales organization. For example, a business-to-business company that flies its CEO to close the deal with a major client must factor in the portion of the CEO's salary that's devoted to sales.
Cost per service inquiry: As demonstrated above, the cost per service inquiry should be based on solving a customer's issue, not on an individual call or email. Companies must estimate or track the cost to service across all customer channels.
Cost per complaint: A subset of service costs, the Cost per Complaint calculates the cost of a service inquiry resulting from an unsatisfactory customer experience. Unlike a normal service inquiry, such as placing an order or paying a bill, a complaint is an inquiry that's entirely avoidable through a

better customer experience. Investing in proper order fulfillment or promotions processing eliminates complaint resolution costs.

Cost to retain a customer: Retention costs should include any and all costs incurred to keep an existing customer, from the costs of the initiatives themselves to the costs of offers made—for instance, the difference between an at-risk customer accepting a discount versus a customer satisfied by an excellent customer experience purchasing the same item at full cost.

In a bit more detail, customer experience cost units fall into four general categories:

Promising the Value of Experience
- Cost of a new customer

  o Brand awareness

  o Leads generation

  o Sales visits

  o RFP response

  o Contract negotiation

Delivering the Experience Value
- Cost of training / full usage
- Cost per issue (call center, web, IVR)
- Cost of a complaint
- Cost of a dispute
- Cost of field service
- Cost of return
- Cost of invoicing
- Cost of legal issues
- Cost of collection
- Cost of special requests
- Cost of repair
- Cost of executive escalation

Communicating the Experience Value
- Cost of value visualization
- Cost of communication
- Cost of loyalty program

Growing the Experience Value
- Cost of retention
- Cost of referral
- Cost of upgrade
- Cost of cross sell

When thinking about these customer-centric cost units, consider the relationship between the cost units and investments in customer experience. We've found that companies that invest in their customer experience reduce their costs. Loyal customers:

- Tend to recommend companies more frequently, reducing the costs associated with lead generation and marketing
- Cost less to service
- Are less likely to complain, reducing the costs of complaints
- Attrite less frequently, reducing the cost of retention

As such, companies have a choice regarding their investments. They can invest in improving their customer experience, or they can increase the costs of lead generation, sales, service, complaint resolution and retention. Either way, investments must be made. Understanding the relationship between customer experience and the costs of running the business helps companies realize that customer loyalty is the more profitable investment.

Summing Up: Sharp Economic Focus

It's imperative that every customer experience initiative be built on the foundation of customer experience economics and not on "common sense" understanding. Organizations should shift toward measuring customer experience from two perspectives:

- **Return on Nothing:** Negative financial outcome as a result of not investing in customer experience. This should factor in both the Business at Risk (current business that will be loss due to a poor experience) and Business at Growth (potential business that is being left on the table due to the current experience)
- **Cost Units:** The cost of serving customers today vs. the future cost after customer experience initiatives are implemented

Using the language of revenue and expenses, any successful customer experience strategy must demonstrate the financial benefits that it will deliver because of customer experience transformation. Deploying the specific methodology I've outlined here helps you translate loyalty and satisfaction benefits into economic terms that will help companies approve transformative customer experience initiatives. Only by looking at a customer experience strategy through the lens of the economics of customer experience will organizations be able to place the topic of a customer experience strategy at the top of the corporate agenda, with the highest sense of urgency.

CHAPTER 4

Innovation of Customer Experience

Businesspeople often talk about "best practices" when designing systems, strategies and solutions. When it comes to innovating the customer experience, I offer but one best practice: Forget best practices—and remember memories.

Best practices are tried-and-true approaches and procedures, but because they're proven, they're also commoditized. The ultimate objective of customer experience management is differentiating your brand. How can you differentiate yourself when you operate in exactly the same way as everyone else out there who has attended the Best Practices 101 class while earning their MBA?

The challenge in innovating customer experience lies in creating the *"Next Practices."* A Next Practice has two characteristics:
- It's an innovative idea that no one else is employing.
- It's an innovative idea that no one else can easily copy and, in doing so, erode it back into being a non-differentiating best practice everyone else will be taking notes on in next semester's Commoditization 101 seminar.

The process of innovation for differentiation requires more than imagination and the old saw about "thinking outside the box." It involves reinventing the box, broadening its borders, and understanding exactly where your customers fit in relation to this new, more spacious box.

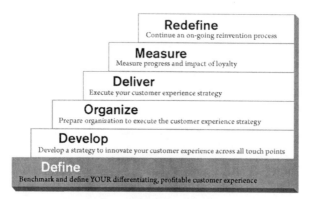

Redefine
Continue an on-going reinvention process

Measure
Measure progress and impact of loyalty

Deliver
Execute your customer experience strategy

Organize
Prepare organization to execute the customer experience strategy

Develop
Develop a strategy to innovate your customer experience across all touch points

Define
Benchmark and define YOUR differentiating, profitable customer experience

Strategic Steps: Define

Innovating customer experience centers around memories. What memory will consumers retain when they complete an interaction with you? What memories will influence the *next* interaction with you—if the memory is good enough to warrant another interaction?

Key elements of innovating customer experience include:
- Defending the core.
- The staying power of memory, and the power of emotion.
- Redefining the customer's complete problem.
- The elements of the total solution.

Let's explore each of these elements in greater detail.

Defending the Core

The evolution of customer experience starts from the very core of the experience you provide today. Your first goal is to defend that core. Defending the core means, on the one hand, living up to your basic promise. But in the context of innovation, it means far more: it means not creating distasteful memories, such as recollections of botched service, indifferent employees and unfulfilled promises.

Many companies are often so removed from even meeting customer expectations that exceeding them becomes wishful thinking at best and the impossible dream at worst. Over the past several years, multiple cost reductions and efficiency initiatives have forced companies to develop myriad processes that ultimately blocked their organizations and employees from being able to simply meet customer expectations. In reducing costs, companies reduced the overall value they provided to customers and dropped their performance below customer expectations. Companies declaring objectives to exceed expectations are often met with laughter by customers still struggling to get those same companies to deliver the basics.

A case in point case comes from a policy once employed by one of our consulting clients: customers were allowed to complain only within 21 days after an event. Customers trying to register their complaint after the official rant period were told, simply enough, "It's too late." Who knew that just like milk, human grievances expire after a short period of time?) The company assumed that they could reduce call center costs by eliminating all the "old" complaints. Yes, throw the rancid milk out, and your refrigerator is sparkling clean. Next customer, please . . .

Other companies have sought to reduce the number of incoming calls by limiting the number of lines to the call center. They must believe they're in the business of delivering busy signals.

Although the aspiration to exceed expectations is admirable, many customers will appreciate the simple art of meeting their expectations. Adding a little humanity and common sense to solving problems will go a long way to building their loyalty. I can understand that claiming "exceeding expectations" does sound a bit more inspirational and exciting as a new corporate mantra (much sexier than, say, "Let's Be Acceptable!"), but in the spirit of listening to customers and defending your core experience, you must start with doing just that. In the trade-off between inspirational and implantable, I choose the latter. Don't heighten customer expectations—and your own—only to fail to live up to them. That's a bigger crime than not meeting lower expectations.

Companies won't reach the level of "exceeding expectations" before they clean up the obstacles they created through restrictive procedures. The first order of business in meeting customers' expectations is identifying those conflicting procedures and getting them out of the way of excellent performance. This is the first and crucial plank on which you build the exceeded expectations. But lacking this foundation, you'll never reach the "exceeding" phase. You can't exceed expectations before you meet them.

In building your defense, ask yourself, *What types of complaints are customers making? What perceptions are they asking you to apply as part of your product and your experience? What is the nature of exceptions and escalations? What fixes and replacements are requested?* In other words, *What explains why customers don't do business with you?*

Review your employee manuals and operational procedures and ask yourself these simple questions:

- Are these the procedures of a customer-centric company?

- Were these procedures designed to protect and delight customers, or to protect and delight CEOs?

- Does it make sense to conduct business this way? Is it profitable?

- Were these procedures designed to address abusers or mainstream customers?

Answers to these questions should allow you to identify the opportunities to change processes and procedures and start designing the way you conduct business from the customers' perspective. If you believe that delighting customers will profit you, you'll soon realize that the customer perspective is your perspective, as well.

Meeting customer expectations is important but not sufficient. It is only the first step. To differentiate and to connect to customers who will stay longer with you, you can't base your initiatives only on rational satisfaction. You must elevate to emotional satisfaction. You must add value that will create a WOW factor. You must make delightful memories.

The Staying Power of Memory

It all begins with a memory. Think back on positive and negative brand engagements that you've personally experienced. How long have those memories stuck with you? If you're like typical customers, you hold memories of customer experiences for years—so you can see the need to shape your interactions with customers around their memories, and to shape new memories for them.

To truly be personalized, differentiating and memorable, each customer experience must be lasting, it must be profitable, and it must evoke emotions. Emotions fuel memories, and the most valuable customer takeaway from engaging with you is memory. The stronger the experience, the longer the memory will last. The ultimate litmus test of any individual experience is whether you're creating ten seconds of short-term memory or ten years of memorable reflection.

To design customer experience for the longest possible memory, you must understand the customers' real problem and the emotions associated with the problem, and then you must apply your learnings.

Innovation, then, begins as a matter of asking yourself, "What emotions are we evoking today, and what emotions do we want to evoke?"

As an example, a customer told a software company I work with, "Your product is too robust." That wasn't a complaint—merely a comment. The company's natural reaction was, "We're delivering a lot of benefit. The product is robust." And that reaction was ignoring emotion.

I said, "Step back and look at this from the customers' standpoint. "They're not praising all the features they're getting. They're telling you the product is too complex and that they can't operate it. They're telling you that you're making them feel stupid by giving them something they can't figure out." As I told this customer, "When you show off all the features in an impressive PowerPoint, each time you click to a slide, you're announcing, 'You're stupid.' *Click.* 'You're stupid.' *Click.* 'You're really stupid.' *Click.* 'Now you're stupid stupid. You can't do any of this and we're smarter than all of you put together.'"

Focus on emotions. When you say, "No, our policy doesn't allow you to do that," you evoke a negative emotion. Work with emotions, and manage for them. Everything you do evokes emotions.

Redefining the Customer's Complete Problem

When looking to create emotional engagement, when looking to exceed expectations, you must reframe the value proposition to include what really matters to the customer. As the old saying goes, customers don't need drills; they need quarter-inch holes. What else do customers need to complete the solution? Maybe they need quarter-inch holes beyond the stretch of a power cord. Thus, the portable electric drill.

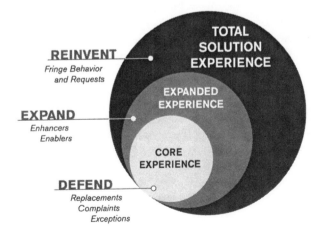

A classic example of redefining the complete problem and defining a complete value proposition comes in the form of the grand success story of Apple iTunes and the iPod. Apple didn't invent MP3 players, and they didn't simply release another MP3 player. They solved a problem. They asked, *What do people want from the music experience?* In this case, people wanted a simple, legal way to get music they enjoy.

On the other hand, other manufacturers viewed their core experience as being in the MP3 player business. To them, music download sources and the legalities associated with them were all someone else's concern. Along came Apple, who said in essence, "We're in the experience business. And the MP3 player is just a vehicle to achieve something else."

Just like most of the rest of the world, Apple didn't have core competence in legal music distribution, nor in music downloads. They knew they would have to search out capabilities, resources, knowledge—and, in fact, Apple was the first to negotiate legal downloads within the music industry. Because all this was outside their core competence, Apple was forced to invest in the key elements of the problem-solution.

Apple made this move even though they knew they would themselves run into legal problems. Apple computers, in settling a trademark suit from the powerful Beatles' record label—Apple Records—had agreed to stay out of the music business. And I don't know this for a fact, but I can almost guarantee you that within Apple, lawyers were expressing nervousness about moving into the various legal territories that iPod was about to venture into. But for the good of the customer experience and the good of the company, they bravely moved forward.

Was it worth it? Billions of song downloads would say, "Yes."

By being willing to expand beyond their core experience of device development, Apple seized opportunity. By taking on extra work and developing new capabilities, they redefined themselves from a product company that happened to dabble in customer experience to a customer experience company that happened to sell products.

Apple's expansion and switch in focus in the form of the iPod involves answering the question, "What else do customers need to complete the solution?", which goes back to a more basic question: "Are we defining the customer experience question correctly?"

A number of innovation elements are at work in the iPod story, elements that lay the groundwork for fresh, expanded customer experience thinking:

Enhancement. *Enhancers* are products or services that complement or individualize the core experience. An excellent example of an enhancer leading to Expanded Experience can be found in specially marked boxes of Special K. In 2000, Kellogg's was facing a number of business challenges that led to slipping behind competitor General Mills in market share—by less than 1%. They decided that if they couldn't be number-one in the world in dollar sales, they could be number-one in volume. As in the contents of a box. Kellogg's responded by offering more of their core experience in every box—50% more cereal without raising prices. They regained the number-one position in terms of amount of cereal sold. Welcome back, bragging rights! The problem, of course, is that delivering more per box meant fewer boxes sold, and the move ultimately eroded profits. In essence, this strategy said to customers, "You don't want my product? Well, OK, then—here's 50% more."

To correct this situation in the light of what customers really need, Kellogg's turned to core experience enhancement. Knowing that customers often topped their breakfast cereal with fruit, they introduced new flavors such as Special K Red Berries, enhancing the customer experience, providing customer solutions to the bother of buying and adding extra fruit, and pumping net income by 52% in 2002.

Enablement. *Enablers are* products or services that make the core experience even more valuable. In the Apple story, the iPod provides the physical delivery of the core musical experience, while iTunes enables the experience by providing a centralized source of a broad range of legal music downloads.

Reinvention. *Reinvention* exploits unexpected, even strange uses of your products. We call these uses "fringe behavior."

When Virgin Mobile entered the U.S. wireless arena, they faced a mature market filled with strong, established competitors. With little name and brand recognition, they knew they couldn't gain a significant foothold on the general marketplace. So Virgin started by segmenting based on age and lifestyle: unmarried 15- to 25-year-olds. The first step was to provide function (the phone and the service) with a modern, cool image. They offered this with no strings attached—no contracts meant independence to a youthful audience craving freedom. But Virgin Mobile didn't stop there.

When Virgin studied phone use among people in this segment, they noticed an interesting phenomenon. Young people going on blind dates would ask a friend to call their cell phone at a predetermined time after the date started. The young paramour would answer, and either chat briefly if the date was going well, or, if a quick escape was in order, blurt something like "Grandma's in the hospital?!"

Virgin Mobile decided to operationalize this fringe behavior. Their first line of cell phones featured a blind date button. If the young paramour decided that the date isn't worth it, he or she discreetly pressed the button. The phone rang, the paramour answered, pretended to talk to someone, and, drat the luck, Grandma's in the hospital again.

Look to your customer touch points for other such clues. Does your call center, for instance, field any unusual requests or questions about how your product can be used?

Extension. *Extenders* are your products that others use to complete their experience. Is your product used to extend or amplify other products? Is it an ingredient in someone else's total experience?—a literal ingredient in this example, once again from the cereal world: The makers of Chex cereals noticed that people were creating snack mixes using pretzels and peanuts and cereals as the primary ingredients. In the 1950s, Chex began promoting a recipe for such a mix using their cereal, and finally developed a separate project—prepackaged Chex Mix—which they began selling in the mid '80s. And now you can get prepared s'mores without having to stage a Girl Scout camping outing, and premixed cocktails without having to hire a bartender. Extension, then, is an offshoot of fringe behavior.

Elements of the Total Solution

Transforming products and services into emotionally satisfying memories requires that the experiences be:
- Personalized
- Expressive
- Authentic
- Relevant
- Customized
- Timely
- Shared
- Lasting
- Clear and conversational
- Valuable before the sale
- Valuable after the sale
- Clearly, visibly valuable
- Emotionally engaging
- Unexpected
- Profitable

When designing a customer experience to address specific touch points, customer segments, or complaints, don't simply fix problems and stream-line processes. Instead, weave as many of these elements into the experience. Map the design of your experiences against this checklist.

Let's examine each item in a bit more detail.

Personalized. Treat the customer as a unique individual. Are you speaking to the "all" in "one-size-fits-all," or are you speaking to specific customers? Don't make the mistake of companies that believe that addressing an email by the customer's first name amounts to personalization. This faint attempt at one-to-one has been around for centuries in internet time. Customers are numb to such commoditized personalization.

Expressive. Create experiences that allow and encourage customers to express themselves. iPod users define themselves not by the device, but by the song list the device holds. It's a digital vault containing songs and memories that the users love.

Authentic. Be real and genuine. The larger your company, the smaller your customers feel. You must make them feel that they matter and that you recognize them. They must see that your company has a human side, which elevates the importance of your associates and their personal cus-tomer interactions. You must humanize the relationships as much as—yes—humanly possible.

Relevant. Design the experiences to relate directly to the customers' needs and desires. Make it relevant to their lives. Virgin Mobile's blind date button touches the personal needs of consumers on a broad scale.

Customized. Tailor the experience to the situation as well as to the cus-tomer. When we talk about customized service, we're ultimately talking about flexibility in processes that allows your employees to customize.

For example, let's say a credit card customer calls the company and asks that his $75 annual fee be waived. The traditional process dictates the an-swer: "No. If we charge the fee, it's likely because we don't want to waive the fee. How else can we help you today?"

In a customer experience environment, the employee opens up the cus-tomer record and views his transactions. If the customer is spending $200 a year, the employee politely explains that waiving the fee isn't possible because that would make the customer unprofitable. But if he's spending $1,000 a month, then the profit is there, and waiving the fee to preserve and perhaps increase that level of spend makes sense. If the customer's transactions are somewhere in between, perhaps the employee can propose a compromise and drop the annual fee to $50. Or perhaps the agent asks about overall use and share of wallet. If your card is the customer's third choice, perhaps the agent can recommend transferring spend to your card, and subsequently waive the fee. In four scenarios, the agent said "No" once and a customized "Yes, with conditions" three times.

You must create an environment where you can treat different customers differently.

Timely. Be fast. The days of customers accepting the concept of "gourmet slow/McDonald's fast" are gone. Customers now expect faster and better.

As an example of innovation in timeliness, the fashion industry traditionally rolls out new lines in two seasons for rolling out new lines: Spring and Fall. Every 26 weeks. Then along came Zara, a fashion company that introduces new lines every *eight* weeks. The time from Zara identifying a new trend to a new shirt arriving in the store is four weeks. This, while producing 20,000 items a year. Such vigorous activity would seem cost-intensive, but Zara maximizes revenues by responding to needs and trends much faster than the competition. Their speed to market and immediate reaction to trends allows them to command better pricing. While the industry normally discounts and ultimately receives 60% of list price, Zara holds that figure to 80%. Believe it or not, some customers pay retail, even today, and fewer discounts help pay for Zara's speed and customization.

Time is critical because of a significant number of factors, among them today's higher customer expectations and less patience, the need to match competitive offers, wider windows of opportunity, and the need to shorten development cycles to lower costs and get items to market faster. The life span of products and services is increasingly shrinking, limiting the period of time in which these products and services can drive revenue and profit. The proliferation of private-label alternatives, web retailers, and shorter product release cycles only accelerates the commoditization of products and services.

Timeliness is not merely an experiential element. It is a product unto itself. Consider FedEx. They appear to be in the business of Delivery, when in reality they're in the business of Time. People are willing to pay for timeliness. In your business, guaranteeing to answer any call within 30 seconds can perhaps be a premium service separate from the basic customer service, and can provide a service model worth testing within your industry.

Shared. Facilitate customer communications. We live in a world where people share—photos, videos, recommendations, experiences, complaints. Allow your customers to share within the context of your brand, be it online customer communities or other web 2.0 tools. Stop trying to protect the flow of information about your brand. Find ways to encourage recommendations. For those who use Net Promoter Score and its gauge of Willingness to Promote, here's an interesting question: If they're willing to promote, why aren't they promoting? To put it bluntly, "If you're willing to promote, give me the referrals."

Provide a platform that encourages customer sharing, not only with each other but also with you. This leads to an important concept of "co-creation"—customers working in tandem with their brands to create their own experiences—which I explore in more detail in Chapter 5, "Customer Experience in the Virtual World."

Part of that sharing is in sharing ideas, and part in sharing complaints and dissatisfaction. Welcome complaints. As I discuss in Chapter 11, "Deliver the Experience," complaints are one of the many currencies of opportunity.

Lasting. Give the experience a life past the actual interaction. The stronger the experience, the greater the level of surprise and delight, the longer a positive memory will last—there to be recalled when making future purchase decisions, or when making recommendations to other customers.

Clear and conversational. Speak using clear language. When you write a document, do you ever ask yourself what memories you're going to evoke? Language is a matter of control, time, trust, respect and clarity.

- *Control:* How many of you understand the terms and conditions of your credit cards? Ask your employees to read your terms and conditions or any other document with similar legal and/or informative purpose, then ask how they feel about what they read. Don't be surprised when they say, "I feel stupid. I went to school but I don't know what this means. I don't understand who's doing what to whom."

- *Time.* If your reps are reading terms and conditions over the phone, I'd like to know how many customers put them on mute and go to the bathroom during the reading. In other words, don't waste customers time with overblown, unintelligible wording.

- *Trust.* Imagine how terms and conditions can be a means of differentiating your company, presenting simplified, everyday language in clear, readable fonts and layouts. Now you're bringing in authenticity, and customers won't be suspicious. If you communicate this philosophy—"You the customer are in charge and we're going deliver on what we promise you, with no loopholes"—customers will trust you.

- *Respect.* The opportunity to instill everyday language into your customer communications goes beyond targeting legalese and ostentatious thesaurus-speak. Puffed-up wording that crops up in a variety of ways signals imprecision, waffling and lack of assuredness. If you use wording such as "by reason of" or "inasmuch as" instead of "because," or "in the event of" instead of "if," you communicate that either you feel you're above your customers, or that you're hiding behind a fog of wordiness. For this point, I'll let the customer address you directly: "Speak to me in a language I understand. Don't belittle me. I'm your customer. Don't make me feel stupid, foolish, helpless or gullible."

- *Clarity.* At the very least, give customers a clue about what you're talking about. People in technology, for instance, *love* to use jargon. They use acronyms ATT (All The Time). Step into any IT meeting and you'll find boxes, arrows, clouds and acronyms. There's never a customer there. Next time you encounter some jargon customers won't be able to decipher in a meeting or in a written document—especially a customer document—turn to the speaker or writer and say, "OSFA." Standing for "One Size Fits All," That's *my* acronym, which I made up to fit in with my clients who use acronyms so frequently.

These principles become particularly important when creating communications that a third party will deliver to customers. Be certain to use language that the middlemen can themselves easily understand so they can efficiently and clearly deliver the information.

Rewrite. Revise. Translate. One language does not fit all. Watch your jargon, terms, and word complexity. In other words, know your audience. You can make the same precise points that speak in a straightforward, clear, comfortable language that honors customers as individuals, instead of belittling them as the masses. Differentiate yourself as the company that speaks directly and honestly. The way we speak and write represents emotions and memories. In this culture of mediocrity, what an opportunity you have.

An example of a company taking that opportunity is English financial firm Abbey National. I was surprised to see this statement in a press release, published in the *Financial Times*, from Luqman Arnold, then Abbey's CEO: "Banks have managed to make money scary, confusing and boring. In talking to customers, we have all been guilty of being patronizing and overbearing. Most of all banks have got in the way of customers and their money." What kind of guts do you need to say this *and* know it will appear in the *Financial Times*? Basically, Abbey was saying that the bank took customers for granted and that they were transforming themselves and, in doing so, they changed the language they use. "We never forget whose money it is, yours," the release said. And the bank was willing to back up this transformation not only through new language, but also with a new advertising campaign, 60,000 extra training days a year for employees, and 600 extra people to service customers directly.

Valuable before the sale. Add value, and then sell. In fact, add value *instead* of selling. Don't try to convince someone to buy something they don't want. You can educate customers; you can inspire them; but don't sell them. If you deliver great customer experiences, you shouldn't have to engage in selling in the first place, because customers will already understand your offer naturally, and the education you deliver will create an attractive positive customer experiences now and forecast additional positive customer experiences should the customer come to you. And in today's culture, selling implies that you're trying to force people to do something they don't want to do naturally. This small but powerful difference implies that your salesperson has no right to meet a potential customer with nothing of value to share. You must teach customers something new, show them something wow that they want to have. Educate customers about your offer and let them make their own decision.

Valuable after the sale. In customer experience, the sale is never over. Add value after you sell, and never reduce value. The smartest companies are applying post-sale value straight into their pricing. They factor in the service as they need to. As long as the customer is using your product, you don't want them to be dissatisfied. That's unacceptable. Either satisfy them, or let them go.

Clearly, visibly valuable. Ensure that customers are fully aware of the value of the experience. Communicate value during the experience itself, but also take opportunity to remind them of your value after the experience and throughout the relationship. Help them visualize value by, for instance, presenting scorecards demonstrating your promised delivery vs. your actual better-than-promised delivery. Take a cue from the Kroger grocery chain and point out specific savings. When you shop Kroger, both the cashier and the printed receipt remind you, "You saved $12.97 using your *Kroger Plus Shopper's Card* today."

Emotionally engaging. Evoke and engage emotions. People don't remember functions. They remember emotional responses. For instance, here's a small but effective moment of emotional engagement that too many companies overlook. Listen for a cue that you should pay attention to—in retail stores, in sales, or in the call center. Customers often will make a reference to family, a vacation, a problem at work. Note how your employees respond to such references. I'll wager that 90% of those references are completely ignored. The customer is feeling, "I opened up to you—I just talked to you about my family, and you just ignored it. I tried to build a connection, and you just ignored it." How many times do your employees use the customer's name? How many times have they mentioned, "Thank you for being a customer since 1997"? "I see that you signed up for our program a year ago. We're celebrating that. Thank you."

There are many things organizations can do on a small but very personal level, and so often they don't even bother. The information is in front of you. Have you ever received a birthday card from your preferred vendor? Or even an acknowledgment of your birthday? What would happen if you were to close this book and say to your spouse, "Honey, remind me when your birthday is again"? How long do you think that relationship is going to last? Send a card, an email, an SMS to customers. Celebrating birthdays, anniversaries, business milestones—it's all quite simple.

Unexpected. Be innovative in the areas in which you innovate. I'm amazed how people chasing the same customer experience issues, in an innovative frame of mind, still end up with the same undifferentiated solutions, created within typical customer experience arenas. They innovate the what and the who and the how—products and personal interactions and processes. How about innovating the where?

Let me rephrase the question: Is your toilet a source of differentiation?

At the Banyan Tree Spa in Sao Paolo, Brazil, I was treated to a massage (highly recommended—indulge yourself). As in the typical spa experience, I was lying face down, staring at the floor. The Banyan Tree Spa decided that this is an opportunity for customer delight, and placed a flower arrangement on the floor. Pleasant—and differentiating. Thinking about guests staring at the floor as an opportunity demonstrates how far the spa searched to inno-vate the experience in the most unusual ways. The spa staff also insisted on turning the shower for me (I'm fully capable of doing it myself) and offered disposable underwear to the self-conscious customers. This is reminiscent of how Virgin Atlantic Airways flight attendants deliver requested blankets to their passengers. They don't simply hand you the blanket. They open it up and cover you. Expensive? Not at all. Small touches can go a long way not only in delighting customers but also in creating true differentiation.

When innovating your customer experience, think place. Think about loca-tions and other elements no one considers intuitively. Look for the unusual places and surprise your customers. Do not follow the common path, even if the path you follow instead leads you to the toilet—and to customer sur-prise and delight.

Profitable. Be certain the experience is making you money.
Well, of course.

The Checklist at Work

Let's take a look at two examples of how companies have innovated customer experience using some of the principles in our checklist.

Commerce Bank dispels the myth that you can't innovate in a mature market. Banking is perhaps the second-oldest profession—it doesn't get much more mature than that. Commerce Bank redesigned their experience top to bottom, beginning with how they defined themselves. They declared that they aren't a bank. They are a retail store. That's *unexpected,* and a case of being *clear and conversational.*

And how do you act like a retail store? For one, you open at 7:30 a.m. and close at 8 p.m., seven days a week. That's being *relevant* to customers' lives. Plus, the branches always open 10 minutes early and close 10 minutes late. I'm sure it's happened to you—you get there just after the location closes, and you begin that game of charades, gesturing trying to get the attention of someone inside. Commerce Bank set the expectations, then exceeded them by a mere 10 minutes on each side. More than that, and the customers blame themselves if they arrive after the location has closed.

Commerce Bank has also built a reputation on something unusual—lollipops. They give out a lollipop every time someone comes in—11 million lollipops a year. They serve doggy treats if you want to bring your dog in with you. That's being *personalized* and *authentic* (and, one could argue, *lasting,* depending on how long the lollipops last).

Where other banks have eliminated coin-counting machines because they make noise in what typically is an atmosphere of library-quiet, Commerce put one in the center of the lobby in each location, and stages coin-counting competitions every Sunday. That's a *shared* and *emotionally engaging* experience, one that delivers customer *value before the sale* (the sale being defined as depositing the amount the machines counted, which totaled $71.7 million in additional deposits in one year). And counted change, supplied as a free service, is *clearly, visibly valuable.*

Commerce placed a heavy focus on education programs, delivering *value before the sale* and *value after the sale.* And they placed phones on their ATMs, once again delivering potential *emotional engagement* should the ATM self-service customer feel the need to speak to a human being.

How can the bank afford to do all these expensive perks? If you want the best savings deposit interest rates, don't go to Commerce Bank. They tell customers that directly, saying, in essence, "We love you, but at a cost. We don't charge you up front, but we build the payment into those lower savings rates."

The lesson here is the power of even small things. Ten minutes here and there. And Commerce Bank isn't doing all this for fun. They're doing it to be very competitive, as evidenced by the $5,000 bonus employees receive if a competitor closes a branch within a certain distance from a Commerce Bank branch.

Harrah's Entertainment— a $9.7 billion gambling conglomerate with 73,000 slot machines in three countries —provides another example. Harrah's is a leader in the practice of loyalty marketing, having created the *Total Rewards* program to allow guests to accrue points for free services based on spending. But Harrah's then leveraged the *Total Rewards* program and the information it gathered to innovate their customer experience. For example, Harrah's knows immediately when high rollers begin to play in the casino, because the customers have identified themselves by using their *Total Rewards* card while gaming. A floor manager immediately locates high-value customers to issue personal welcomes. That's *personalized* and *emotionally engaging.*

Utilizing a sophisticated business analytics system, Harrah's calculates the spending of guests to ensure they don't go over their "comfort level." If the system detects a losing streak and overspending on video slots, for instance, the casino can display screen messages like "You win—a free dinner at the hotel, if you claim it in the next 15 minutes." They're giving customers a choice—they aren't sending the security people to drag them away for their own good. They're doing it gently.

Again, this is *relevant* and *emotionally engaging.* Harrah's is also managing memories. Instead of customers walking away remembering big losses and blaming the casino for them, they walk away with memories of special treatment and personalized care.

In this situation, the answer to the customer's problem was not functional, nor was it necessarily intuitive. Such a problem is not a case of "The invoice is wrong—fix it." This is an example of turning an emotionally negative customer situation into a positive memory and a loyalty-building opportunity.

This example also illustrates another important factor in creating and executing delightful customer engagements: Customer experience doesn't necessarily produce immediate return. At some point you're going to face this moment of truth: Do you choose to lose short-term gain for the promise of long-term relationships and greater profits? Do you make money or make memories? If you chose the latter, then you will make both.

Memories in the Making

In the process of design—whether for the whole experience or for individual touch points—your first question, and your *driving* question, is,

"What is the memory?" Because the memory lies at the core of innovation, the memory should define innovation. And you cannot leave those impressions to chance, launching experiences and then letting them play out in order to define the memory. You must define the target memory and work back to innovate the experience that will deliver that specific memory.

Use the following exercise to map experience innovation at every touch point. In building this map, use the chart below as a guide. These elements will give you the cornerstones for designing a disciplined process, and for covering all necessary components of experience design.

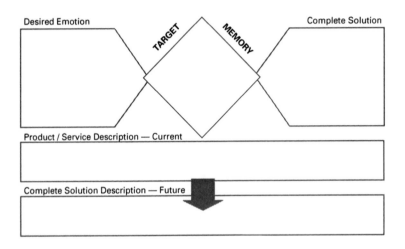

1. Define the target memory. Of course, the target memory varies from company to company. Iberia will have a different target memory from budget carrier Ryanair. If the memories you target resemble the memories generated by your competitors, the design has missed its goals. Employ emotions to define this memory. Approach the target memory for your company in this way: Imagine that you have solved a problem, made a sale, landed a new customer, answered a question. Now, imagine that the customer writes a thank-you letter. What will that letter speak to? What has impressed the customer so much that he holds a memory and is inspired to thank you? The greater the memory you envision and build to, the stronger your overall design will be. Record this in the top center of your map. Insert pictures and words that describe the products and services you currently provide.

2. Describe the emotions you want to evoke. What do you want the customer to feel at the end of the individual experience with you? With Ryanair, the emotion is happiness for getting a deal. It's all about sense of value, saving money and getting a deal that no one else got. Finding that deal is part of the adventure. Record the target emotions for your customers in the top left of your map.

3. Define the problem that you are solving, from two perspectives:

- What is the commodity problem or goal? In the case of our Apple example, listening to music on an MP3 player was the commodity.

- What is the total experience problem or goal? In other words, what problems are you really solving? What business are you really in? The answer that defined the total experience in Apple's case was convenient access to legal digital music. Record your solution on the top right.

4. Distinguish the solutions:

- *Commodity Solution:* For Apple, this possible solution was designing another MP3 player. What is your Commodity Solution?

- *Total Experience Solution:* For Apple, the selected solution was weaving legality, ease of download, and playability into something much bigger. What is your Total Experience Solution? What items will be in your complete solution? What characteristics? After this examination, if the solutions sound similar to the list of the products and services you already have, you didn't ask the right question. Many companies typically make this mistake.

5. Document what you're doing now from a commodity standpoint. Record this in the second row of the map. Estimate the gap between the current solution and the total experience solution you have defined. If today you are solving only 10%, 20%, 50% of the problem, you're not delivering customer experience. Here's an example of visualizing how you might estimate the gap. Suppose a customer is throwing a party, and has a checklist of 43 preparation tasks, from creating the guest list to sending invitations to baking a cake to cleaning the house to welcoming the guests with a smile and having fun. If you were a supplier of party paraphernalia and solutions, you could estimate your service cap on such factors as:

- You sell the cake ingredients. You're delivering a commodity, providing 10% of the solution and leaving the customer feeling overwhelmed with 42 other tasks.

- You sell a ready-made cake. You're delivering a service, providing 15% of the solution and leaving the customer feeling stressed.

- You sell the pre-made cake and all the party theme items. You're delivering enhanced service, providing 30% of the solution, and leaving the customer feeling busy.

- You sell a complete party setup, start to finish. You're delivering total experience, providing 90% of the solution, and leaving the customer feeling relieved. There's that smile—and there's your profit, based on what you can charge for the complete solution vs. piecemeal contributions.

6. Redefine the problem. How much of the customer problem do you want to solve? What would you add to achieve the future solution? Include in your evaluation services and capabilities that you don't have today. To obtain those services and capabilities, you might acquire them or outsource them. Identify what you currently lack to execute each step:

- **Products.** List missing features, complementary services, unique requests, and so on. What do your current products lack that's necessary to deliver the total experience solution?

- **Procedures.** What processes must be changed? What obstacles stand between your current situation and the ability to deliver the total experience solution? What conflicts must be removed to assure employees' ability to deliver? What's holding employees back?—which is a question answered in greater detail in Chapter 8, "Employee Experience."

- **People.** Is your incentive and recognition consistent with your targeted customer experience? If you pay people based on productivity, they give you productivity—even if it is stupid productivity that isn't based on quality.

   - *Education*—How much do your employees know about how to deliver experience? Do you create the service guidelines that allow them to deliver great experiences? Did you ever spec an experience?

   - *Evaluation*—Do you base evaluations on delivering customer experience or on interaction skills? Just showing empathy on the phone isn't sufficient. Are you rewarding employees on WOW or on OK?

- **Paper.** Do you deliver information clearly and conversationally? Do you detail your service in confirmations and billings to allow customers to visualize your value? Do you engage in continuing communications, such as sales or service follow-up, and, if necessary, apologies and explanations? And as we've discussed, do your communications employ simple, attractive and easy-to-understand language?

At this point, describe the solution as a narrative. Write it like a story, visualizing the ideal engagement. The customer comes to you with a problem—write what you do to solve the problem, and how the customer feels when he or she comes away from the engagement. Identify:

- How the customer will approach you.

- The reason for the customer's approach.

- How you will greet the customer.

- How you will probe to better understand the customer's needs.

- The options you will make available to the customer touch point.

- The freedom and empowerment you make available to the customer touch point.

- How the engagement concludes. This approach allows you to establish the detail that leads to a complete specification of the experience, designing the total experience solution step-by-step.

A Word About Six Sigma

In designing and redesigning processes, many companies today continue to turn to Six Sigma, a management strategy that relates quality of input to quality of output. The goal is to eliminate "defects" in a system that could lead to customer dissatisfaction. As in the customer experience mapping process I describe above, Six Sigma uses a clear set of steps and practices to achieve results. I recognize that you will encounter Six Sigma, and perhaps people within your company will try to apply Six Sigma to solving customer complaints. But I must warn you—don't be tempted to apply Six Sigma to customer experience solutions. It won't work.

Six Sigma is based on two assumptions:
1. You have high predictability of input
2. You have high predictability of output
With such predictability, you can designate an outcome and design a process that creates the outcome.

In the customer business, these two assumptions will work very well . . . if you eliminate the customer. You have low predictability of who will call next, who will write you next, who will come into your retail store. You can't predict their state of mind, their emotions, their memories. You can't predict their desired outcome. Therefore, trying to apply Six Sigma to customer experience means imposing a mindset of one-size-fits all.

The number-one question to ask any Six Sigma Black Belt (the name for an expert in the process) is "How do you handle exceptions?" Once when I asked this, the Black Belt responded, "We eliminate them." The problem is that customers are exceptions, and the number of exceptions they bring up is growing, because each customer wants to be treated individually. Reduce customers to parity and, perhaps to the satisfaction of a Black Belt somewhere, you eliminate them.

Six Sigma is effective for eliminating dissatisfiers, addressing customer complaints, creating uniform processes, addressing touch points that aren't designed to delight and surprise, and treating different customers in uniformly. Six Sigma was designed for repetitious manufacturing processes and not highly unpredictable human-based processes. Six Sigma is less effective when addressing complexity and diverse resolutions, dealing with human behavior issues, creating new ideas, innovating the experience beyond parity, and treating different customers differently

If you seek to engage customers in emotional, experiential, personalized ways, you must provide flexibility to those serving the customer. You must become the very exception that Six Sigma seeks to eliminate. In Six Sigma, the process is the end goal. In customer experience management, the customer is the end goal, and the process only a means to the goal. If the process works, use the process. If the process doesn't work, use your brain. Right now the corporate world is hammering employees with the message: "Don't think. Follow the process. If the customer doesn't fit the process, that's the customer's problem, not ours."

Embrace diversity. Six Sigma seeks to minimize diversity. The problem is that diversity and exceptions will come back in the form of complaints, escalation and other types of exceptions. And the problems aren't going to go away unless the customer goes away.

Memories at Every Touch Point

Strategic Steps: Develop

Customer memory of interactions with your organization is built on the whole of the experience, the sum total of purchase engagement, inquiry response, problem resolution and even receipt of invoices. All touch points must work together—and yet, they must avoid complete consistency of experience in order to truly work together. Just as teams need players with different talents and roles, touch points must deliver experiences specific to their function. You must build an overall memory for your customers while still understanding that customer expectations are different at different touch points. When you get to the level of sophistication that you can start differentiating between the different touch points, you will have built a powerful vehicle for surprising and delighting customers as they encounter your various silos.

Touch point experience is a large topic, from its innovation as discussed here to building buy-in from the stakeholders at each touch point to designing and executing metrics that build a common financial language that unifies silos and functions. We explore this continuing strategy, critical to building the overarching customer experience and contributing to the success of customer experience management, in detail throughout this book. For the moment, consider these starter thoughts for innovating experience at specific customer touch points:

Sales. Sales is about delighting and solving. It is not about selling. Everybody likes to buy, but they don't like being sold. Redesign the sales process to make sure customers don't leave their experience feeling that something was taken away from them, but instead that they were being delighted by something being given to them. Be ready with all relevant information for any customer. Offer choices, and let customers, not you, choose the appropriate solution. Listen actively and ask questions to ensure solution compatibility.

Marketing. When marketing your brand, never stop personalizing. The technology available today for personalization is both powerful and useful. Customers want you to speak to them, and not to one-size-fits-all. Use information such as consumer demographics and purchasing patterns to add value and knowledge. Speak to customers via their preferred channel and encourage customer response through multiple channels. Inform customers about geographically close store locations, contact details, hours of operations, etc., and speak to them as you would to someone you know.

Customer service. Acknowledge time sensitivities—reps must resolve customer challenges yesterday, not today. Educate your employees with financial data, skills, common sense, sensitivity and role-playing. Redesign complaint and exceptions resolution processes. Put customers in the driver's seat by providing alternatives. Recognize customers both by name and by transaction history. Keep customers informed—communicate anticipated delays and time frames for resolution. And thank customers for their business with specific mention of the duration of the relationship.

Also, be aware of an important trend that customer service must prepare for in this self-service world. When someone uses your web site for self-service, and then calls the customer-service center, why are they calling? They have a problem. By sending your customer to self-service, you have just outsourced Tier One. When they call you, it's an automatic escalation. This makes it even more imperative that you have employees who can break the rules, not repeat them.

You must be prepared with two elements: People who can solve my problems and solve exceptional issues, and people who can deliver exceptional service. It's a design completely different from how customer service is defined today.

Finance and Billing. Treat the customer with respect, and communicate with clarity. For instance, look at your invoice. Do employees understand what the invoice says? Just what are the inherent messages and the emphasis of the invoice? Does the invoice celebrate your customer's patronage? Or does the invoice say, "Pay up, buster." Do you help the customer see the value in what they received and are now paying for? Does the invoice instill a sense of control or value, or does it only dun them for money, and send it along as fast as possible, please? Where does the name of the customer appear? Are you trying to make this communication experiential? Because it is, after all, a moment of truth.

Picture a customer subscribing to a service like Vonage, which charges $29.95 for unlimited usage that otherwise would have been billed minute-by-minute. What would usage in a given month total? Without detailing per-minute costs customers don't have to pay, those customers don't necessarily know if they got a good deal. Maybe they think they overpaid at $29.95 while racking up 700 minutes, and won't realize otherwise until you allow him to see your value.

Retail. We live in a multichannel world. Customers often shop at the retail location, and then buy from the web. Sometimes they shop the web but place a phone order. Because of this, you can't pressure retail to concentrate only on consummating actual purchases. The retail experience legitimately is only a showcase, leading to deals completed by the call center.

When customers step into a bricks-and-mortar location, they're looking for theatre. They want a show. They want direct experience with products and people, experience they can't get on the phone or on the web. Your frontline people are actors in retail. On this retail stage you can present demonstrations, product trials, and celebrations. Product launches become local events. Do you have customers who drop by the store regularly just to play with the products? Embrace them. Turn them into evangelists who can showcase your products to other customers. Make them part of the show.

Legal. I'll cover this in detail elsewhere in this book but my advice for this often-overlooked customer touch point is to make certain that you have a target memory that makes customers feel that you are protecting them, and not just you. The worst memory you can leave with customers is the memory after they've gotten off the phone with their lawyer because they needed someone to translate what you're saying.

Recognize the emotions. Customers are making a serious financial commitment to your organization. Understand their feelings and the likely anxiety and fear that they harbor when dealing with things legal. Build confidence in the transaction.

Summing Up: The Experience Opportunity

In review, here are questions to keep in mind when innovating memories within the customer experience framework:

1. What is your *experience journey?*
2. How does your experience provide a *total solution?*
3. How do you *surprise* your customers?
4. How do you *exceed* customer expectations?
5. What *words* should you use in your customer experience?
6. Is your experience built for the *long term?*
7. How does your experience deal with customer demands for *speed?*
8. How *generous* is your experience?
9. How do you deliver *tailored* experiences?
10. How do you enable your customers to *visualize the value* you deliver?

Finally, when it comes to innovating the customer experience, keep two things in mind:

First, you must manage innovation as a process. Creativity without management is irresponsible. Set up platforms for devising, gathering, evaluating and implementing innovations. Make this part of your corporate mandate.

Second, innovation comes from multiple sources. It isn't the job only of the guys with the Einsteinian hair and eyebrows down in that mysterious lab in the southwest corner of HQ's basement. Innovation comes from salespeople, front-line employees, and behind-the-scenes customer experience enablers. And it comes from customers—their emotions, their desires, and their overall needs.

Start to look at the customer from a lifestyle standpoint to identify more opportunities as opposed to the one-size-fits-all to build the total experience. Always remember that your product serves as part of a bigger solution. There is always a gap between what you sell and what the customer is trying to resolve. That gap is your experience opportunity.

CHAPTER 5

Customer Experience in the Virtual World

The world as we know it has ended. Again. I need to start setting my watch to the end of the world.

This latest apocalypse is unraveling us marketers in a familiar way: A new technology is taking over and the marketing world as we know it is coming to an end.

What am I talking about? *Twitter?* Maybe. *Facebook?* Getting a little dusty. *Blogging?* Old stuff. *The web?* Prehistoric times. *Television?* As you see, our marketing world, crumbling with each new media wave, is pretty fragile.

When Twitter—the technology that allows individuals to broadcast short messages of up to 140 characters anytime, anywhere—popped onto the scene, pundits again proclaimed that customer relationships as we knew them were over. I confess that I'm a bit tired of such punditry, particularly when it's all too apparent that people are simply glorifying a new means to an end, rather than the end itself. Just as they did with Facebook and MySpace. Just as they did with the internet. Just as they did when "moving pictures" were about to put live theatre into its grave.

Once upon a time when direct marketing exploded, many experts predicted that the role of the retail channel would be drastically diminished. When email and web chat blossomed, many projected the demise of call centers. Too many analysts surmised that speech technology would replace traditional interactive voice response (IVR) units. However, as we all know, direct marketing, email, web chat and speech technology today live side-by-side with the retail channel, call centers and traditional IVRs, which remain alive, well and a critical component of the customer experience.

The flaw in reacting to Twitter and other web 2.0 innovations as sea changes in the world of marketing/communications/transactions/fill-in-the-blank is thinking that somehow the mediums change the customer. Yet, customers were socially networked human beings before MySpace. They sought to compare and research products before the internet. They passed notes in high school class before texting.

The sea change actually lies in how consumers go about connecting with each other and, far more significantly, with you and your brand. Unlike the past, you can directly and interactively touch customers' core emotions and needs to build strong relationships beyond face-to-face engagements. You can empower customers, engage them, and reinforce their need to stand out as individuals. And, in fact, you must do all these things, because today's web-savvy consumer knows you have the capabilities, and will expect and even demand them of you. You must stop appealing only to utilitarian customers, those who seek expediency over experience, and connect with tribal customers, those who connect with those around them—their networks of support and friends—like a tribe. Utilitarian customers and tribal customers are often one and the same, but, in general, web efforts have forced the tribal to act in utilitarian fashion in the virtual world.

Therefore, to fail to use the virtual world's new tools in the context of customer need and experience is to anchor your brand in the past or push it into an unachievable future straight out of a science fiction story in which robots do all your selling. Or better yet, all the buying, too.

After a video of two Domino's Pizza employees committing some, shall we say, dubious actions hit YouTube, TV news coverage quoted a web 2.0 expert saying that the company itself was negligent "for not having a Twitter strategy." While I'm no doubt aging myself here, I distinctly remember thinking that I'd never heard of a Twitter strategy and couldn't fathom how opening a Twitter account represented a meaningful strategy of any kind.

Though companies in virtually every industry have accounts through various social media with thousands of "friends" and "fans," many of these companies are slowly recognizing that social media simply reflects a new (perhaps more personal) communication medium. So now, in addition to websites, newsletters, direct mail, email and web chat, companies also have Facebook, MySpace, YouTube and Twitter and whatever new golden-haired medium has surfaced by the time you read this. The proliferation of social media doesn't reflect a strategy as much as it reflects adoption of additional communication tools. Companies still require resources, personnel and actual strategies for managing and incorporating such media into their customer and communication strategies.

No doubt some of you are shaking your heads, thinking that I am naïve or short-sighted because I fail to internalize the "potential" of social media. Yet I would posit that when companies analyze their core customer experience and relationship challenges, they quickly recognize that the lack of Twitter or YouTube strategies is the least of their problems. The use of this or that communication medium will never be sufficient if the content, format and timeliness of information shared with customers are not customer-centric.

Companies across every conceivable industry utilize one or another form of web 2.0, including social media sites, blogs, forums, wikis, and podcasts, some to great effect. Zappos.com is but one of the many organizations utilizing today's web capabilities to achieve their objectives. Zappos has used Twitter to build fanatical customer support, solicit customer testimonials, generate high-quality leads, and engage in permission marketing. The benefits of effective use of social media are endless. But, with apologies to Marshall McLuhan, the medium is *not* the message.

Besides, all media tend to evolve from the world-shattering to the practical. Cable television was to be the source of, other than clear reception in remote areas, focused community narrow-casting. *The Sopranos* were never part of the vision. eBay burst into awareness as a communal commerce platform that empowered individual users to control their own pricing and shopping experience, and now much of eBay resembles traditional e-commerce, as much as you can call e-commerce traditional. YouTube dabbled in pay-per-view. Napster transformed its service because of legal challenges. These changes demonstrate how media evolves, often innovatively and intelligently, to serve basic customer needs.

We will see similar evolution in the social media d'jour, both present and future. Your task is to monitor and leverage that evolution to bring those basic human needs for community, conversation, control and recognition more deeply into your company's customer experience.

The key here is to think Customer first, then adapt the new Tools. This approach will help you rise above the misdirection of a generation of web use that thought Product first and then applied Tools, or that thought Tools first and tried to figure out how Tools could benefit Processes. "Wow! This new Information Superhighway thing is pretty cool. Let's get a website up by Tuesday. On Wednesday we'll figure out what to do with it."

What to Do With the Information Superhighway

Such concentration of medium over message and means over end led us to stagnation, parity and missed opportunities in Web 1.0. Web 2.0 allows us to finally reach out personally to distant consumers and, in turn, invite them in by creating virtual experiences in two areas we'll call *Self-Service 2.0* and *Conversation 2.0.*

Self-Service 2.0 gives customers control over not only managing such functions as online purchases, but also customizing and even controlling self-service—all the way to the point of designing their own products.

Conversation 2.0 allows deeper customer-brand communication, in the form of blogs, forums and, yes, Twitter.

Both of the experiential areas broaden the total customer experience and lead to even more powerful total solutions. But both require a significant shift in corporate attitude away from control and direction to participation and contribution. Companies want to maintain close control over branding and potential legal matters. "It's our brand, it's our space, it's our way or the Information Superhighway."

But by yielding some of the control they traditionally held, companies are trading logistical efficiency for a high degree of customer commitment and loyalty to the product and the brand, and in many cases are obtaining a premium price in doing so. If you ask me, this is a great trade-off.

Consider some of the advantages of a customer-centric Web 2.0 strategy:

- **Increased engagement.** A customer spending three hours on the web but only two minutes on your website is a missed opportunity. They spend only two minutes because organizations have transferred old processes to the web without creating new reasons for customers to stay with the sites. They've presented no opportunity to do something interesting. Interesting is 2 hours and 58 minutes elsewhere—a videogame site, a news feed, a competitor. Web designers speak of "stickiness," the ability to hold consumer attention. Stickiness is important, but you must also seek addiction. You must make your website experience so personal, and so interesting, that consumers feel that they must return to you. Each minute someone spends on your site signals that the consumer is deriving value from you, and it's a minute not spent at a competing site. One of the more important statistics in American football is Time of Possession: how long the home team maintained control over the football versus how long the visiting team did the same. Generally, greater time of possession correlates directly to winning the game. What's your time of possession in the virtual world?

- **Memorable engagement.** The delight and emotional engagement in the tribal web experience weds the customer to your brand.

- **Greater profits.** Customers are willing to pay for personalization, particularly of product design.
- **Word-of-mouth.** Delighted customers talk about their delight. If those customers have created personalized products, such as the customized shoes I will discuss momentarily, they can show off their delight in public. Some product co-creation sites even allow customers to archive their designs so others can see them, or email their designs to friends.

The transition to sharing power with customers isn't easy. It has more to do with ego and traditions than with actual product design. Many executives can't accept the fact that they must share power with customers. This denial forces them to refuse to accept the fact that their customers can reach millions of people today via websites and other modern tools. In terms of reach, these tools place customers almost at the same level as your company, which has the ability to reach millions via such corporate tools as mainstream advertising.

Don't get me wrong: The issue of consumer control vs. brand control is by no means black or white. The degree to which you give up some measure of control is relative and must be carefully thought out. Different companies will be able to give up varying degrees of control based on their unique products and services.

As well, this transition needn't be made immediately. Take baby steps. Start by allowing customers to select or create the external design on their own. Then gradually incorporate greater levels of design creation with customers to reach the ultimate personal platform status.

As an example of the need for baby steps, I've been asked, "When is the best time to get started with a blog—when do you know you have a critical mass of positive customer perceptions and things to say to customers that will propel a successful conversation platform?" I smile in response, and think about the male stereotype of "problems with commitment." Prospective grooms may be ready to get married, but they always have one more trip to take or one more person to see or one more job goal to achieve. You must commit much more quickly. A blog is not a prize awarded to you when you become great. As with many of the concepts I discuss within these pages, a blog and customer conversation is part of the customer experience journey of continual improvement. The moment you've established a customer relationship, you're ready to engage that customer in conversation and co-creation.

Think of a blog as a conversation—and the question then becomes, "When are you ready to speak to your customers?" It had better be soon. Every day that passes without your customer engaging with you through your blog is a day your customer spends on someone else's blog. Perhaps the competition's blog.

Company objectives when deploying customer experience in the new virtual world aren't surprising—enhance customer loyalty, increase customer insight, reduce customer attrition, and increase customer purchase size and frequency. To meet these objectives, you'll do well to act as you do when entering foreign markets. Learn the rules, customs and culture to ensure that you will be welcomed as a guest. So rather than asking yourself if you should tweet or blog or Hulu, determine if you have an underlying reason to do so, and if you're willing to do so under your hosts' guidelines. If so, prepare to receive citizenship in this foreign land.

The Utilitarian Customer vs. the Tribal Customer

The first step is to understand the way that initial attempts at leveraging the web tried to force customers into a company-serving corner, corralling the utilitarian customer. Even though the web is a medium full of personal discovery, emotions and interactions (for example, through social networks), self-service sites often manage to produce the opposite experience.

In the new virtual world, organizations must move away from being a price-driven interaction channel to being a destination and a platform that generates passionate experiences. While companies have focused almost exclusively on the emotionless utilitarian customer, a new type of customer, the tribal customer, is steadily making his presence known. The tribal customer seeks emotionally engaging web experiences and craves emotional interactivity and personal expression. These customers are often self-expressionists who want to connect, interact, personalize, co-create, share and, above all, express themselves.

Whereas the time-starved, utilitarian customer seeks to minimize time spent doing functional shopping on websites, the expressive tribal customer wants to spend more time on websites that offer emotional interactivity, personalization and self-expression. The tribal customers will grant loyalty to those companies (and websites) that provide such experiences.

Let's put the virtual world in context with one simple statement: It is not a channel. The web experience is misdirected if it's used only to reduce the costs of interacting with your customers, which is exactly how most companies approach it today. It's engrained in the current web's DNA.

Because companies recognize that driving customers to web self-service would reduce costs significantly, the earliest generation of self-service efforts (and the self-service sites still being offered by most companies) focused on simplifying the customers' web experience. First-generation self-service sites made several achievements in the pursuit of customer experience simplification:

1. Data source consolidation. Prior to the focus on self-service, corporations designed their web presence with a "brochure" mindset—and in fact, industry jargon for such sites was "brochureware." Organizations posted their products and services on their websites for customers to see and review. Companies started making critical information publicly available with the aim of increasing the ease of conducting transactions. Brokerage institutions enabled customers to buy and sell securities on their own. Retail companies allowed customers to directly place orders and view inventory status while logistics companies enabled customers to track personal shipments. The access to information sources necessitated the consolidation of a variety of internal data sources to reduce the time of transaction.

2. Usability and user interface. The shift from basic web presence to self-service functionality required better design of data capture and transaction forms. Concern about usability and transaction efficiency resulted in reducing the time that customers were required to spend on the site.

3. Availability of insightful information. The epitome of such information-sharing was and remains the airline industry. Airlines were willing to avail customers to seating plans so that they could choose their own seats. In general, customers enjoyed greater diversity of information, which allowed them to personalize their selections and ultimately shift their transactions away from the call center to kiosks or other self-service channels.

4. Around-the-clock service. The ability to access information and conduct transactions 24/7 benefitted busy or traveling customers accustomed to conducting business at odd hours. This feature also benefitted customers unwilling to wait in line for an agent. The 24/7 availability created a sense of convenience that attracted customers to self-service. Banks allowed customers to transfer money, airlines enabled its customers to book flights, and retail outlets facilitated product purchases at any time of the day. Moreover, this service eliminated the need to staff call centers with late night and weekend agents and the higher wages they commanded, further driving down call center costs.

5. Basic recognition. Websites allowed customers to build a profile of preferences and then recognized customers and preferences each time they returned, saving time for customers and reducing the time necessary to complete a transaction.

All well and good, but the downside is severe. Designing self-service for the utilitarian customer accelerated the commoditization of products and services. Customers were left to determine their own differences and to find any element of uniqueness in the vast printed catalogs presented to them by vendors.

Self-service sites treated the utilitarian customer as someone who sought to conduct transactions as quickly as possible and then move on to other activities. (Applying this line of thinking to retail stores has led some bricks-and-mortar retailers to replace people with automated kiosks that could place customer orders.)

Yet, when Strativity's *Customer Experience Consumer Study* (2009) asked 1,994 consumers to identify the drivers of exceptional customer experiences, they pointed to human interactions with their favorite vendors. Such self-service channels as web and IVR didn't show strong correlation to loyalty and future purchases. The consumer verdict was very clear: exceptional customer experiences are rewarded with premium price, longer relationships and larger purchases. These results have been validated in multiple customer experience diagnostics we've conducted with clients in the last several years. Although self-service channels are required to be easy to use and intuitive, consumers do not attribute loyalty to interactions through these channels.

I would go a step further to state that by shifting customers to self-service channels, companies are trading cost-savings for loyalty. Following the cost-reduction path comes at a hefty price most companies are not aware of. Consider the following statement: "We can reduce calls into our call center by 10,000 customers a month. This will result with $30,000 savings a month. However, such a move will also reduce the likelihood of these customers from buying from us again by 45%." How many CEOs would approve such a proposal? Yet this is exactly the sort of loss you risk when you don't measure the impact on customer loyalty and view the cost reduction in the context of the complete customer relationship.

On the other hand, our survey respondents ranked traditional human interactions at retail locations and call centers as having a high degree of correlation with customer loyalty and future purchases. The reason was quite simple. These channels represent experiences in which customers feel that the company served them, added value and delivered value unique to the customer.

In Self-Service 1.0, the entire approach was to treat customers as utilitarian. A customer zips in, conducts business, and exits as quickly as possible: e-commerce as drive-through window. Nowadays, customers spend hour upon hour on the web, but how much of that time is devoted to your site?

Two minutes? One minute? Most designs emphasize finishing that transaction as soon as possible. *Snap snap! You're wasting electrons!* And the customers wander off to Facebook and YouTube and companies competing not only for the customers' share of wallet for your product or service, but also for their overall share of budget. These customers, because they see no difference between the companies, take their business, their time and their attention elsewhere.

When companies created Self-Service 1.0, they simply migrated existing processes, layered on a bit of information, and set the customer off to do their work for them. This amounts to little more than extending a customer service rep's work screen to the generally available web. As we mentioned earlier, we have outsourced Tier One to the customer without paying them for their efforts, and some companies took all this by actually charging penalties to customers contacting the call center, as a form of deterrent.

Replicating existing processes on the web wastes the web's greatest opportunities. In taking this approach, organizations failed to realize that if their companies are just a series of processes, then they are no different from the competition.

Take the banking world, for instance. Retail banks now allow customers to access their account information online and carry out such transactions as account transfers, bill payment, wire transfers, and foreign currency transactions. These are great services, but they're still Self-Service 1.0. Any teller can conduct these transactions. What's more, if, say, self-service loan origination doesn't differ from Bank #1 to Bank #2, if the process for checking my credit card account doesn't differ from Bank #1 to Bank #2, then what's the difference?

Treating the web as a channel to replace other, more expensive channels— for instance, migrating call center activity to the web—misses what the web is all about. And, in fact, this migration accelerates your commoditization. Here's why: On the web, your brand is exactly the same size as your smallest competitor. The customer's point of reference is a screen that doesn't change size from site to site regardless of corporate assets, history of being in business, quality of products, and so on. What's more, you've lowered a barrier to entry down to the level of your smallest competitor, as well. Technology is easily available to all and, in many cases, competitors can deploy such efforts as YouTube casts as easily and as cost-effectively as you can.

And perhaps the saddest problem of all is that, ultimately, the utilitarian customer was merely a figment of efficiency-hungry managers' imagination, and that serving that mostly imaginary customer has accelerated the race to parity at best. Self-service sites are seldom a competitive differentiator. Their presence simply acts to eliminate competitive inferiority.

And in the absence of rich, emotionally engaging experiences, self-service sites drive customers to define preferences primarily based on the lowest price. The commoditization factor is exacerbated by the customer's ability to switch to the competition. The barriers are as small as a mouse-click, meaning that companies hardly get a chance to make their pitch. Customers are in full control as they shift from one site to another at speeds never previously experienced.

To apply the concept of the tribal customer to the web experience, let your customers customize your website for themselves. Let them dictate what they see, where they see it, and the form they see it in. If you insist that your site look exactly the same for whoever visits it, you have created nothing more than the electronic version of one-size-fits-all. If you allow customers to make their web experience their own, they will invite their friends. But to enable this platform, you must be willing to relinquish the control that brands so often cling to.

Don't be the same website for me and for my grandfather. Guess what? I'm going to go to the competitor's site that is *not* for my grandfather. Do you remember that classic ad campaign—"This is not your father's Oldsmobile"? In the world of the web, when I go to a website, the site should be saying, "This is not your father's website." For my father, it should be saying, "This *is* your website."

Self-service is more than researching troubleshooting tips for products that don't work, submitting a purchase order, or getting a book of first-class stamps from the kiosk outside the post office. Self-service is now collaboration.

Self-Service 2.0

Begin the journey to a virtual experience that attracts and serves the tribal customer by allowing customers to self-segment and to introduce their own variation on your site—variation in language, colors, font sizes, content, and any other element that, when you put the control in their hands, makes them feel like a more integrated part of your company. The Bank Machine in East London once experimented with ATMs whose instructions were written in Cockney Rhyming slang. Need some cash? Select "Sausage and Mash."

Follow through by allowing them to co-create the total experience via that now-personalized platform, letting them select and design everything from how you communicate with them to how they communicate with other customers to the features and look of the product itself.

This is Self-Service 2.0. This is self-personalization. Customers are still doing some of your job for themselves but, in this case, they are taking over the personalization that you as a brand must instill into their experience.

To succeed, Self-Service 2.0 must design and execute:

- **Self-Personalization Experiences,** which give consumers control over the look, feel and personal elements of interactions with your brand.

- **Self-Expressive Experiences,** which puts the consumers' individual stamp on your services and your brand—in essence, co-creating the value proposition you deliver to your customers.

- **Lasting Experiences,** which both evoke and preserve memories that lay the foundation of all future customer interactions.

Self-Personalization Experiences

"If you want it done right," goes the hoary old saying, "do it yourself." If you are to make self-service work for your customers and your company, you must return to the core concept of self-service: "Make it my way." Such personalization creates happier, more engaged customers who have taken it upon themselves to differentiate your brand specifically for them.

Savvy companies are making progress in offering collaborative models where customers can determine what they want and how they want it delivered, uniquely tailoring experiences to each individual. However, companies aren't yet taking full advantage of the capabilities of personalization. Let me give you an example in the banking world: Keeping in mind the typical banking Self-Service 1.0 features I described above, including checking account balances and making loan payments, I presented the next step to HSBC in Asia as part of a client engagement. HSBC wanted its customers to stay longer on their website, but weren't hopeful, claiming that customers had no reason to linger after they'd checked their balances. I nodded, then offered this scenario for deep personalization of the online banking experience:

The moment I as a customer sign in to my online banking account, the song "I Love Money" begins to play. It's a song I've chosen myself. It might have been Pink Floyd's "Money" or The Four Tops' "Money Money Money"—or any other song I enjoy. When I navigate to the page displaying my savings account details, I see the picture of my kids I've selected to appear next to the account balance. After all, I'm saving for my kids' future. Over on the mortgage summary page is the picture I uploaded of my house, reminding me of why those mortgage numbers exist in the first place. Another goal-oriented reminder—a picture of a beach and palm trees— sits on the summary page of the account I've set up for vacation savings.

Such a scenario is easily achieved with today's technology, even with yesterday's technology, which has rarely been put to such use. Most companies don't think to allow customers to even approach this customized approach. Consider it a transformation from banking statement to personal statement, from personal Checkbook to checking Facebook.

Some banks have taken steps in this direction with co-brand credit cards sporting the logos of their favorite sports teams and such, and some even allow customers to place a preferred picture on the face of their card. Before that capability, consumers could order personalized checks with designs they picked themselves and, before that, there was personalized money (well, George Washington was one of the few who could swing it, but still). But these are only a couple of steps in the potential of immersing the customers in their own worlds while interacting with your company.

Other businesses that provide good examples of providing customer-generated personalization include:

- MyShape.com's "Your Personal Shop" asks questions about customers' shapes, styles and fit preferences and measurements, then picks among seven body shapes to consumers can shop according to their shapes.

- Jones Soda allows its customers have a personal photograph featured on to one of its soda bottles.

- Steve Madden's "Design Your Own" feature allows footwear customers to, yes, design their own shoes, a privilege that costs about 25-30% more than a similar non-customized shoe, according to *USA Today*.

- The Capital One Card Lab experimented with allowing cardholders to select the card features and attributes important to them—for instance, opting for a slightly higher interest rate to increase the rewards earn rate.

The check-in self-service option provided virtually by all airlines today is a great example of a successful self-service channel. Customers who selected this option benefited from greater freedom. They were now able to see the complete seating arrangement on the plane and selected their preferred seat. This option was not available through airport check-in or the call center. The airlines were willing to trade off more power to customers in exchange for cost reduction and greater satisfaction.

The self-service customer experience on the web truly is about self. Although you want the customers to run the experience their way, it doesn't mean that customers suddenly become call center agents for you. It means they're going to shape the experience to their preferences, so that they can serve themselves completely differently.

Self-Service 2.0 changes the whole foundation of what self-service is all about. The website is no longer a destination. It is a platform that allows the customer to co-create with you. Customers are saying, "We won't simply be visitors—we'll join in creating our own web experience."

The change to Self-Service 2.0 requires a fundamental shift in corporate thinking about customer relationships. Again, the sea change I mentioned earlier is not in the customer. The change is not in the medium. The change is in corporate understanding of the customer and corporate willingness to leverage innate but until now unsatisfied customer interest in collaborating with each other and, yes, even with brands.

That's why you can't treat the web as a channel. Channels imply that the brand controls the medium and customers just come to visit, do your work for you, and go away.

Self-Expressive Experiences

People express themselves and their uniqueness through the products and services that they use—witness the huge popularity of Izod Lacoste sports shirts (hint: think alligator) in the '70s. Now, imagine the power of enhancing that self-expression by enabling customers to co-create the product or service they receive.

Footwear companies are at the leading edge of offering collaborative product experiences, including customized brand-name shoes from NIKEiD, Converse One, Vans and Timberland; painted shoes from PunkYourChucks; custom and personalized baby shoes from Darling Baby Shoes, and Soft Star Shoes and Moccasins; and custom high heels from Shoes USA. Let's look a little more closely at NIKEiD:

In chapter 4, we discussed innovation through adaptation of fringe behavior. Nike noticed that third-party designers advertised shoe-personalization services. Send your Nikes to these designers, choose your favorite colors, and the designers would ink the shoes and return to you one-of-a-kind footwear. Instead of clinging to absolute control over their brand, Nike decided to operationalize this fringe behavior into a co-creation platform called NIKEiD. Co-creation is a concept critical to maximizing the potential of the web and to securing the loyalty of the tribal customer.

The web-based NIKEiD service allows customers to design shoes to their own specifications. The customer selects the colors from the toe to the laces to the heel and sole and down to the Swoosh itself, producing the look that best expresses their identity. The customized shoes are, of course, more expensive than the Nike shoes anyone can buy in-store. However, customers consider the additional expense a small price for the personal expression it delivers. And important from Nike's standpoint is the delight and emotional engagement that they bring to their customers, from the fun and challenge of designing their own look to showing off that look once the shoes arrive.

NIKEiD customers create shoes that are very personal and, in fact, part of their identity. The NIKEiD shoes are becoming more than just an external product they share with millions of others around the world. The shoes are as unique as the designer (a.k.a. the customer) and reflect each person's individual taste, preferences, values and personality. This level of intimacy between products and customers achieves the highest level of customer experience.

Consider the numerous benefits to Nike:
- They capture what would have otherwise been third-party business.
- They command higher margins with the increased price of the service.
- They reduce returns—customers are less apt to return *their* shoes than they are *your* one-design-fits-all shoes.
- They personalize their customers' experience with a co-creation platform.
- They appealed to the tribal customer by allowing customers to share their designs with their friends—via the website.
- They potentially opened up a test laboratory to watch for other fringe behaviors and fuel further innovation.

Perhaps most important of all, Nike lets the consumers take control over a product that in and of itself is a personal statement. This is now more than a matter of personal expression via the brand someone wears, and broadens to an instance of self-expression that tribal customers can talk about personally. "Look at my cool Nikes. I built them myself. You can, too."

Look for opportunities to follow a similar path in your web efforts—because at the level of co-creation, the product becomes the platform for expression. Companies relinquish the dictatorial position of "we know better" and embrace the position of "let's share ideas" and "you participate in the process."

Co-creation is a strong element in the iPod phenomenon that I detailed in Chapter 4's discussion of innovation. What made iPod successful, in my opinion, is not the cool device but rather the unique play list created by each customer. In fact, the device lacked a clear outlet for a social element, and was merely a platform for each person to create a unique song playlist that reflects their individual taste and personality. In this case again, the product becomes a platform. Apple allowed customers to create and reflect their identity by enabling them to create their own one-of-a-kind playlist. Compare this to the predefined song lists contained in CDs sold worldwide and you can clearly see the difference in approach. The record/CD labels determine the product for customers and force them to purchase 10-12 pre-selected songs versus the ability of customers to select only the songs they like. Trends such as eBay successfully reinforce products as platforms by allowing customers to obtain the oddest products they wish to buy and not settle for products preselected by buyers of large store chains.

Some other examples point to how co-creation can enrich the customer experience and the brand relationship. Take Stony Creek Wine Press, which allows its customers to co-create their wine labels. In the arena of durable goods, a growing number of car manufacturers allow customers to go to the web to choose design features such as colors and leather interior and a variety of products such as OnStar. And on an everyday personal level, consider a refrigerator offered by an Israeli company, which allows customers to create the external design of their refrigerator to complement their overall kitchen design. The refrigerator arrives painted with art to match the overall kitchen look. This new service is, of course, offered at a premium price and is distinguished from the regular refrigerators offered in the stores. The more customers become involved in the design and creation process, the more intimate their commitment will be to the product and the company. The products become a natural part of the customer's identity and are woven into their lives. This is another example of how co-creation can increase prices and create greater margins.

All this is co-creation for customer benefit. Chapter 11, "Deliver the Experience," will discuss co-creation for the benefit of your brand when I introduce best practices for managing customer complaints as ideas instead of nuisances, and for managing and operationalizing product, service and procedural ideas brought to you by your customers themselves.

Lasting Experiences

As we've established, customer experience is founded and built upon memory. Customers want to preserve their personal memories in ways that reflect their individual and unique experiences. Web 2.0 allows you to go beyond designing customer memory by bringing them into the co-creation model to create the memory in the first place, and then to preserve that memory.

For example, SharedBook has created a publishing platform that allows users to extract, create and manipulate data and content, then distribute their unique "MemoryBook" online or offline. In the tourism business, Regent Seven Seas Cruises employs this technology to enrich customer memories while at the same time generating extra revenue. When we travel, we tend to take a lot of pictures, and we've all found ourselves with a lot of shots that clip subjects' heads off, that are blurry or dark, or that missed the Eiffel Tower because of the large construction worker who stepped into the shot as you took it. Regent offers its passengers *The Regent Commemorative Album,* which weaves the best of your tour pictures with striking standard shots of your destination in a professional layout. Using a web interface, you create your individual title, write your own dedication or select from a range of standard dedications, and choose the cover photo and your own vacation shots that you want included. You can even select which ports-of-call from your trip that you want and don't want included.

The result is a very personalized and very specially presented memory. Of course, you'll want to show the book to your friends and, in doing so, share not only your memories but also the Regent Seven Seas brand.

When customers consider the next vacation while paging through this striking album, they remember not only the fun and glamour of the cruise, but also the brand that delivered that fun and glamour. This deepens the customer experience and strengthens the brand relationship.

Would all self-service channels be candidates for co-creation? Probably not—in the same way that not all self-service channels are differentiators. Many of these channels can be and should be differentiators if you rethink them from the perspective of customers and co-creation.

It is time to rethink self-service with a target of not just easy and intuitive experience, but as a delightful, differentiating experience. That will require placing customers at the center of the design, allowing them to contribute to the design and individualize the outcome. You must measure and determine the success of the self-service channel in the context of creating future loyalty and not just in the context of reducing complaints. And in some cases, you may have to accept the fact that self-service might not be the answer. In some cases, you may discover that human interaction is the right way to go to create differentiation and future loyalty.

Conversation 2.0

In years gone by, "conversation" with customers amounted to a pair of one-way streets that rarely crossed. Companies spoke in advertisements, press releases, newsletters, invoices and statements, and a variety of other mechanisms pushed out from their offices. Consumers responded in letters of complaint, calls to the customer-service center, answers to surveys, and nodding their heads in focus groups.

Web 2.0 merges those streets. But like young drivers facing cross-town traffic for the first time, companies fear moving off those cozy, well-worn boulevards and facing the challenges of heavy traffic.

A big question today in the world of the virtual experience centers on the need for and art of Web. 2.0 conversation. "Should we allow blogs and invite comments?"

In a sense, this is the same conversation as the puzzling "Twitter strategy" we encountered at the beginning of this chapter. The question is not "Should you blog?" Instead, it is "How can you meet the needs of the tribal customer via Web 2.0 conversational tools?", of which a blog is one.

My discussion here will refer mostly to blogs, but the concepts relate to any platform on which brands and customers can interact. Such exchanges can take the form of chat rooms, Facebook postings, Twitter feeds, community forums, or the display of any content and tools—from text to video to podcasts to widgets—that encourage on-site feedback and further conversation. Indeed, blogs are not one-way communications, but conversations in which the brand makes the first statements and then invites comments.

Many companies have hesitated in their web conversation strategy because of such disadvantages as:
- Maintaining such communications streams requires investment, including time, staffing and energy.
- Everyone is privy to what you say—including competitors, who might get a competitive view into your brand.
- The space suddenly opens up to negative feedback and commentary.

Companies must move beyond such objections. In the case of investment, we need only point to the Return on Nothing covered in Chapter 3. The second and third objections, on the other hand, are mired in product-centric thinking, and overcoming them requires a fundamental shift in corporate thinking.

The tribal customer seeks open communications and distrusts attempts to control or overtly steer avenues of conversation. The tribal customer wants to talk about both delights and disappointments, and if you approach Web 2.0 conversations boldly, openly and intelligently, the tribal customer will do much of that talking directly with you.

If something goes wrong your brand, what are the chances that the internet-enabled world won't learn about it? Zero. For all practical purposes, assume that the truth will come out. The question is when and where it will come out. It can be revealed on another website over which you have no control, where someone can blast you with no chance of your responding. Or you can seek to manage the message and deliver a positive, constructive response.

Companies approach blogs with the same fear with which they approach the web itself. Blogging is kind of cool, and it's an inexpensive means of communication, but, ultimately, guests can come in and say what they want and fuss and fume and complain. However, many rarely take into account another possibility: The Good Guys will come.

If you create a dynamic, differentiating customer experience, the good "customers will visit and tell you—and everyone else—how great you are. Corporations fixate on the negative impact of the web because they're trying to control the message, the relationship, and everything that happens with customers. The web represents loss of control. But conceding some control doesn't mean relinquishing it. It means opening up the conversation.

In that context, do *not* make the common mistake of letting your public relations people write your Conversation 2.0 communications. They will approach the job with their PR perspective, stripping this communications channel of all authenticity. People seek honest conversation. You cannot turn it into a commercial by jumping into the conversation—yours, or the conversation on other sites—and expounding on your corporate point of view. When the experience allows for a personal voice to be expressed— both from the customer and from the brand—the experience becomes authentic.

Some companies have created such positions as Director of Cyberservice. These employees monitor what's going on in cyberspace, and step in with comments about complaints—and about praise. If you consider employing such dedicated staffers, they must be trained carefully in the etiquette and conventions of conversing on the web in blogs and in forums.

Always work under the assumption that every piece of material that you send out—whether electronically in such forms as email or in print, such as a letter—will ultimately be showcased on the web. If you make a mistake, take a misdirected action, say something silly, establish a new policy—it's going to make it to the web.

This makes instilling web acumen into all employees who are communicating with customers imperative. There is a famous call to an AOL customer service center attempting to cancel an interaction. The AOL agent attempted to cross-sell/up-sell/prevent the customer from leaving, making a couple of gaffes along the way, including asking to speak to the customer's father. The call ended with the agent saying, in essence, "When you're ready to listen to me, then we'll talk. Until then, I'm not canceling anything. Calm down and call me when you're ready." The customer, of course, had recorded the call, and subsequently posted the call to the web. One call exploded into people's attention, leading all the way up to mainstream TV interviews. That's *exactly* what the press is looking for. Ironically, the agent was following script. The script is called "World-Class Service for Customer Cancellations."

Understanding this assumption, have you set response mechanisms in place? More important, does your mechanism bring the complaint to you so that you can exercise more control over the situation on a personal level before it balloons into something unmanageable? With no options to complain or converse with you, your customers are forced to go elsewhere. Don't believe me? A slew of websites are named by combining a company's name with the most severe of curse words. That sort of elsewhere you don't need.

Remember, there are parts of the customer ecosystem that you have no control over. Let it go. The questions are, *Are you smart in the way you interact? Are you smart in the way you contribute to the conversation? This conversation is going to occur—does it occur on your turf or someone else's?*

To succeed, Conversation 2.0 must design and execute:

- **Relevant, Authentic Experiences,** which demonstrate to consumers that caring human beings populate your portion of the new virtual world.

- **Shared Experiences,** which allow the tribal customer ease and delight in connecting to their friends and others on their network.

- **Evangelizing Experiences,** which leverage the passion and power of loyal tribal customers moved to recommend you to those in their networks.

Relevant, Authentic Experiences

Customers are human, and as such, they crave personally relevant and authentic experiences. Conversation 2.0 allows you to instill authenticity into customer-brand interactions. The problem in the corporate world is that the larger the company, the less human it becomes in the eyes of the rest of the world. Blogging and other Conversation 2.0 communications allow you to humanize the company by putting a face behind the brand. In fact, in this market, not having a blog is communicating that you are unwilling to converse, and to be authentic.

A great example of authentic interaction can be seen in the Web 2.0 communications from Sun Microsystems. Sun uses Twitter, Facebook, LinkedIn, and Second Life to carry out technology discussions, collaborative publishing, product development, market research and public relations. In particular, Jonathan Schwarz has proven to be a very successful blogger for Sun Microsystems. He's not out of the PR department—he's the company's CEO.

As well, Sun employees in general are invited to blog on the company website. On that site is a web page entitled "Sun Guidelines on Public Discourse," and it notes, "Many of us at Sun are doing work that could change the world. Contributing to online communities by blogging, wiki posting, participating in forums, etc., is a good way to do this. You are encouraged to tell the world about your work, without asking permission first. . . . By speaking directly to the world, without prior management approval, we are accepting higher risks in the interest of higher rewards." The guidelines page is very specific and very instructional to companies that similarly want to open up mutually beneficial dialogue with their customers.

Sun's communications guidelines, by the way, are instructive to all of us. You can find the page at http://www.sun.com.communities/guidelines.jsp

Another example of designing authenticity into the customers' web experience comes from Dell. The Dell Community, particularly in the case of the innovative IdeaStorm initiative, allows customers to interact with each other, read blogs, and suggest and vote on ideas for product and service improvements. IdeaStorm helps Dell transform complaining customers into idea-generating customers. I cover more on the power of idea-generating customers, and more on the specifics on IdeaStorm, in Chapter 11, "Deliver the Experience."

Companies like eBay allow users to post and read comments about products, and even rate them, usually on a 1-5 scale. eBay specifically allows users to ask questions of eBay merchants. And buyer feedback directly impacts the ratings of sellers.

Some companies and organizations have encouraged brand participation up to the level of inviting customers to submit their own commercials—the NFL, for example. NFL invited people to submit ideas for Super Bowl commercials. Winning ideas were made into ads by professional agencies. Also realizing the power of word-of-mouth in such matters, particularly the Super Bowl, Doritos runs an annual "Crash the Super Bowl" ad contest inviting consumer-created videos. A 2009 consumer-created entry was ranked by Super Bowl viewers as the most popular in a real-time Ad Meter measure—beating out professional ads from top brands, winning the creators a million dollars from Doritos parent Frito-Lay, and garnering immense publicity for Doritos.

Shared Experiences

The mark of an enduring and memorable experience is that it can be shared with family, friends and colleagues to allow them participate directly or indirectly (at some time in the future).

For example, when you search for a nearby bricks-and-mortar location on the Barnes & Noble bookstore website, the site asks you, "Would you like a friend to come with you?" The site allows you to send an email to a friend. The email invites the friend to join the customer at the location. Notice the transition here. Barnes & Noble embellished a personal experience—the physical bookstore—with self-service on the web, where customers can browse and buy without any human contact. But then they employed the web to not just encourage a return to the physical experience, but also to extend the experience to the consumers' social circle. Here, the co-creation lies in the customers' ability to engineer the personal experience, while at the same time giving them a choice of shopping channels to use to get their books.

Sharing is an integral part of today's web experience, from the social-networking sites like Classmates.com to evite, a party-planning and invitation site that offers a photo center where users can share party photos and view other guests' photos. At a more day-to-day level, news websites allow readers to email news stories to friends and family directly from the stories.

Refer back to my section on "Lasting Experiences" earlier in this chapter, in which I discussed the *Regent Commemorative Album* customized for Regent cruise guests. The resulting personal album is created on the web, and can be shared with others via the web. But it also has a physical component. Passengers can order a hardcover or paperback version of the memory book, further bringing the quality and the passion of the brand to life.

How will you encourage and facilitate sharing on your website?

Evangelizing Experiences

The web provides an incredible opportunity to generate referrals, and the corporate world has not yet begun to leverage this potentially powerful source. Here is your opportunity to create authentic evangelism. Stop thinking of your customers as utilitarian transactors and start thinking of them as partners. This is not only opportunity but also payoff—an easy and immediate payoff.

It's one thing to ask the customer, "Are you willing to recommend?" It's another thing to actually collect a recommendation—which you can do quite easily on the web. Customers are connected to friends, colleagues and acquaintances on Facebook, MySpace, LinkedIn, Plaxo, and so on. All *their* friends, colleagues and acquaintances are linked. These connections lead to a tremendous opportunity to create recommendations. In doing so, you create a positive force that validates you.

You can tap into consumer evangelism right now on the web, but because of the narrow concentration on the web as a channel instead of a co-creation platform, many organizations don't even consider the opportunity. They also hesitate because of the fear and the fallacy that everything on the web can attack them. Some companies are starting to discover a little secret: If products and services are designed to delight customers and not just to deliver "me too" value, relationships, repeat business and, yes, evangelism will develop naturally. The people who will speak positively about you are out there, and you can help give them voice. To build a movement of people who will talk positively about you, design the web experience with collaboration in mind. For example:

- Appoint a cross-functional committee responsible for maximizing the power of word of mouth. Establish mechanisms for aggregating customer discussion content and acting on it.

- If you're delivering great experiences, invite customers to read what their peers are saying in an objective environment. A site that exhibits a way to build positive promotion is Yelp.com. Yelp is a platform inviting consumers to rate local businesses—restaurants, cleaners, and so on—positively or negatively. Many small companies have begun sending customers to read reviews of the companies on Yelp as a means of natural and authentic promotion.

- Provide customers with a forum for discussing products, services or the actual company among themselves.

- Cap positive customer care calls in your company by saying "Don't forget to link to us on your Facebook page" Or with "Don't forget to mention to your friends that you're one of our customers."

- Design a Facebook button consumers can easily integrate on their social-networking pages.

- Consider paying customers to advertise your company on Facebook and other platforms.

- Encourage customers to contribute ideas for improving products, services and service. Celebrate customer commitment to making your company better. Reward and recognize customers for their ideas—for example, place a picture of a contributing customer on the corporate website.

- Celebrate 5-, 10-, 15-year customer-relationship anniversaries right on your website. Show the individual customers involved how proud and appreciative you are of the continued relationship, give them some public star treatment, and demonstrate to your other customers how much you value those who do business with you. That will get some positive conversations started.

- Create a referral program and enroll every person who patronizes your company. Reward all references and referrals. Hype the program—for example, you might run annual referral drives to drive awareness and results. Surprise top referral customers with added incentives and recognition.

Companies are beginning to realize the immense financial benefits of customers who are constantly connected and who share their opinions and experiences with "friends" who in turn share it with their friends. These friends can number into the thousands and even hundreds of thousands. Product evangelizing, customer recommendations and the spread of good will by people who have bought your products or services are invaluable. As well, these customers may provide competitive information and offer ideas for new products and services. Reduction in customer attrition, repeat purchases, increase in referrals, and customers' lifetime value will shortly follow.

Mobile Marketing: The New Rules

In something of a convergence of internet, social media, co-creation, Self-Help 2.0 and Conversation 2.0, mobile phones and smartphones bring new opportunities and new dangers in dealing with the tribal customer.

As we argued regarding social media, the mobile revolution presents an opportunity as an emerging channel—but far greater opportunity as a vehicle for adding value and enhancing customer engagement. When mobile phones first began to proliferate, many organizations immediately approached them as a marketing tool. (What else? Isn't selling the main purpose of our existence?). But in reality, mobile devices provide organizations with a broader and more powerful engagement opportunity. Beyond simply selling to customers, the mobile devices may complement the customer service function, as well as serve as an excellent customer-feedback tool. Before rushing to copy how your competitors utilize this device, examine your unique brand promise and the nature of your customer relationships, and then ask yourself how mobile relationships can enhance the customer experience.

The customers' relationship with their phones not only provides opportunity to extend both Self-Service 2.0 and Conversation 2.0, but also demands such extension. Consider what your phone means to you. Could you survive without it? For how long? What information do you keep on your phone?

If you're like the billions of other mobile phone owners, your phone is very personal to you. Understand how you feel about your phone when engaging in mobile marketing. Your customer shares your feelings, so you must act as a customer as you plan your mobile campaign.

I was chatting about customer experience and loyalty with a young woman in a coffee house. She argued that her generation of Millennials weren't loyal to any particular any brand. As she stated it, "We are loyalty-free." As she turned away to glance at a passer-by, I slipped her iPhone off the table out of her view. When she noticed it was gone, I had to quickly return the phone to prevent her from suffering cardiac arrest. I said, "Instead of being loyalty-free, you've just shown that you're very loyal indeed—to brands and devices that you believe represent you and express who you are." With that tenet in mind, you can see the unique opportunity to leverage the intensely personal relationship customers have with their phones to engage people with customized experiences and relevant content.

When designing mobile engagement, remember that the customer is still the purpose of all your activities. We're not talking channel engagement or device engagement; we're talking individual engagement via a very personal medium. When designing your approach, then, consider these guidelines.

- **Focus on your customer.** Nothing says "me" more than the mobile phone. Customers invest in customizing it in so many ways, from ring tones to custom screens to music selection to apps and games. Because the tool is so personal, your approach must be deeply personalized.

- **Be respectful.** You are a guest in this device. Act as such. Don't be inhospitable, and don't betray customers' trust.

- **Be authentic.** Create communications as unique, personalized and meaningful to recipients as the phone itself is to those recipients.

- **Add value and enrich the customers' lives.** The mobile device is a life tool for customers. In any potential mobile engagement, consider what customer wish or aspiration you will address, and whether this wish or aspiration will motivate the customer to respond to your offer. To do this:

    o Make the customers' life easier.
    o Provide special opportunities to experience something unique.
    o Provide experiences worth bragging about.
    o Offer with money-saving opportunities.
    o Enrich customers with special knowledge.

- **Gadgetize.** Much of the consumers' relationship with mobile revolves around the factors of cool and new. "My phone is cool, therefore I am cool." Design your approach to accentuate the cool, with content, offers and communications that take advantage of gadget fascination so that customers not only enjoy the experience, but also brag about it to others.

- **Think freedom.** The mobile phone is about movement, flexibility, freedom. Design your approach to complement this mindset.
- **Save time.** An integral benefit of—and attraction to—using mobile phones is efficiency and time-savings. Design your approach not only to respect this attitude, but also to support it and enhance the time-saving experience your customers seek. And never waste customers' time with irrelevant engagements.
- **Enable connection.** Phones are about communication and connection with loved ones, business colleagues and new friends. Design offers, campaigns and communications that assist your customers in making new and meaningful connections.

Mobile marketing is about new channels of communication and engagement. From location-based offers, mobile web, mobile web promotion, text messaging, social networking or voice, new channels of engagement are opening up. All these new channels present an opportunity to connect with customers in new places and at new times. The authenticity, engagement, relevance and respect must however remain the same. You must design content that adds value, solves customer problems and delivers exceptional experience.

Summing Up: The Future, Version 3.0

Granted, web 2.0 is exciting, and its growth is nothing short of breath-taking. Here's an interesting stat: According to Facebook and the Socialnomics blog, "If Facebook were a country it would be the world's 4th largest between the United States and Indonesia." Other stats are equally impressive, and equally fleeting because of the rapid developments on the web, so I won't try to detail them here.

Used effectively, as a strategic means and not as a jump-on-the-bandwagon trend, social media can benefit company-customer relationships. From one standpoint alone, companies of all types can communicate and interact with customers and prospects at speeds previously thought to be impossible.

However, given historical trends, what remains unclear is the extent to which social media and web 2.0 will influence the customer experience. Companies seeking to develop or enhance a social media strategy should carefully consider social media guidelines and determine if they are truly ready to accept them. As you pursue the social media realm, consider the following questions:

- How will you foster customer collaboration?
- What degree of collaboration are you seeking?
- What will make your approach authentic and real?
- Are you prepared to receive critiques and negative comments from customers?
- What parameters will you establish to ensure that the customer is truly equal?
- What value will you provide to customers through social media that you're not providing with "traditional" communication mediums?
- How will your organization modify its web presence to facilitate customer personalization of their experiences?
- To what extent are you ready to share control with customers over content, messages and resolutions?
- What ground rules will guide your social media strategy?
- What new channel in the virtual world is suitable to support your experience?
- How should you build interactivity with customers?
- Do you need to look cool? If yes, why?
- What elements of your experience can you open to co-creation with customers?
- What potential customer misbehavior should you be ready for?
- How do you allow customer insight exchange to support your experience?
- How do you encourage customer recommendations through the web?
- How do you allow experimentation by customers on the web?
- What involvement of your employees should you include in the virtual experience?
- How does your virtual experience support your overall differentiation goals?

Customers embrace Web 2.0 technologies as personal tools for their own social needs. You must embrace them in the same spirit—that they are *customer* tools. As such, it's critical for companies to recognize that entering personal and social domains—from social networks to the screen of a mobile phone—requires a great deal of sensitivity and adaptation.

The web and other new communication media are not channels, and they are not means for reducing the costs of customer interactions. As a whole, they constitute an environment that allows tribal customers to thrive in interacting with people important to them, and sometimes with people they have never met. Are you going to join the conversation? Or are you going to stand outside and achieve irrelevance? Will you embrace and leverage the tools? Or will you try to behave as if the world has remained stagnant and pretend that you still have control over every aspect of the customer relationship?

Above all, remember that it will soon be time to set my watch again. The marketing world will "end" again with the arrival of new technologies, new means of communications, and new pundits to tell us how the latest revolution is "changing everything." Just remember that whatever waves of "the next big thing" wash over us—mobile or web 3.0 or 4.0 and be-yond—human beings will continue to function as human beings. In what-ever future we face—whatever channels, devices or platforms—always focus on the experiences and value you are seeking to achieve. The tools change. The channels change. The underlying "language" of marketing changes. You must simply learn to use them to complement your goals of customer delight.

CHAPTER 6

Different Experiences
for Different Customers

An old marketing maxim describing the difference between product features and benefits goes like this: "Customers don't want quarter-inch drills. They want quarter-inch holes." Although that's a proper step away from product-centric thinking toward experiential thinking, it doesn't go nearly far enough. One customer may want more-efficiently drilled quarter-inch holes as an equipment upgrade to further a home-renovation business. Another customer may want quarter-inch holes to build her daughter a playhouse. Still another customer may want quarter-inch holes when hanging his own paintings in the art gallery that he dreams of starting. And then there's the one who can't figure out how to drill quarter-inch holes, doesn't care to spend a few minutes with the instructions, and actually rather enjoys calling the manufacturer to gripe endlessly about his problem.

Different customers, different goals, aspirations, and transaction frequencies. And different experiences. One customer is a professional, with service-efficiency goals to help him maintain productivity. Others have lifestyle goals in which the drill becomes a tool for displaying self-expression. Clearly, the one size that does not fit all is a quarter-inch. One of the most important leaps from product-centricity to customer-centricity is learning to discard one-size-fits-all and begin treating different customers differently.

Key to differentiated treatment is segmentation—assigning customers to broad, clearly defined groups with common attributes that help guide your design and execution of customer experience. Personal differentiation and delight is your ultimate goal, of course, but first understanding customers in broader terms provides a crucial foundation for achieving customer experience on the individual level.

Segmentation can come in many flavors, but two have particular relevance to the design and execution of effective and profitable customer experiences. Those flavors are Financial Segmentation and Lifestyle Segmentation.

Financial Segmentation allows you to identify your most profitable and potentially most profitable customers and to allocate customer experience resources where they will have the most impact. Lifestyle Segmentation allows you to develop experiences that will truly delight those with high present and potential value.

Financial Segmentation

Segmenting customers based on their financial contribution to the organization is both traditional and essential. And a solid customer experience initiative must employ clear and objective views into customer revenue; otherwise, the initiative will find itself spinning its wheels, unable to gain traction with customers most able to make the initiative succeed. After all, to continually exceed customer expectations, you must follow these two rules: The experience must be pleasant and delightful, and the experience must be profitable.

Customer financial segmentation allows you to differentiate your value proposition and deliver experiences to different customers. You design different strategies for customers who deliver revenue and profits, and for customers who cost the company.

When you commoditize all customers, you reduce them to the lowest common denominator, and you fail at delivering differentiated, personalized experience. This, of course, has financial impact—the impact of Return on Nothing, as we've discussed. Customer commoditization results in higher customer churn rates, lower employee morale, and ever-decreasing margins.

Focus on customer profitability requires focus on the right customers. Often, organizations do business with the wrong customers in the name of market share and at the expense of the right customers. Picture the trap that this practice leads toward: The right customers are the only ones who can truly appreciate the experience and will reward a company by paying a proper premium price. You can't deliver an experience that warrants a premium price if your resources are scattered. Focusing on all customers distract efforts and focus. This forces companies to waste resources in the wrong places by trying to please customers who don't fit their value proposition.

When I speak of financial contribution, I'm not referring to level of spend, or to pursuing top dollar. Instead, concentrate on frequency and profitability. As we're about to see, your top customers aren't necessarily your most profitable customers. We truly believe that you'll find that some of the largest customers are the least profitable. That's why when I refer to frequency, I mean frequency of spend rather than frequency of contact, because multiple contact without spend is a money-loser.

When developing this level of customer transparency, some companies we work with segment their customers in this way:

- **The Moneymakers—The Frequent and Profitable.** We like these people. They pay the bills, and then some. For them, we provide special considerations; for instance, with customers in this group, we don't dare to allow functional measures like average handling time trump excellent service. For them, there's no such thing as average, there is either generously spending on customers or trying to win them out. We will bend the rules for them if it means making them happy. With this group, we want strategies in place to increase their transaction frequency even further to increase profitability. When they call, drop everything.

- **The Misunderstood—The Infrequent and Profitable.** We like these people, too, because though they don't contact us as often, they're still profitable. They earned the name because we tend to believe that, because they're not so frequent, they're cost us money. Don't be misled—perhaps these customers are giving us the lion's share of business within our product category, yet the nature of their business might not require frequent use of what we supply. They, too, are targets for increasing frequency and, therefore, profitability. We drop everything for them, too, and show them great attention, because if we can increase their frequency, we can move them into the Moneymakers segment, with the financial benefits that result.

- **The Lost Souls—The Infrequent and Unprofitable.** Unlike the Misunderstoods, the Lost Souls do indeed cost us money because of their infrequency. They live at the Moneymakers' expense, draining resources each time they contact you. They reside in this segment because they have no other place to be. They're lost. We might be able to find them again with marketing efforts to move them into the Misunderstoods by addressing the cause of their unprofitability. But do so carefully, examining the ROI and success rates of any initiatives directed to this group, as many Lost Souls are Lost Causes, and might very well profit you best by remaining lost. If you can't convert them up, convert them out.

- **The Candidates—The Frequent and Unprofitable.** We like to call them "the F.U.'s"—and I'll let you read into that what you will, because it is within this segment that problems begin. F.U.'s are your abusive customers. They're demanding but don't spend a lot of money. They call ten times a day. They use resources meant for the Moneymakers and the Misunderstood. They came in during the promotion, the special. They are price-sensitive. They expect everything for the little they paid. We need to either upgrade the Candidate to Moneymaker or send them to the competition.

Imagine this scene: An F.U. phones the call center. The agent, recognizing the caller ID, gets up, and stretches the phone line so he can reach a window, which he opens. As he answers, he opens a petty cash drawer installed near the window specifically for such occasions. As he begins the conversation, he takes a few of the dollar bills and tosses them out the window. He nods, attempts to get a word in edgewise, and tosses more dollars away, and more until he whispers to a colleague that he's run out and needs a resupply of cash to toss out the window. At least it's safer than setting the money afire, but it has the same effect. And that's what you're doing when you spend time with F.U.'s.

The F.U.'s cost you twice. Once because they aren't profitable on their own, and twice because they're snitching resources from the Moneymakers. When you find yourself facing strained resources, remember that your actual problem may be not total resources but resource allocation. In such a case, the answer lies in different services to different customers. Right now we're running our Moneymakers, our Candidates, our Misunderstoods and our Lost Souls all at the same level. We're under-servicing the Moneymakers who paid for and expect better treatment, and over-servicing the Lost Souls who have paid you very little. The result: Vanilla service and experience that doesn't apply to anyone. Allocating resources to the wrong customers and then wrapping it up with average makes no one happy.

A customer-service study we undertook for a car manufacturer revealed a segment of what we called "inherently unhappy customers." These customers represented only 5% of the customer base but occupied 45% of the service department's time—and I don't know a single investor who would give a company permission to do that, let alone a single profitable customer who would allow you to use their margins to delight someone else. The inherently unhappy were likely customers who were sold cars at the end of the quarter by some salesperson motivated by an aggressive sales-incentive program. Because of these service costs, the company was literally shifting revenue from profitable customers to service unprofitable ones. What impact does this kind of imbalance have on your margins?

How did we handle these unhappy souls? We offered to buy their cars back, and then we suggested that they try the products of a competing manufacturer.

That's the ultimate win-win when dealing with F.U.'s and other unprofitable customers. Send them to the competition. Tell them specifically who can serve them—give them the address and phone number and primary contact of your competition, somewhat the way Santa recommended Gimbels while working at Macy's in the classic movie *Miracle on 34th Street*. But in the real world, you're being Santa to yourself when suggesting the competition to your F.U.'s. In fact, you win twice. Your competition is stuck with the wrong customers, and you have greater capacity to deal with the right customers.

Ask yourself, "What customers should I neglect?" As a policy, which customers will you turn your attention away from? Because at this moment, your customer database is contaminated with unprofitable customers. I know what you're thinking: Letting customers go, when the focus of your company has been on acquiring customers for so long, would likely confound and possibly infuriate your CEO and your CFO. And, in fact, firing the F.U.s or even simply saying no to a customer in the appropriate situations is impossible in some corporate cultures. It is this very impossibility that gets those companies in trouble with F.U. customers—not to mention the profitable customers, as well. Saying no to the customer is the first step in realizing and declaring that you are not all things to all people. If you're all things to all people, you aren't providing specific special worth to the right people.

The Moneymakers and the Misunderstoods are the ones you can satisfy and delight. They will respond to more focused customer-centricity. Remember that relationships are reciprocal. Good customers give you something back for your efforts; bad customers are just using you. Isolating a subset of inherently unhappy and unprofitable customers and gently nudging them to shop with your competition can have an immediate impact on your margins. Stay faithful to the faithful.

Segmentation Differentiation

To fully leverage Financial Segmentation:

Flag incoming! Once you classify customers according to their frequency and profitability, establish mechanisms that allow customer touch points to identify the status of each customer. Agents in your call center, for instance, must know immediately if they're speaking with a Moneymaker or an F.U. Caller ID at the call center can access customer profiles and alert agents to the status and importance of the caller, who can then adjust the customer treatment appropriately. Either that, or keep the cash drawer near the window unlocked. When a Moneymaker calls in, the Gold flag should start waving. When an F.U. calls, perhaps a Jolly Roger is more appropriate.

Employ identifiers at other touch points, as well. For example, web sites can identify existing customers either by log-in or cookie identification. Extend the sort of customization your site already employs in customer-specific content and product display. Give Moneymakers and Misunderstoods access to offers and areas of the website unavailable to other customers.

You might even program the site to alert a service rep when particularly good customers log onto your site; this rep can address the customer directly with an instant-chat feature.

As well, identifiers such as loyalty cards can alert associates to customer status. Customers frequenting Harrah's Casinos use their *Total Rewards* cards when gaming and using facility services. As discussed before, when upper-tier customers arrive at any of the many global properties and use their *Total Rewards* card, the staff is alerted, and a manager is dispatched to personally greet the customers and attend to any special needs.

At early stages, the segmentation can be very basic. What's important is that frontline employees begin differentiating services right away. As with all elements of customer experience, these employees must be trained in the precise nature of the segmentation and differentiation, and they must be given permission to handle the F.U.'s with utmost efficiency. Here, the average handling time metrics still apply, and must even become more stringent. Instilling service skills and soft skills into employees who have no tools to determine when to use them at their most impactful is wasted effort.

Align your resources with the segment. Adapt not only your products and services to different customer personas, but also the level and type of contact made at every touch point in your organization. Take, for example, the sample grid that appears on page 121. Your sales department can tailor its efforts based on the expected types of return that financial segmentation reveals to you. The Lost Souls are left to wander your website and other passive sales vehicles, at little cost to you. The Candidates are pushed to self-service mechanisms, where they can talk to themselves and not to you. The Misunderstoods get an increased level of attention—some directive consultation about the overall benefits you can bring to them. The Moneymakers command your eye contact, your ready availability, and your personal attention.

So it is with all other points of customer interaction. Using a blank grid, conduct a benefit exercise for these four segments across all your touch points. These examples are generic—complete such a grid for your organization, function by function, following this model.

	MARKETING	SALES	CUSTOMER SERVICE	FIELD OPERATIONS
The Lost Souls	Generic Awareness	Web based / faxed orders	Basic service Cost effective	Investigate referrals to competition Basic service Cost effective
The Candidates	Direct Marketing	Recruiting Efforts – new customers Self service	Service with up sell efforts	Investigate upgrade possibilities
The Misunderstood	Loyalty Program	Consultative Selling	Problem solving Recognition	Provide additional incremental value
The Moneymakers	Special/ Customized Offers	Personal Attention	Preference White glove service	Enhance overall experience preference The next new thing

Shift your resources. Financial segmentation is not a cost-cutting exercise. Yes, you will be able to trim expenses. We once refused to work with a company because its database was so deeply contaminated with the wrong customers that we knew our contribution would be ineffective. The company looked at the numbers, made the hard decisions, and spent a full painful quarter firing its unprofitable customers. At the end of the quarter, their margins had increased by 25%. Instead of an exercise in cost-trimming, financial segmentation is an allocation strategy. You can't simply clean out the money-losing segments or pare down attention to the low-profit segments. That's just the first step. Reallocate cost-savings to the Moneymakers and, as appropriate, to the Misunderstoods. Sending marketing and experience-creation dollars their way not only maximizes ROI, but also demonstrates clearly to the customers who deserve and demand special treatment that they're receiving above-and-beyond value in transacting with you.

Build segment strength from the ground up. The best way to eliminate F.U.'s and Lost Souls is to keep them out of the pipeline in the first place. At HP, when interviewing job candidates for my software division, we asked a significant qualifying question: "When do you walk away from a deal?" The last answer we wanted was, "I won't walk away from a deal. I'll stick with it until we make the deal work." We didn't hire candidates with such answers, because we were realistic about the products and the experiences we provided. Our offer wasn't right for everyone. No offer is. And forcing customers into offers that aren't inherently beneficial only leads to unhappy, unprofitable customers. You're feeding the realm of the F.U.

Similarly, beware the trap of market share. We've all heard the earnest clichés time and again. "The customer is number one! The customer is always right!" We hear this almost as often as we hear upper management intoning, "We must control market share." And in that case, it seems, both the customer and the CFO are always right. Or so they would like us to believe.

To illustrate the lengths companies will go to retain customers at all costs, a major foreign car manufacturer called me a couple of years back. "Mr. Arussy," the caller said, "we hear that you have great training programs, and we'd like to engage your training to reduce our employee turnover." When I asked if they knew what might be leading to turnover, he replied, "The customers are screaming at them." I explained that I didn't know how I might be able to solve that problem. The caller said, "We want you to train them to like it."

I thought I'd missed something in translation. I said, "Let me get this straight. Customers are upset because they're not satisfied with their cars. The employees don't like to be screamed at. And you want me to convince them that being screamed at is a good thing." When I heard that I had indeed gotten it straight, I politely declined the opportunity.

This manufacturer was shackled by "The customer is always right," to the point of ignoring the cost of high employee turnover, and other profit-eating consequences of serving F.U.'s. By the way, if you haven't guessed already, this is the same car manufacturer who discovered those 5%/45% metrics exhibited by the inherently unhappy in its customer base. When we convinced the company that the customers and not the employees were the problem, they hired us to conduct training beyond mere employee scream-appreciation.

One of the most valuable aspects of financial segmentation is the ability it provides you to define the mutual value proposition with the profitable segments. Once you've identified the Moneymakers and the Misunderstoods, define precisely what you're trying to achieve from them. Moneymakers, for instance, make more than money—they generate opportunities, as well.

Too often, companies think of a customer interaction as a one-time proposition. They chase the sale, but have no plan for what happens afterward. They ship the new clients off to customer service and expect that silo to take full responsibility, while they go off and chase another sale. When companies don't think of customers in terms of long-term relationships, resources for nurturing those relationships can dry up, or be diverted to the kinds of aggressive sales tactics that bring F.U.'s to them in the first place.

Also, opportunities can slip away. For example, technology suppliers generally look for referrals and case studies from best customers, and often wander back to make such requests after the work is done. Build such requests into the contract. When you're negotiating discounts and contract details, take the opportunity to negotiate for and specify future interactions. The technology supplier might formalize an agreement that, in exchange for a price break or other considerations, the supplier and the customer will cooperate on a joint press release, a case study, and mutual appearances on-stage in industry conference presentations. What opportunities can you leverage—a discount for agreeing to provide referrals and studies, for instance?

When you get to the point where you can flesh out what you want from customers, you can then fully understand their potential, employing loyalty measurements, LTV metrics, and so on. The killer statistic that convinced the foreign luxury car-maker to make such bold moves as buying its cars back from dissatisfied customers is that average luxury car buyers own 20 cars in their lifetime. In one revelatory instant, that customer suddenly jumped from 75,000 Euros of value to 1.5 million Euros of value. That's a small dealership in one customer. For 75,000 Euros, my financials would have one set of margins dictating how much I can invest in courting the customer's business. For 1.5 million Euros—now *that's* interesting. And then extend the impact even further by considering the customer's social and referral network. How many other potential customers will that satisfied owner of 20 luxury cars possibly direct your way?

Right now, your service people are taking calls from unprofitable customers instead of doubling the time that they have with the profitable customers that present such interesting long-term futures. You can't afford to let that continue. You need all available resources to focus on the right customers. Fire the unprofitable customers. Turn away from abusive customers. The right customer may always be right, but the wrong customer belongs to your competition.

Lifestyle Segmentation

In order to engage with customers, your employees must know much more about them than they know today. In the product-centric world, employees know customers only at a functional level. This is a traveler checking in. This is a package recipient. This is a guy using tools. They're not people— they're not individuals.

The intermediary step to knowing customers as individuals is to understand them as personas, as representatives of specific lifestyle segments that describe common goals, aspirations and motivations for consumption. Flesh out personas so you can connect to the customers that the personas represent. Learn their preferences and tastes beyond even product and service, as deeply as to discover their favorite websites, their role models, their goals, their piques and frustrations.

In developing the persona perspective, you're seeking to fulfill two goals:

- Understanding the customer base so you can design products, services and experiences that touch customer needs and aspirations, and not just product uses. What motivates customers to buy? What exactly do they want to buy? And how do they want to buy it? Answering these questions reveals the special ways you need to serve them, communicate with them, and delight them.

- Arming employees with insight that will allow them to build personal interactions with customers. Knowing overall customer characteristics and concerns allows employees to connect with the customers, to at the very least strike up a conversation. Without such background and perspective, all your associates have are piles of numbers—accounts and transactions and dates—and none of that explains who the customers are, why they're transacting with you, and what they're ultimately seeking to accomplish. As one example, customers' credit scores provide useful information, but they tell you nothing about the people behind them and how to engage with them emotionally.

Start your lifestyle persona exploration by working to understand the customer's world from the perspective of consumption and not product.

In an engagement with a major European hotel chain, we convened a focus group of the organization's top-performing London employees—the highest-rated reception clerk, bellboy, chef, and so on. During the session, Paul, the premier reception clerk asked me, "Lior, can you explain to me what's wrong with the Americans? French guests never present me any problems, and the same with the Germans. But Americans are always grouchy and upset. They're fussing and wasting my time. I get so fed up with them that I automatically place them in the room block over the dance club. These guys will never sleep."

This gentleman was concerned only about getting the customer checked in—that's how he'd achieved his top rating—by winning the hotel's check-in-check-out-check-in competition. How many keys can the front-line clerk issue, without ever looking up to see who the customer really is? Had he looked up, Paul might have seen the results of jet lag. "The German and the French were at home last night," I explained. "They went to bed at their usual time, woke up at their usual time, took a one-hour flight to Heathrow Airport, and checked in relatively fresh. The American, due to cost-cutting mandated by the CFO, was sitting in row 66B, with a chatty octogenarian on one side, and a baby who screamed all the way from Los Angeles to London on the other. He has a business meeting in three hours. He is tired. He doesn't care about your product. He doesn't care about check-in-check-out. He isn't renting a room; he's renting peace and quiet, and the opportunity to regroup before heading off on a hectic business schedule."

Paul had engaged in a bit of customer segmentation of his own, but it was missing the mark widely. In fact, when we investigated further, we found that the Grouchy American was a distinct representative of one of the hotel's customer segments, the Business Traveler, with a specific range of expectations and aspirations. Had Paul viewed the Grouchy American from the perspective of *that* segment instead of the segment he made up on his own, he could have delivered distinctly anti-grouchy delight.

To understand the customer's world from the perspective of consumption and not product, engage in a process we call "Customer Experience Mapping" as another way to provide different experiences to different customers.

Designing the Customer Experience Map

The reason we were speaking with Paul's particular hotel in the first place was, ironically, that the chain's upper management wanted to build customer loyalty while differentiating pricing and customer experience. To do so required that they overcome a clear obstacle: their core product was consistent for every customer (well, except for maybe the rooms above the dance floor). All the rooms were the same and all the food was the same and so on. When we began the conversation by asking what business the chain was in, we heard, "The Bed and Breakfast business." That's a basic, common-sense view, but it's a limited view.

We discovered that this hotel, as most large hotels do, serves four different customer segments. Each segment is interested in features—usually physical attributes, such as a bed in a hotel room. But more important, each segment exhibits certain emotions and holds specific aspirations, the things that worry them, keep them happy, and occupy their thinking and dictate their approach to life.

When we started to look at the emotions and aspirations of this chain's customers, we discovered a huge gap between how the company defined their business versus how the customers defined their needs. For each segment, we found that the hotel is in a different business, solving a different problem. Same room 501, same toiletry, same towels—completely different consumption. And then through customer experience mapping, we found that for each segment, the hotel has different competitors for the customer's time, attention, interest and money.

Here's what we found:
- **Meeting Attendees and Planners** need meeting space, food and accessories. Their concerns, fears and emotions center on losing money, confidence, embarrassment, and teamwork. The hotel enables

these customers to do their business or job better. For the hotel, these customers are important because they control a considerable amount of spend, but the reverse side is that they're not returning next year unless they're independent contractors arranging events for multiple clients. Individual conferences are usually held in different places each year.

- **Business Travelers** want a bed, food, a health club and an internet connection. But most of business travelers' emotions and aspirations revolve around loneliness and being in the best position possible when they go to their meetings. The hotel's real business for this customer segment? Executive effectiveness and confidence—making the customers feel welcome and connected, and providing an environment in which they could prepare and be confident.

- **Leisure Travelers** want something completely different. These travelers talked to us about escape and about building relationships. They talked about marriage boredom and about being with family. The true business of the hotel for these customers was marriage extension and providing the opportunity for bonding with loved ones.

- **Non-Residents**, people who come for a meal or for coffee but don't stay overnight. Non-residents are often entrepreneurs and small business owners who arrange to meet important clients in surroundings more impressive than their own offices. They purchased an upgraded image for the price of a cappuccino. The true business of the hotel for these customers was image upgrade.

So the hotel chef who bakes the croissants is using the same flour for each of these customer groups, but is sending them out for different reasons— business enablement, executive effectiveness, marriage extension, and image support. Same hotel, same guest room, same kitchen, four different businesses. For example, housekeeping's business is not simply delivering clean rooms. Housekeeping is delivering job security for meeting planners who depend on the hotel to please *their* customers. Confidence and focus in a calming atmosphere where the businessperson can prepare physically and mentally for important business. And marriage extension for the couple whose clean and well-appointed room provides no frustrating distractions.

Identify your lifestyle segments. Some segments are obvious and clear-cut—the types of guests the hotel in our example entertains, for instance. But even when the segments appear to be straightforward, investigate further to find hidden surprising segmentational gems— because we're in the business of pleasant surprises, after all.

Through data analysis, focus groups and other voice of the customer mechanisms, discover commonalities in attitudes, aspirations and motivations behind consumption. For example, in working with a credit card company, we sought to develop personas with a simple customer survey studying attitudes toward financial-services' core product: money. We asked all customers to complete one sentence by selecting from a number of options: "The future is not certain, therefore . . ."

Based on this customer view, we were able to identify, flesh out and clearly validate four personas:

- **Power Users**, who use their financial achievements to assert power and prestige.

- **Obsessive Shoppers**, who can't stay out of stores and can't stop spending.

- **Dream-Makers**, who use capital to create new businesses or establish legacies through charitable participation

- **Strict Savers**, who believe that every penny must be preserved.

This attitude analysis allowed us to see that, although the credit card company's core product was short-term lending, the company was actually in four different businesses, with four different customers displaying different financial understanding, requiring different communications and demanding different types of respect.

Innovate your lifestyle segmentation. What range of characteristics is integral to your customer base, in addition to goals, job duties, recreational interests and so on? In some cases, for example, we've begun mapping call center personnel to *geographic* segments. Customers calling in from various parts of the country are diverted to specific agents trained to handle the regional differences in attitude, stress levels, and so on. Midwesterners are different from Californians who are different from New Yorkers. They speak differently, they operate at different paces, they have different expectations of transactional conversations, and so on. Companies often treat the U.S. as a homogenous market, when in truth certain customer and cultural characteristics can vary within the States as widely as between some countries globally.

As another example, one of our clients routes incoming customer service calls to agents calls based on the age and gender of both the caller and the agent. This client's studies show that, within their customer base, young female customers respond better to older male agents, older men respond better to young women, and younger men respond better to older women, and older women respond better to older women. The company's CTI—the tech initialism for computer-telephony integration routes the calls based on these characteristics to match the right customer with the right call center agent.

These are the types of surprising segmentational gems that can result from careful analysis. These reach deeper than other customer views, although more traditional views are hardly unimportant. Remaining in the financial services arena, take three more traditional views of banking customers by way of example—the small business operator, the kid fresh out of college, the person eying retirement. Each customer might have the same bank account balance, but their goals are far different. So are the ways you communicate with them, the offers you make them, and the experiences you deliver to them.

Also, be aware of the potential intersection of lifestyle and demographic groups. The person eying retirement is likely but not necessarily a Strict Saver, and the small business operator is likely but not necessarily a Dream-Maker.

Introducing Persona Portfolio Management

Once you have targeted lifestyle segments within your customer base, you must deploy formal management of those segments. Just as you have individual brand managers, dedicate budget and personnel to governing portfolios. Task individual portfolio managers with developing the persona experience strategy on the front end, and with monitoring, nurturing and invigorating the strategy as time goes on.

The portfolio manager's first step is to define and flesh out the characteristics and needs of the assigned segment to establish differentiated service and experience for those within the segment. You have innovated and benchmarked for customer experience in general, and now you can move to the next level: innovating for each lifestyle.

Portfolio discovery and management involves this key process:

Identify the features each persona seeks. When you get into the customer mindset and recognize the variety of mindsets that customers can bring to even a single product, you begin to unlock the opportunity to bring new levels of products and services to your clientele. Within each segment, picture one of your customers. List features you offer that this customer would be interested in. Remember, features are more physical. They are the bed and the towels in the hotel, the checkbook in the bank, the quarter-inch hole from the power drill.

Identify the customer's emotions and aspirations. Think of the customer you have pictured. What does he think about or worry about? What makes him happy? What keeps him up at night? Back to our power drill example, one customer is seeking a more productive and more profitable business, and another aspires to artistic expression. In the business-to-business world, a complex bit of machinery can mean job security to the organization's equipment buyer who seeks to be assured that he has made the most effective choice for his organization. To a young technician in the company, it can mean the experience and credibility that comes with the wherewithal to use the product effectively. To the executives in charge of operations and finance, it means potential promotions when corporate efficiency goals are met and bested. Although all are asking for the same SKU number, they are asking for different things from that SKU. They each have different expectations.

Identify your real business for this customer. What problem are you solving for him or her? Describe the business are you truly in—from the customers' perspective, not yours. Build on emotions and aspirations when determining your true role in your customers' lives. Let's take, for example, a customer who runs his family-owned business. Is he a Dream-Maker, or are other factors at work? You observe that he's a control freak and a micromanager, not trusting anyone to get the job right. Overall, you might determine that you're in the business of building his ego—he runs the show as much for the prestige as for the profit—and that you're in the business of security, assuring him that things will go right. How can you assure him that you are providing just those services (not in so many words, of course)? And what other products or services can you provide that satisfy those needs?

As another example, ask a bank what business they're in, and you'll get answers about lending and financing mortgages and keeping resources safe. That's not the business they're in, because money is a very personal and very emotional item. To most people, it represents status and self-worth from one viewpoint and security from another. On the one hand, people likely don't know how to handle financial issues—are they saving enough, investing properly, making smart decisions? And on the other hand, the emotions involved in the financial arena are intense. When a bank thinks about finances only in terms of checks and interest rates and other things fiduciary, they miss the whole point, as well as the opportunity for connection.

Identify your competitors for this person's time, attention, money, and interest. What standards do they set for delivering on the true business you're conducting with this customer? How do you exceed those standards?

Remember that competitors for your customers' attention and spend based on lifestyle dimensions encompasses a wider scope than just your own industry. For example, a manufacturer of video games who targets a "Young Adult Escapism" lifestyle segment must look beyond other video game companies, and consider all other suppliers of entertainment for that audience, including recording companies, concert promoters, sporting venues, and the internet.

Lifestyle segmentation and dedicated persona portfolio management allows you to differentiate and innovate your overall value proposition to fit different customer expectations of the complete experience, and to adapt your product or services, your experience and your brand to customer viewpoints.

The Persona Portfolio Manager refreshes the innovation process described in Chapter 4 through the lens of a specific customer viewpoint on a daily basis. Your portfolio manager for the Business Traveler, for instance, is devoted each day to how they can delight such travelers tomorrow.

As an example of employing such portfolio management, let's look at Groupo Banco Popular, which is the third-largest banking group in Spain. Banco Popular is recognized as a pioneer in what has been termed "relationship banking"—using a loyalty-program model to integrate customer interactions across multiple banking products.

Banco Popular, in developing its relationship banking initiative, sought new growth opportunities through customer segmentation and new product offers. In analyzing lifestyle segments within its customer base, the bank identified unique needs of a growing portion of the Spanish population: a ffluent senior citizens. This target group indicated that they valued personal security and the convenience of personal concierge services. Banco Popular responded by establishing "Club Senior"—customers who chose direct deposit of pension checks were entitled to special discounts on restaurants, travel and car repair. They also received access to a dedicated customer hotline, and a 24/7 health line was dedicated to Club Senior customers. Banco Popular went on to expand the service to foreign retirees living in Spain.

Another example of lifestyle segmentation comes from Korea's Hyundai Credit Cards. This organization's business challenges included creating new growth opportunities in the face of a mature market and customer caution after the credit market bubble burst. Hyundai decided to focus on simple identification of cards and unique value; smaller, well-defined lifestyles, and a customized offering for each lifestyle. Their lifestyle offerings included:

- The M Card for Hyundai and Kia car owners, featuring discounts on gasoline and car insurance
- The S Card for shoppers, offering unique discounts at users' favorite stores
- The T Card for telecommunication customers, with unique offers on cell phone services
- The U Card for students, featuring unique offers based on education-related needs

Marrying Financial and Lifestyle Segmentation

As you may have noticed through the analyses presented here, lifestyle persona programs are not revenue-based segmentations. However, the intersection of personas and financial segmentation can reveal considerable information about to whom to deliver customer experience, at what level, and with what specific goals and approaches.

Analyze overall characteristics of your customer base to identify such potential customer pockets that need individualized attention.

And take it a step further. Which of these lifestyle segments is most profitable? Data mining can tell you on which lifestyle segments to concentrate and invest resources. Which lifestyle segments are your Moneymakers, and which are your Misunderstoods? Which are your F.U.'s?—certainly this group shares lifestyle elements that you likely won't want to try to leverage in marketing, but perhaps those lifestyle elements can help steer your initial customer approach—or lack thereof.

In fact, data mining might help you identify critical lifestyle segments in the first place. Data analysis of your most profitable financial segments can identify shared lifestyle characteristics to give you an even clearer picture of your customers to which of those customers to devote resources and how best to engage them. If you have lifestyle transparency into your Moneymakers, you can more effectively engage them when they call in and that Gold flag begins waving. If you have such a transparent view into your Misunderstoods, you can develop points of leverage to help elevate them into the Moneymakers segment.

Similarly, you can discover leverage points by finding the intersection of customer segmentation and other elements of your business. For instance, in Chapter 12, "Measure What Matters," I discuss how to identify the touch points that are most important to your customers, the functions where they expect delight, and where delight has the most overall impact. As you begin to apply demographic information to the analysis of the important touch points, further personas begin to emerge. Different sets of customers will view the various touch points in different lights.

Summing Up: The Heart of the Customer

When you begin to understand financial segments and identify persona elements, you open up an entirely new set of opportunities to create individualized customer experiences. And this is an opportunity that most companies have thus far failed to leverage.

Like your customers—and like you—those companies have motivations and aspirations beyond simple purchase transactions. Yet, they'll fall short in achieving those aspirations because they don't see beyond the product. They don't understand the power of delivering not just quarter-inch holes, but the dreams that the tool can fulfill.

Understanding the heart of the customer, you have that power.

CHAPTER 7

The Diverse Universe of Customers

Perhaps the most pervasive misperception about customer experience is the perception that it doesn't exist at all. Most suppliers of products and services outside of the consumer arena don't believe that the people they deal with are customers at all. Yet, customer experience applies to all types of services and products. Each consumer is actually many different customers, because every product or service represents a distinct, individual experience to its consumer. And the people in line for driver's-license renewal, for example, are just as much customers of the Department of Transportation as they are when they're in the checkout line at Best Buy with a new DVD in hand. And those in a dentist's waiting room are just as much customers as they are when shopping for apparel in Macy's. The purchasing agents at large industrial companies are as much customers as they are when they purchase Disney World travel packages for vacation. And as long as there is a customer, there should be a customer experience.

In whatever realm you operate in—B2B, governmental, medical, and so on—the fact that your customers also visit Starbucks or are spoiled at a Ritz-Carlton hotel creates new operational ground rules. Let's examine the range of experiences customers expect and demand in their dealings with various types of suppliers:

The Consumer Experience

We all know this customer. **The Consumer** purchases goods and services for personal use. He travels and enjoys foods and merchandise. Whenever he engages with a vendor, he expects that the experience delivered to him will bear several characteristics. The experience should:

- Deliver the complete solution to his needs.
- Remember him and treat him as a unique individual.
- Be customized and personalized.

- Be emotionally engaging.
- Be available through multiple, easy-to-use communication channels.
- Provide simple and easy interactions.
- Be relevant.
- Be timely.
- Speak in easy-to-understand language.
- Exceed expectations and provide a surprise.

The Consumer is usually the sole decision-maker and his objective is total satisfaction. He often pays the price of the experience. And the Consumer turns to friends and other consumers to help him determine his final choice of product or service.

The Business Buyer Experience

Business-to-business marketers often mistakenly believe that customer experience is irrelevant to B2B relationships. In reality, considering the size and the longevity of the typical business-to-business relationship, customer experience is even more critical to ensure profitable business.

The Business Buyer operates within an organization or a business. She acquires, for example, new equipment or technology to the benefit of the business. As a human being, she shares the same expectations as the Consumer. However, several characteristics are unique to the Business Buyer experience. This type of experience often includes multiple stakeholders, such as influencers, the purchasing department, the VP of finance, and the end user of the product or service. Each represents a different perspective and interest that must be satisfied by the overall customer experience. Sometimes these interests will actually conflict with each other.

The Business Buyer experience bears these characteristics:
- A long term-relationship—sometimes over a matter of years.
- A long, complex decision process.
- Multiple decision-makers involved in the purchasing decisions.
- Sometimes different stakeholders reflecting different and potentially conflicting perspectives and expectations.
- An operation focused on research and development leading to product-centricity with little regard for customers.
- Multiple end users of the product or service.
- Less emphasis on emotional engagement.
- Purchase of big-ticket items.
- Greater risk of failure.

- Greater emphasis on a product that delivers to specification without any surprises.
- Greater scrutiny of performance.
- Demand for measurable results.

Another common mistake is assuming that the Business Buyer experience is cold and calculated. Our research demonstrates that although Business Buyer expectations tend to be more rational than Consumer expectations, the Business Buyer experience involves a great deal of emotional engagement. Consulting with a large technology company, we discovered that several deals had been lost because, as the customers said, "The competition was warmer and more eager." The relationship may technically be business-to-business, but, in reality, the relationship remains business-to-people at its core. People pay close attention to the attitude that company representatives bring to the discussion, watching for clues to how the relationship will be shaped after they sign the contract.

There are many ways to demonstrate the experience that will create engagement. Such engagement includes:
- Proactive willingness to assist in solving unique problems.
- Demonstrating the eagerness for partnership.
- Flexibility and willingness to customize.
- An overall proactive approach that ensures the Business Buyer success while using your product and services.

Due to the nature of the Business Buyer experience, it's even more critical that the experience will be well designed and executed to ensure the most profitable revenue.

Unlike the Consumer environment, however, the B2B environment employs not customer experience, but customer *experiences* in the plural. You have multiple decision-makers, multiple clients when selling to another business. Each decision-maker has different needs and presents different experiential opportunities. Map what's important to each separately, and then gauge where the differences are. The head of retail, for example, might require the most advanced product available, while the purchasing agent needs to keep costs under control. In cases where the decision-makers' goals are not compatible, address their needs as a team, and ask for clarification of priorities. Make sure you understand the connections between the principals. For one B2B client, we mapped the decision-makers for one of the client's customers, and discovered 20 of them, each with a different perspective. Mapping is very important because these disparate stakeholders are forcing the fragmentation of the organization-centric customer on your business.

The Internal Customer Experience

"We do not do customer." I heard this once in a meeting with a human resources department. The phrasing may be unusual, but the attitude behind the comment is alarmingly typical among workers in internal services departments (often called "shared services"), including human resources, information technology, purchasing, finance, legal and facilities, to name a few. "Internal services" refers to the fact that employees in these departments don't deal directly with the organization's external customers. But that fact doesn't diminish their role in the overall customer experience.

The Internal Customer is a consumer of shared services and, as such, must be treated the same way as external customers. The Internal Customer experience exhibits these characteristics:

- The customers are "fixed"—shared services can't pursue new customers and new customers can't pursue different shared services.

- The relationship is often acrimonious because neither side selected the partner in the relationship.

- The assumption that the Internal Customers are employees may reduce internal services' sense of urgency and importance in serving those customers.

- Operating out of a cost center, those in shared services face limits on what they can invest to delight customers.

- The work of shared services may not be appreciated by those employees they serve.

- Internal Customer satisfaction has no real consequences, but is rather a nice-to-have.

We often equate the Internal Customer experience to a fixed marriage where both sides spend their time trying to prove how dysfunctional the other side is. This type of unproductive relationship exhausts both sides. The Internal Customer deserves an experience that will free him to create a great experience for the organization's external customers. The Internal Customer experience must be complete, customized and proactive, following the same principles of customer experience. It's often helpful to create a line of sight between internal services and the external customer to illustrate the importance of their work, because their work influences the value to the external customers. If IT won't ensure that the latest technology is available, companies will miss on new opportunities to engage with customers. If human resources won't work to understand the external customer, their hiring won't bring in employees who fit requirements and the overall company's customer experience will suffer. As such, those who service the internal customers are enablers to the performance and experience the external customer receive. They must fully understand and embrace this role and be as customer-centric as their external customer-facing colleagues are.

E.ON UK Business Services

E.ON UK Business Services is a shared services group within E.ON UK. Parent E.ON is the world's largest investor-owned power and gas company. UK Business Services supports 17,000 internal "customers" (employees) in five primary areas: Asset Management (Fleet and Real Estate), Change Management, Finance, People Process, and Supply Chain.

THE CHALLENGE

The Shared Services environment typically fostered a contentious relationship between customer and service provider, as the internal customers felt that they're "hostages" lacking a choice in vendor selection. This acrimonious relationship was fertile ground for complaints and lack of cooperation.

What's more, E.ON companies through Europe were about to offer choice of shared internal service groups.

Because of this combination, Business Services' need to deliver greater value became imperative.

THE STRATEGY

A new corporate business strategy called "Changing Energy"—focusing on "Planet & Society, Customer and People" as guiding principles on which to maintain a sustainable business—necessitated a uniform customer strategy within Business Services—the first ever such strategy. Among the many tenets of the strategy were:

- **Complete mapping of the customer experience journey**. E.ON deployed the initiative in eight phases, including leadership alignment; diagnostics of the gap between current employee performance and customer expectations; quantitative experience inventory of customer needs; current customer strategy assessment; redesigning the customer experience; "Capturing Hearts and Minds" so employees could own the changes they would help implement; gathering organizational recommendations; and creating a sustainable action plan.

- **Dedicated execution.** The transformation included developing a Customer Experience Team and a Customer Engagement Team, and creating a Stakeholder Manager position. Cross-functional initiatives are handled by a BSLT (Business Services Leadership Team), and customer experience Action Plans are consolidated and coordinated Business Services Partner Experience Plan (PEP). Derek Parkin (Managing Director of Business Services) and Nicki Akhavan (Head of Customer Experience) provided the leadership and sponsorship for the initiative.

- **Tailored engagements.** E.ON created a Premier Service for executive support to service the Top 60 managers in the business units.

- **Proven seriousness behind the initiative.** E.ON conceived and implemented a "You Said, We Did" marketing campaign to demonstrate listening and action to customers—and specifically what was changed as a direct result of their feedback.

- **Reward for desired activity.** E.ON emphasized annual bonuses based in part on "customer" targets based on achieving customer satisfaction scores. This was in addition to the new enterprise-wide "Business Services Heroes" program recognizing colleagues who have gone the extra mile, becoming a "Hero" or a "Superhero" based on customer feedback.

THE RESULTS

E.ON, UK received a Bronze award in the Organizational Transformation category of the Gartner & 1to1 2009 Customer Awards. The project generated improvement in their Net Promoter Score from -30 to 54. As E.ON Business Services notes: "Our key brand message is providing excellent service and intelligent solutions that save our customers time, cost and carbon. This made it easier for customers to understand how we can help them and how they can contact us, and has also has created a sense of unity and pride amongst our people."

The Citizen Experience

The drivers behind the Citizen Experience evolution come from both private Citizens and the public sector organizations that serve them. While Citizens and public sector organizations have different underlying reasons for requiring innovative services, both groups have reached the same conclusion: Innovating or, at the very least, improving the Citizen Experience is imperative.

The Citizen Customer is a consumer of numerous public sector services. Education, electricity, fire and emergency service, gas, health care, transportation, public housing, town planning, waste management, water services, public information and social services are but a few of public sector services that governments provide their Citizens. For years, most governments treated their constituents as subjects of the state who should feel privileged to receive public sector services. Interestingly, the Japanese take a different approach to the Citizen Experience. In Japan, Customers and Citizens alike are known as *kamisama*—"king" or "god"—and everyone is chartered with visiting and listening to them. In most countries, because Citizens had no choice in selecting service providers, they could do little to materially affect the experience provided by their governments. However, in recent years, Citizens have begun voicing criticism and demanding that their governments treat them like valued customers rather than subjects of the state.

The superior experiences and greater respect that customers receive in the private sector are increasingly influencing them to demand equal, if not better, experiences from their public sector service providers. More and more, Citizens simply refuse to distinguish between private and public sector services, and demand consistency in the quality of experiences provided by these two sectors. The good news is that governments are beginning to listen. In the United States, the Environmental Protection Agency (EPA) created an online knowledge base to support the growing volume of email communication. The agency now handles 90,000 emails per month and responds to 80% of questions without any human involvement. Citizens are more satisfied with the speed of response, while the EPA is delighted by the 70% reduction in emails that require human support.

During periods when every dollar must be stretched to the maximum, citizens want to be assured of receiving top value for their taxes. They no longer view taxes as fees for services that are often seen as inefficient and overly time-consuming. Citizens increasingly take a free-market approach to public sector services, seeking and demanding ever-better value for their tax dollars.

Although the evolution of the Citizen Experience follows that of the Customer Experience, there are distinct differences between the two in strategic, relationship, operational, legal, measurement and cultural arenas.
These differences manifest themselves in the design, innovation and delivery of an effective Citizen Experience, and preclude weaving several Customer Experience principles into the Citizen Experience.

The distinctions between the two experiences include:
- **Strategy: Effectiveness vs. profit.** Unlike the private sector, public sector organizations don't exist to make a profit. In the absence of a profit motive, public sector organizations are limited in the quality of experience they may wish to provide, because they can't charge customers accordingly. Since private sector experiences are predicated on this profit motive, organizations can invest in and deliver more costly experiences with the knowledge that they can simply charge their customers for them. This absence of a profit motive requires public sector organizations to balance experience efficiency and effectiveness with "reasonable" costs.

- **Relationship: Absence of choice.** Customers choose to conduct business with a given vendor out of their own free will. In the public realm, Citizens lack any substantive alternative to utilizing public sector services because there are no private sector competitors who provide identical services. The element of choice so prevalent in the private sector sets the relationship between customer and vendor on a completely different path—one where the customer feels in control of the relationship. The absence of choice in the public sector often leaves customers feeling helpless and trapped in relationships from which they desperately want to escape. Thus, even when experience quality is poor, customers have no alternative but to continue doing business with their public sector vendors. This "forced" relationship often brings with it a strong sense of entitlement among Citizens who, knowing that their tax dollars sponsor government services, demand to be treated like valued customers. This implied or expressed sense of entitlement contributes greatly to the tenuous public sector-Citizen relationship.

- **Operations: Lack of robust delivery infrastructure.** While public sector service providers often serve the same Citizen, they rarely, if ever, share information between themselves. Each organization focuses on its own services, and measures its performance against a narrow set of internal objectives. Because government agencies don't view and treat Citizens holistically, Citizens must establish a relationship with each government entity from which they receive services. Furthermore, poor delivery infrastructures and limited information sharing not only increases citizen frustration but also leads to a perception of wasteful and costly inefficiencies. While opinions in different countries vary, according to the Pew Research Center a majority of Americans agree that "when something is run by the government, it is usually inefficient and wasteful."

- **Legal: Prevalence of privacy concerns.** While private sector organizations increasingly share information across their departments, legal issues often limit such information sharing in the public sector. These concerns greatly inhibit large numbers of government employees from viewing Citizen information, particularly where such information is highly sensitive.

- **Culture: No track record of a service culture.** Since private sector vendors strive to delight Customers, they are often available to address Customer challenges and complaints on a 24/7/365 basis. Public sector service providers generally have restricted "operating hours," usually between the hours of 9 am and 5 pm. These organizations are committed to Citizens only during the hours in which they are open to the public. This restricted commitment impacts the way the public sector approaches citizens. Historically, public sector companies wouldn't receive service training, or measure Citizen satisfaction. They would, therefore, provide sub-standard service. Because Citizens had no alternative, these organizations had little incentive to elevate the quality of their experiences. They exerted total control over the Citizen-government relationship and would consequently treat citizens as "subjects," rather than as partners. The absence of a service mentality creates a significant cultural barrier to designing and delivering delightful Citizen experiences. However, this barrier must be overcome if public sector companies will ever succeed at delivering delightful Citizen experiences.

- **Measurements: No track record of measuring Citizen satisfaction.** Every organization gauges its performance against pre-defined measurements. Employees "follow the numbers" and strive to perform according to the metrics against which they will be measured. In most if not all cases, employees will follow and adhere to processes even at the expense of upsetting the very Citizens that these processes were meant to satisfy. In the private sector, many companies utilize Net Promoter Score and other loyalty measurements to gauge performance. In contrast, public sector measurements typically focus less on Citizen satisfaction and more on adherence to budget and compliance with internal processes and policies. The failure to link public sector performance with Citizen satisfaction leads to unrealistic Citizen expectations and lower public sector quality of service.

When comparing the Customer Experience to the Citizen Experience, another significant difference emerges. Private sector relationships have two primary stakeholders—the Customer and the Shareholder. Public sector relationships have five stakeholders with varying interests and agendas. Because of multiple and sometimes conflicting interests, designing and delivering an agreed-upon experience can be daunting. Public sector organizations must balance agendas that often appear to compete and diverge in order to satisfy, to the extent possible, all stakeholder needs and wishes.

Let's examine the different stakeholders and their primary interests.
- **The Consumer Citizen.** As the primary stakeholder, the Consumer Citizen is the recipient of government services. These individuals are often taxpayers who finance the delivery of the service. During interactions with government organizations, the expectations of Consumer Citizens are similar to those they have with private sector companies. The Consumer Citizen's expectations include:
    - Listening to and understanding citizen needs.
    - Respectful treatment.
    - Adapting resolutions to unique situations.
    - Delivering complete resolutions.
    - Treating issues in a timely manner.
    - Demonstrating empathy and caring.
    - Delivering value for tax payments.
- **The Service Provider.** This is the public sector organization chartered with developing and delivering a specific service to Consumer Citizens. The interest and agendas of these Service Providers include:
    - Developing and delivering efficient and effective services.
    - Minimizing customization to streamline processes.
    - Developing strong accountability over service processes.

- o Adhering to budgetary guidelines and constraints.
- o Developing relevant policies that meet the organization's charter guidelines.

- **The Taxpayer**. The Taxpayer is any citizen or resident who pays taxes, regardless of his or her use of a specific service. Taxpayers finance the services delivered by government and are concerned over the effective utilization and allocation of tax dollars. In this sense, Taxpayers are similar to stockholders with the principal difference being that Taxpayers don't choose to invest in government entities, but are required to do so. The primary concerns of Taxpayers, regardless of their use of services, include:
    - o Utilizing tax dollars effectively.
    - o Demonstrating value delivered for the tax dollars.
    - o Allocating tax dollars fairly to all requisite services.
    - o Avoiding misappropriation of tax dollars to certain causes.
    - o Providing logic behind the usage and allocation of tax dollars.
    - o Accepting accountability for spending tax dollars.
    - o Reducing the tax burden to support government services.

- **The Community.** The Community reflects the larger social context in which a government operates. The Community primarily incorporates social concerns such as environmental organizations and government watchdogs who claim to be operating for the common good. While the Community is not a direct consumer of public sector services, it may have concerns and agendas that supersede those of specific Citizens. As such, the Community will often pressure government to consider those broader societal issues when designing and delivering the Citizen Experience. The Community's primary concerns regarding the citizen experience include:
    - o Treating people equally.
    - o Investing in the environment.
    - o Investing in long-term projects.
    - o Acting in the best interest of the Community, not the individual.

- **Political Leaders**. These individuals guide public sector organizations according to their strategic vision. Most important, though, they determine and allocate budgets. However, unlike corporate executives in the private sector, Political Leaders aren't motivated by revenue and profit. Their motivation stems from their ability to make an impact on society and their constituents. Their primary concerns regarding the Citizen experience include:
    - o Aligning with the overall mission of the organization.
    - o Delivering greater influence and impact on society.
    - o Supporting long-term goals.

The Patient Experience

"You ask me if I have a God complex. Let me tell you something: I am God." Spoken by Alec Baldwin portraying a doctor in the movie *Malice*, these words define for me the challenge of the Patient Experience. Patients are customers of medical treatment. But because of their vulnerable position and the doctors' all-knowing attitude, they're often treated as if they have no choice. No experience factors into their treatment, and being assigned a caring nurse is a matter of luck. This trend is changing—more hospital and medical treatment providers are taking notice and applying customer experience principles to the overall treatment they deliver. However, several fundamental differences must be recognized when designing the Patient Experience.

- **It is about the process, not about satisfaction.** Unlike traditional customer engagement where the goal is total customer experience, Patient engagements can't set such a goal. Every Patient will experience a different outcome. Stating otherwise is a false promise. As such, Patient Experience efforts must adapt in order to focus on being a pleasant partner on the Patient's journey while recognizing that each Patient engagement will have a unique outcome.

- **The family is part of the Patient.** The Patient's loved ones are integral to the full definition of "patient," and therefore integral to the Patient experience. Every experience design must incorporate family into the overall consideration.

- **Well-being is holistic.** The Patient does not bring his body to the treatment; he brings his complete being. As such, the caregiver must respect and support religious, social and other spiritual elements that support the patient on their journey.

Just as it is with traditional customer experience, Patients seek a complete one-stop-shop solution for their needs. Patients want to feel in control and not helpless in face of jargon-speaking medical professionals. They want to understand what's happening and gain some sense of control over the treatment decisions. They want to be treated as human beings with feelings and emotions and not as a set of symptoms to be addressed by the exact combination of chemicals. That is where emotional engagement plays a critical role. When being treated, Patients want to feel as if they're the only Patients that matter. This is the sense of individuality and personalization that was reflected in the original definition of customer experience.

Summing Up: The Universal Customer

Although a customer of government services may be the same person seeking treatment at a hospital in another instance and the same person purchasing supplies for business, his or her customer experience expectations will differ based on the setting. Because we're speaking of the same individual in different customer roles, the demands and the standards that you must exceed remain high.

CHAPTER 8

Employee Experience

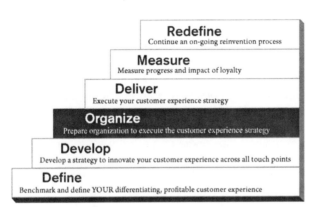

Strategic Steps: Organize

In the *Times of London* in 1913, one Sir Ernest Shackleton is said to have placed this advertisement: "WANTED: Men wanted for hazardous journey. Small wages, bitter cold, long months of complete darkness, safe return doubtful. Honour and recognition in case of success." The ad and the wording may be apocryphal, but Sir Shackleton's search for volunteers for his expedition to Antarctica was not. Over 5,000 people applied to Shackleton. Now *that* is occupational passion.

When your company posts a job, do people line up for the chance to dig in, go to work, and make a difference? Do you attract people fueled by occupational passion, eager for the experience of delivering customer experience?

I ask these questions because while working with clients to define the necessary steps toward customer-centricity and customer experience, I've noticed something interesting. Several top executives I spoke with were receptive to only 50% of my message, while choosing to neglect the other 50%. These execs fully appreciated the importance of redefining their value proposition and creating fascinating customer experiences. Yet, they were reluctant to concede the necessity to do the same for their employees. They believed that customers, having more choices, need persuasion and courting, and that employees don't have the same needs.

The flaw in this thinking is so substantial that I prefer that these executives decline the first 50% of my message and not initiate a customer experience strategy at all.

Employees create the customer experience. Without delightful employee experiences, there is no customer delight. You cannot initiate one without the other—it's that simple. Either through product and service innovations, or through exceptional customer service, employees cement customer relationships.

The executives mentioned above believed that employees will simply follow orders. And worse, they believed that following orders was *all* employees needed to do. A job, in the eyes of these executives, was merely a set of processes, one after another, like an automobile assembly line. Therefore to them, spending extra to delight employees is unnecessary. Why do you need to delight a cog? Yet, employees aren't robots. If you order them around, they function only at partial capacity. They will conduct the transactions they were trained (like dogs) to do—but (unlike dogs), they won't care.

An organization is the sum total of its people—for better or for worse. In a product-centric organization, employees are cogs, and the sum of the employees is a faceless machine. In a customer-centric organization, employees are builders of the experience, and the sum of the employees is an atmosphere of employee delight—and, therefore, customer delight. *There is no customer experience without employee experience.*

For harsh evidence of this fact, consider that Circuit City, the nation's second-largest electronics retailer, filed for bankruptcy and shuttered all of its 567 stores in part as a result of a 2007 decision by Circuit City executives to fire 3,400 seasoned salespeople and replace them with a new, lower-cost sales force. The company defended its decision by claiming that since customers were already loyal to the brand, a sales staff shuffle would have little to no impact on overall customer loyalty. This logic and the decision to replace sales personnel would prove to be disastrous. The move came at a time when its arch rival and the nation's largest electronics retailer Best Buy was investing in and nurturing the relationship with its own sales force. What happened to Circuit City following the replacement of its sales force was inevitable. Consumers would show up at stores and seek the salespeople with whom they had built a relationship. When told that their favorite salespeople had been replaced, customers would seek price discounts to justify their loyalty (and compensate for the perceived deterioration of service). Circuit City failed to recognize that its core strategic asset was its employees—not the logo, not the product selection, not the store location.

Loyalty is a human trait that can be established only through a relationship involving at least two human beings. Loyalty is ultimately given to someone who creates or reinforces value. For this company, the differentiator and source of customer loyalty was its people. Undermining this source of loyalty proved to be fatal.

Focusing employees' efforts on conducting transactions and completing tasks will deplete the company of its best available resource, the passion and willingness to care and help. Issuing the paychecks will go as far as buying their robotic functioning, but it will never reach their hearts. You will never unlock their passion, their comfort in taking risks, their willingness to work in teams, or their ability to excel or lead change. The key to unlocking their hearts is in their experiences.

Reengineering the employee experience requires the same commitment and resources that redesigning the customer experience requires. The justification to invest in such reengineering lies in the factor of 10x you will achieve in employee innovation, in employee productivity, and ultimately in customer commitment and loyalty. Creating a culture of employee delight will deliver not incremental impact, but geometric impact. Passionate employees put you on the fast track to revenue growth.

The economic benefit motivated employees can deliver is not only external, creating a stronger customer base and greater incoming revenue, but also internal. A greater fit of employee passion and employment roles lowers turnover, increases productivity, and generally lowers personnel and HR costs.

The components of a culture of employee delight include the following, which I will explore in greater detail throughout this chapter, as well as in Chapter 9, "Readying the Organization and Developing a Culture of Change":

- **Recruiting.** Do you hire people who pursue missions and not vocations, who love their work and your products?
- **Education.** Do you educate them to care? Do you teach them the skills to resolve problems?
- **Procedures.** Are they empowered to solve problems?
- **Tools:** Do you provide the tools to help them excel?
- **Evaluation.** Do you evaluate productivity or quality? Is the customer part of the evaluation compensation?
- **Compensation.** What are the criteria by which employees are compensated?

- **Rewards.** Do you treat employees with star treatment?
- **Growth.** Do you provide them with opportunities to advance in the company, and are they aware of those opportunities?
- **Executive Responsibility.** Where is top management in building and implementing the customer strategy?

These points add up to one overarching question you must answer: *Why aren't people lining up to work for you?* Design your customer experience with one goal in mind: To create an environment that employees would volunteer to work in, to thrive in. Borrow a chapter from the nonprofits, where people work for passion and most members of the workforce donate their time.

When I worked for Hewlett-Packard, I began to notice that my top performers had something in common. They subscribed to an arcane publication called *Dr. Dobb's Journal.* This is a completely "lunatic" magazine for tech freaks (said with every ounce of respect for these valuable folk), filled with numbers and formulas. To those who read *Dr. Dobb's,* a broken server was not a job, and not even a challenge. It was a calling. *Dr. Dobb's* subscribers would tear apart that server and get it humming for the fun of it—they'd do it for free. The correlation between subscribership and performance was so consistent that eventually I made subscribing one of my hiring criteria.

After all, it all starts with a motivated individual. Just as emotions underlie customer needs, emotions can fuel the passionate employee's mission.

The Foundation of Employee Experience

Ultimately, the employee experience begins with the employees themselves, and with hiring those who will appreciate and thrive in that experience. To find such employees, you must first look within the individuals themselves. There, you must find passion.

Here's an example of that passion at work. Not long ago, friends and family had gathered at a Johannesburg chapel to celebrate the wedding of Barbara Boegner and Gustav Myburgh. The couple hadn't yet arrived by the time the ceremonies were to begin, so the celebrants waited patiently. Fifteen minutes, a half hour, nearly an hour. They likely weren't particularly worried—probably nothing more than a traffic jam.

Well, the delay indeed involved traffic, but not quite in the way the wedding guests likely envisioned. You see, while driving to the chapel, Barbara and Gustav spotted three armed men holding a truck's driver at gunpoint. Even though they were dressed in bridal regalia–the bride in her white gown and the groom in his smart suit—the couple confronted the hijackers, who jumped into a truck and fled. Barbara and Gustav chased the hijackers and eventually caught up with them—resulting in their arrest.

It's an inspiring story, yes, but particularly so for those of us in customer experience—because Barbara Boegner and Gustav Myburgh are law-enforcement officers on the Johannesburg police force. On that special day, they faced a difficult choice—carry on and continue to the church to get married, or deal with the gunmen. Their personal allegiance to their work guided a difficult decision, made in a split second.

Barbara and Gustav represent a different type of employee—the one who comes to work to fulfill a mission, the one who relates to the job as if on a personal calling. Such derive personal meaning and fulfillment from their work, not merely a salary. The Johannesburg police force is blessed to have Barbara and Gustav among their law enforcement officers. Your organization—in order to rise above your competition—must be similarly blessed.

Three broad groups populate the employee ranks:
- **Job People.** The question most on their minds is "What is my next job?", leading to high turnover and negative impact on business. Their motivation is survival.

- **Career People.** With "What's in it for me?" clearly on their minds, Career People are identifiable through the stack of papers they always carry and an attitude that seems to speak, "I'm in a meeting, therefore I am." Turnover of such people is average as they work to climb the corporate ladder, and their ultimate impact on business, because of the more selfish attitude, is neutral.

- **Missionaries.** The true contributors are those who have elevated themselves to a mission. With a commitment to higher purpose—helping others, solving problems, making people's lives easier—drives them, and if they can believe in what your company does, turnover will be low, business impact will be positive, and their commitment will energize not only their work but also the organization itself.

Here's an example of a missionary that approached his job as a calling: a bank's mortgage loan officer received a call from an inspector working on a loan. The inspector reported that the house he'd just inspected needed work before the loan could be approved. After making a couple of calls, the loan officer discovered that the buyer doesn't have the money to handle the needed fixes right away. Now, from a functional standpoint, the loan officer could simply have said, "It's not my problem." From a missionary standpoint, he instead thought, "I'm in the business of putting people in homes. My job isn't done until I've put that person into a house." The loan officer took his own tools to the house, checked out the needed fixes, spent seven hours of his own time making the fixes, and approved the transaction the next day. He didn't break the rules—he didn't approve a loan on an unacceptable house. He simply made good on a personal commitment to his business of putting people into houses.

Your job—your mission—is to bring in the missionaries, and then provide them an occupational environment in which they can thrive and excel.

Building a Delight-Enabling Staff

Take a moment to assess the passion level of your current employees. Ask yourself:

- What would your employees do when a pressing professional need conflicted with a personal need (without the gunmen, of course)?
- Which calling would your employees follow when faced with stressful time-sensitive decisions—a higher mission or personal enjoyment?
- Do your employees limit their commitment to their jobs to working hours?

If you need time to think about these questions, the answers are clear. Welcome to the world of interchangeable employees. Your staff shows up to make money and then go home to spend it. They work for you only because they didn't inherit Paris Hilton's trust fund or win the lottery. These employees are on your payroll because they have to be, not because they want to be. At least they're not out hijacking trucks.

The business implication of such reluctant employees is quite serious. At a time when products and services rapidly become commoditized, employees who don't create differentiation for your business are counter-productive. Reluctant employees don't care about delighting customers or creating innovative products; they are there to conduct transactions and complete interactions.

Each time the reluctant employee touches a customer, you not only lose an opportunity to differentiate your products and create loyalty, you clearly risk reducing loyalty by providing careless service and boring experiences.

At this point, you're probably thinking, "Aren't all employees like that? Aren't they all there to exchange stated services for a paycheck?" Sure they are, if those are the people you hire. Obviously, Barbara and Gustav are not like that. And there are many more Barbaras and Gustavs out there. But you must search for them. You must create a culture that, once you have them, will nurture their passion rather than stifle it.

The right passionate people are the building blocks of your company. Without them, you are a commodity that will always fight for the next sliver of margin. To put yourself on the fast track to revenue growth, take these steps:

Change the way you think about your workplace and the profile of people you seek to attract. A product-centric company doesn't care about passion—they only need people who can operate processes. You take a call and 2 minutes and 30 seconds later the call is done. But if you're in the emotionally engaging experience business, this is no longer enough.

As a rule of thumb, people who can work for you *and* for many other companies (not at the same time) are probably technically proficient, not passionate. They can conduct functional tasks, but not elevate a transaction to a memorable experience. They lack a differentiating level of passion.

Design customer experience around the employee. One of the most common mistakes is focusing on customer experience strategies while taking employees for granted. No matter how carefully you plan the elements and execution of customer experiences, employees who don't find meaning in their jobs will doom your customer experience strategy to failure. People do business with people. People create experiences.

Design the experience around *all* employees, whether or not they are customer-facing. Everyone in your organization is in the customer experience business. Either they create the customer experience directly, or they support the experience creators and enable them to achieve excellence.

Recruit for passion even above skill sets. According to studies, 23% of employees are classified as engaged. They fully believe in the company, they want to contribute, take initiatives, and go above and beyond. 59% are not engaged (reluctant, courteous employees), 17% are negatively engaged. This means that less than 30% of the workforce cares about what their employers do and want to do the best job possible. This is where the crisis starts—the mismatch of skills against what customer experience is all about.

Employees can't deliver passion to others if they don't have it within themselves. Let's take a smile, for example. Can you force someone to smile? Say "cheese"? No. You've all seen faked, forced smiles on airplanes. They're more likely to upset you than to soothe you. Fake smiles are equivalent to forced sincerity. And, in fact, anything artificial—a smile, a reassurance, a nod of sympathy—can communicate precisely the opposite. The fake smile says "I dislike you" instead of "How can I serve you?"

Disingenuous passion can't possibly be transmitted to others in real life—no matter what training you put your employees through. Genuine passion can be supplemented with trainable skills. First Direct is HSBC's phone-based bank in the U.K. Their experience definition is "Caring," and, they had one instruction for the HR department when they started out: "Do not hire a single banker. We don't want bankers here. You're going to hire nurses and social workers. They are people who care, who have made personal sacrifices to care."

Hire for brand passion. And more specifically, seek people who are passionate about your specific product. Have they even used it? I had an argument with an executive with a major wireless provider, who claimed, "All my staff have passion for my phones." I made a bet with him. He allowed me to survey his employees, over 500 in the main building—15% used phones from another provider. Surveys can be more informal: take a look at the parking lot of any car company; what do the makes and models of the cars parked there tell you?

I can't stress enough the need to redesign your educational process, and the importance of fully instilling the goals of your brand in the people who touch customers. They must live and breathe the brand. A standing joke within the Orange telecom company, known for its innovation and customer service, is, "If you cut us, we bleed Orange."

And if not passion specific to your brand, at least to the product or service category you work in. I was doing an analysis of problems FedEx was facing with outsourcing in India. In a focus group, an employee thought he understood the core problem. "The customers are very arrogant," he said. "They have unrealistic expectations. Why do they feel that they're so important? We have a high percentage of complaints just because the package doesn't show up the next day. In India, we're happy if the mail arrives two weeks later. One week, excellent! They want it the next day? What kind of customers are they?" He had no direct sight into the customer, and his own experience prevented him from understanding the customer's concern.

The lesson: You can't develop a superb customer experience and then deploy it in the hands of people who don't live your brand every day. You must intensify the training so that employees do live the brand. Customers don't care where the customer service comes from. It's about the tools and the education you give the employees.

Hire for attitude in addition to passion. Most hiring criteria today are based on skills and not on attitude. And just as with passion, you can't train attitude. You must hire it in, and nurture it. One of the best hiring questions I've ever seen comes from online retailer Zappos.com. "How lucky do you consider yourself in life?" because if life is not fair to you, do it in another company. Feeling lucky is a great attitude. Zappos.com's hiring practices and general atmosphere of employee delight landed them on *Fortune*'s list of "The 100 Best Companies to Work for" for the first time in 2009—at #23, they debuted at a higher position than any previous newcomer to the list.

Virgin Atlantic Airways classifies job candidates into one of four categories:
- Victims—are never at fault (and therefore also never at cause)
- Cynics—are the only smart people in the world, and they'll let everyone know it as sourly as possible
- Observers—are detached; they tend not to act nor to care
- Players—are the ones having fun, and the ones being hired by Virgin Atlantic

Look at your current staff with Virgin's classifications in mind. What percentage of your workforce falls into each group? And what will you do about those who either don't contribute to customer experience, or who only succeed in eroding it? Absolutely do not put the victims, the cynics and the observers in front of customers. And perhaps more severe actions are in order, as explained in this next tactic:

Cut bait. As told in his book *Four Seasons: The Story of a Business Philosophy*, Isadore Sharp realized he couldn't build the world's best hotel chain if he retained the existing hotel properties and employees that failed to live up to his vision, so he cut them loose. Only those employees who could transition and fulfill Sharp's vision of excellence kept their jobs. The vision of excellence extended not only to the physical properties but also to the employees who directly or indirectly would be delivering the Four Seasons experience to customers.

This was indeed a serious and courageous shift in strategy, and one that answers a question often posed to me: Can an organization change its product-centric culture and DNA? People who pose this question generally fall into one of two camps:
- Those who ask the question rhetorically, as if there is no answer. They're seeking any excuse to avoid change, preferring familiarity and the status quo over the new and unknown.
- Those who understand and internalize the need to change, but lack the guidelines, strategy and action plan to effectuate such change. They generally don't, however, lack the courage.

While I wish the first camp much luck in their attempt to stop the wheels of time, it's to the second camp that I offer my support and encouragement in their efforts.

Mr. Sharp's story clearly illustrates that companies can change their DNA, and highlights the principle that one can never compromise on standards to reach illustrious goals.

During our many years helping organizations undergo significant cultural transformations, we have observed employees at all levels unable to find or maintain their passion under the new direction or vision of their companies. When this occurs, it's incumbent upon these organizations to let these individuals go so that their misery, contempt or skepticism doesn't influence other employees.

Letting them go respectfully is the most effective way of allowing them to search for an organization where they can find their passion and be happy in their professions. It's simply a matter of matching goals and passion, rather than a judgment of capabilities. While employees may not thrive in one environment, in another they may flourish.

Companies can transform their cultures if they're willing to make the tough choices and stick to their principles. To that end, they must clearly define the new standard, and the associated criteria for hiring or retaining those individuals that will help get them achieve it. Organizations can never compromise on such criteria, because if they do, commoditization and price pressures will surely follow.

Cut bait as quickly as possible. In an extreme yet highly efficient example, Zappos offers $2,000 to new hires right after they complete new-employee training—*if those employees leave the company then and there.* This practice identifies and weeds out employees motivated only by money, the type of employees you don't want talking to your customers. By the way, most Zappos recruits stay.

Creating a Culture of Employee Delight

Support the results of experience-oriented recruiting and decruiting practices by immersing your employees in a culture of delight. Employee experience is the sum total of the supporting environment enabling employees to perform. Building the right culture is difficult—like that smile you expect of your employees, it must be authentic.

Designing employee experience is not a matter of slogans and empty pats on the back and cheery thank-yous in an internal newsletter. Employee experience is a matter of building a truly nurturing environment in which to perform and to exceed goals and expectations. Employee experience utilizes a combination of obstacle removal, inspiring tools, and education for success.

Again, look outside to see if a line is forming. If it isn't, it's time to get started, using these tactics:

Focus on executing extraordinary experiences and not on merely completing the ordinary tasks. Raise the bar from executing everyday performance to devotion to excellence. An employee can come in with the proper attitude but be worn down by continued managerial focus on tasks.

Empower employees. In your company, is the power to act independently a concept or a mode of operation? Empowerment is one of those odd concepts that every manager claims to deliver but no employee feels they actually receive. Managers claim that they delegate and that they never micromanage, but most employees roll their eyes when they hear such boasts, knowing full well that this empowerment has never reached their desks. Authority to execute is crucial. If you don't trust your people, don't hire them. If you hire them, don't tie their hands and disable them from doing their job.

I discuss employee empowerment in greater detail in Chapter 9, "Readying the Organization and Developing a Culture of Change," but within the context of creating great employee experience, it's critical to note here that if you give employees the power to help someone, to solve problems, to make people's lives easier, you will continually energize them and their passions.

Educate—and teach the right things. Do you *train* or do you *educate*? Traditional training is about controlling employees and holding them responsible for executing procedures. Education is about teaching them the business ground rules and then allowing them to use common sense to delight customers. The former approach sends a message that the employees' primary focus must be on following the rules, while the latter approach bestows your staff full responsibility to solve customers' problems, and to care.

In a real example, a customer called the help desk of a large printer-service outsourcer. His printer was broken. The customer service representative consulted the service level agreement for that printer, which outlined promised response time depending on the number of people affected: 1 person affected, response in 72 hours, and on up to a 4-hour response if more than 25 people are affected. The CSR asked, "How many people are connected to the printer, sir?" When he learned that only the caller was connected, the CSR promised resolution in 72 hours. The problem was that actually 22,000 people were affected indirectly, in that the caller needed to print 22,000 paychecks that day. But with one connection, the CSR was following the rules. He wasn't thinking. There was no reason to think. He was given very specific service criteria, and he acted to the letter of those criteria—the commodity service.

Review your training program and weed out unnecessary rules and regulations. Replace them with commercial guidelines that allow your people to understand your business and financial considerations, and then apply that understanding as they service customers. Educate employees on the importance of treating different customers differently based on their total business and profit level they supply the company. Make certain that they understand your margins and annual customer value so they can select the right compensation for certain problems. Instead of controlling employees, free them to execute through better understanding of the business principles. Again, see the next chapter for further detail of this critical topic.

Clearly define customer experience standards and goals. This is not a job description or a task list—it is a solid foundation for actions that employees might take to delight customers. Some companies simply fail to define customer experience outright, leaving employees to at best make up things as they go along without knowing if what they're doing is what the customer wants, and at worst, do nothing at all. Don't leave the customer experience to chance.

We conducted a three-year study with 32,505 participants, 42% of whom were customer-facing and noncustomer-facing employees from five companies in B2B, B2C and services, and 58% of whom were the customers of those employees.

Participants were asked to rank the quality of the customer experience they provide or receive. Both employees and customers were asked to respond to the same questions. While 78.2% of employees responded with strong conviction that they exceed customer expectations, only 27.4% of their customers agreed with the same statement. Similarly, 88.3% of the employees strongly believed that they use their common sense and discretion in the way they deal with customers. Only 40.0% of their customers agreed with the same statement. In the area of defining the experience, employees consistently ranked their performance higher than their customers did, with an average gap of 43.0%. The study clearly demonstrates that employees and customers have completely different definitions of a great experience, leading to unacceptable results.

The problem was that customer experiences were never clearly defined for the employees who participated in the study. There was no common definition of what the customer experience should be. The experience was left to the personal interpretation of each employee, which created misunderstandings and discrepancies in performance. While employees may be trying hard, they often lack the guidelines and directions to deliver a top-notch customer experience.

Here's where guidance and training again becomes critical. Although tool skills and transaction handling are taught in great detail to prevent any misunderstanding, experiences and customer knowledge are often vague and undefined. While 66.7% of the employees in the study were convinced that they understood the customers' pains and issues, only 24.6% of customers agreed with the same statement.

Close that gap by defining the experiences you want your employees to deliver based on customer expectations and what is defined by the company as a profitable value proposition. Provide them with the customer knowledge they need to achieve that delivery. These steps form the core of breaking the deadlock between employees' and customers' perceptions of the customer experience. Customer experiences should be treated like products, accompanied by defined performance descriptions, clear measurements, and comprehensive employee education programs.

At a time when customer experiences are the next competitive battle, you can no longer afford to leave your employees guessing what experience your customers want. This approach results in denial and diverse versions of what the employees believe the experience should be. At a time when every employee's actions can build or destroy loyalty, employees must operate from a clear experience execution guide to ensure maximum customer delight and profitability.

In my travels, I've encountered various corporate slogans claiming total commitment to the customers. "Taking you more personally," declares Qatar Airways. "Emotionally yours" is the promise of the Indian airline, Sahara. These slogans are no different than many others produced by ad agencies trying to dress up their clients with more customer-centric messages.

When encountering such slogans, I like to approach employees of these companies either in their retail outlets or through the call centers and ask them what the slogan means to them. The employees are usually confused and embarrassed as they try to explain. I do this not to be mean but to examine the heart of the issue. Are the people at the front lines committed to the message? Do they understand it? Do they live it? Like purchased advertising space, these employees were plastered with the latest slogan and commitment without any expectations. They are expected to smile and spit the slogan out upon request. Meaningful mission statements are motivational, instructional and achievable, as we'll see in Chapter 9, "Readying the Organization and Developing a Culture of Change," but short of that, if your employees don't understand the latest slogans, let alone believe and live them, then you have failed the first credibility test.

Create product and service excellence employees can be excited about. You can't sell substandard service or experiences with WOW employees. Nor can you continually expect WOW performance if you communicate to employees that you will accept being OK with customers. When Henry Juskiewicz acquired Gibson Guitar in 1985, he faced a company with a great heritage near collapse. One of his first steps was to end the practice of selling scratched guitars as seconds—profitable as such a practice was—to enforce the concept of product excellence. To dramatize the decision, Juskiewicz took a faulty guitar and in the presence of the company's employees, smashed the guitar and declared that, as of that moment, any guitar that would not meet the standard of a first-class Gibson guitar would not be sold to customers. "This guitar says Gibson on it, and it's not Gibson quality," he said simply. To emphasize his seriousness, he instructed employees to smash each faulty guitar themselves, and at the end of each week, Juskiewicz would take a chainsaw to what remained of the seconds.

While destroying guitars with a chainsaw might seem a bit theatrical, this action sent two critical messages to employees: 1) To ensure that customer expectations and experiences would be exceeded and delightful, anything less than perfection wouldn't be tolerated 2) By destroying faulty guitars, Juskiewicz was destroying any attitude of taking customers for granted.

At Gibson, prices had been declining 20% a year—yet, to the astonishment of employees, Juskiewicz not only raised prices, in some cases, he doubled them. And sales volume increased. By inspiring employees and offering a product that delighted customers, Gibson could significantly raise prices as customers reaffirmed their conviction in the value delivered by their premium-priced products.

Invest in passionate employees. Consider investment in passionate people as important as an investment in research and development or in the quality of your products. Consider it as important as important as investment in top talent.

Passionate people may command higher salaries. They may also accept lower salaries in exchange for the opportunity to exercise their passion. Don't be tempted to take advantage of that willingness—pay the appropriate salary. It's the underlying attitude—that they might even be willing to do the job for free—that you seek. Either way, well-paid passionate employees bring a much higher return in the form of more business with higher margin. They don't merely conduct business; they increase your value.

The Circuit City episode, while sad and unfortunate, is one from which we should all draw the necessary conclusions. The temptation to eliminate high-paying jobs when under pressure to reduce costs should never outweigh the impact of such layoffs on the customer experience. These employees will only be perceived as "costly" when ignoring the value they provide customers and, consequently, to the organization. Employees that create and reinforce customer loyalty are assets to be cherished, not liabilities to be discarded. Therefore, it's incumbent upon CEOs to ensure that cost-reductions don't impair corporate value and reduce customer loyalty.

Continually celebrate devotion. Share stories of excellent performance in your organization. Publicly reward those who deliver such performance.

At centers of exceptions, companies align employee performance with incentives that appropriately reward desired performance and encourage other employees to strive to obtain these incentives.

The size and type of the rewards and how often you present them correlates with the performance standards you've established. If your company seeks mediocrity, the occasional pair of movie tickets will deliver precisely the level of mediocrity to satisfy your goal. If your company seeks to establish or maintain a center of excellence, you must go much further and celebrate employees like the stars they are. If they're recognized and treated like stars, they'll give a star-like performance for your customers. If the incentives are inspirational, employees will aspire to do even more.

Leave incentive programs for functional motivation, not fueling passion. Don't fool yourself into believing that you can incentivize creativity, caring, and leadership. Such qualities can't be instilled in people if they're not there already. You can reward for exercising those qualities, as we see in detail in Chapter 9, but passion won't follow a carrot on a stick. In informal terms, you can't throw a plasma TV at employees and get caring in return. You can get faking, but not caring.

Set WOW goals to fuel WOW passion. At the InterContinental in Atlanta, all employees are instructed that if they don't get an unsolicited compliment from the customer, they didn't do their job. For the purposes of definition, "Thank you" is not a compliment. A compliment is, "You surprised me. This was unexpected. This was WOW." Right then and there, management is setting the bar higher than that of the rest of the industry.

Innovate your employee evaluations. When dealing with passionate employees tasked with delivering delightful customer experiences, you'll very quickly realize that your evaluation form today is a template for parity. And if you evaluate for parity, why do you expect employees to give you more than that? Do employees understand how high you're asking them to jump? Are you willing to judge them on the highest level, or are you compromising the level? The goals that you demand of your employees and the questions that you ask of them employees will determine whether you will get to the WOW.

Surround passionate employees with passionate employees. Let's consider two hypothetical employees: Jenny, who is consistently excellent at her job, and Richard, who is consistently mediocre at the same set of duties. Customers interacting with Jenny will raise their expectations, and when those same customers speak with Richard, the resulting disappointment dips their satisfaction level below where it was before speaking with Jenny in the first place. You don't want to subject customers to such rapid rises and falls. If you have only a few heroes, you'll give customers a heart attack.

Now, consider the impact on Jenny and on your culture of delight. Jenny isn't isolated—she works within an ecosystem. If she is surrounded by Richards, she will lower her standards, or she will leave.

Allow passionate employees to help shape the experiences themselves. Walk the road less traveled and approach your operations people before making brand promises to customers. The questions should be, *What can we do or change to become a more customer loving organization? What processes should be changed? What impact should we have on the way we produce and deliver our products and services? What else can we do to delight customers?* Operation and execution are at the core of the challenge of becoming customer-centric. There is no point in raising customer expectations through over-promising communication if there is no organization to back up those promises.

Removing the Roadblocks to Employee Experience

As you approach the process of reengineering your employee experiences, you will very likely encounter obstacles to accepting and creating such initiatives. These obstacles extend beyond the half-acceptance from top executives that I described at the beginning of this chapter. The obstacles are often from the employees themselves.

When hearing of yet another internal experience initiative, employees will very likely be suspicious, skeptical, cynical—or all of the above. They deserve to be. After being told during the 1990s that they were the company's critical asset, employees saw a different story told to them by actions in the early 2000s. A cold, faceless company gave employees the cold shoulder as it focused on cost reduction and treated them as another source of cost. It takes time to rebuild the trust. You must demonstrate that you are launching a program that will last with investment, not just another round of T-shirts and posters. But if your efforts are sincere, your employees will eventually believe you and buy into it.

The obstacles extend to the employees' ability to deliver customer experience. Anything that removes one of the key elements of employee experience—whether the tools, the empowerment, the education, and so on—weakens the ability to keep not only customers but also the employees themselves.

Take, for instance, our visit to a client's call center, where we saw customer service reps in headsets and microphones hunched over their keyboards, typing furiously—even though their computer monitors displayed the command "No input allowed." Because the reps were handling customer complaints after an internal deadline had passed, they were blocked from further input into their files, and thus were forced to position their microphones near their keyboards so the customers could hear the keyboard clacking and believe that their complaints were being recorded.

Such obstacles can lead to not only skepticism but also complete lack of faith in the company—again, because of the implicit message delivered to employees: *We don't care about you.* One of my friends did a study on why employees leave a company. He read and analyzed 20,000 exit interviews. His conclusion: only 11% left for better pay, 89% left because they don't believe in the company anymore. Over the past few years, as companies focused on efficiency programs, they did so at the expense of their employees. Employees resented the price they were required to pay and as, a result, lowered their commitment level to the company. This lower commitment level is just the tip of the iceberg. Employees also witnessed the devaluation of the products and services at the companies they worked for. They observed how bureaucratic accountants stripped the products of value and turned them into vanilla commodities not worth the asking price. Additionally, companies sharply reduced their human resources, and therefore, their ability to deliver products and services to customers in a satisfactory manner. All these activities eroded the employee/company relationship.

Throughout the cost-reduction and efficiency-building process, employees lost their faith in the very products and services they represented, sold and delivered. The result: they simply can no longer look their customers in the eye. They know better than to try and deceive their customers. And yet, deception is exactly what they feel they are practicing these days.

Roadblocks such as these can be hard to dislodge if they are emotionally ingrained in the employee or institutionally ingrained in the company. But dislodge them you must, as soon as possible. Among the tactics you can employ:

- **Start simply, directly and aggressively.** The key to smoothing the little speed bumps and dismantling the forbidding battlements is to identify problems at levels large and small and address them immediately. Do so publically, so that employees see that you're serious about making the improvements, and that they'll be heartened by the improvements themselves.

- **Put some teeth in the effort.** Designate a Chief Obstacle Removal Officer whose job is to learn, and to respond. Invest this position with authority to act, and to hold people responsible for delivering suggested improvements.

- **Address cynicism point blank.** Don't try to guess what might make employees cynical about new initiatives. Ask, "What makes you cynical?" We've posed that question to employees during several of our projects, and always benefit from the directness of their responses. Employees can't very well respond cynically to being asked what makes them cynical, now can they?

- **Identify and leverage disguised passionate players.** Imagine a meeting in which everyone at the table agrees with all decisions and conclusions the group makes—except for one smart aleck whose only contribution is the occasional wisecrack. Most would find this employee to be little more than a disruption, but look at him through a different lens. The smart remarks might come from misguided passion—a true caring about what happens in the company, and deep-seated disappointment that the company isn't fulfilling its promise. Again, approach such individuals point blank. Recruit them as allies and tap the passion and the perspective they still harbor.

- **Provide tools to do the job right.** Imagine a help desk devoted exclusively to handling employee challenges with BlackBerrys. Now imagine that help desk with nary a BlackBerry in sight. We couldn't imagine it, until we'd seen it for ourselves. During one of our customer experience audits, we discovered this very situation—a BlackBerry help desk where service representatives have no access to BlackBerrys for training and reference purposes.

  o Companies planning to empower their employees to deliver great customer experiences must first grant those employees unfettered access to the tools and information they need to answer customer questions and resolve their challenges. Only a fully informed employee base can turn a traditional customer service department into a center of exceptions.

  o Knowledgeable employees can answer and resolve complex queries and problems. Uninformed employees will look utterly helpless in front of customers—not exactly the impression that most companies wish to convey to those who keep them in business.

  o Do your employees have the proper and most up-to-date tools to do their jobs effectively? For instance, do employees have access to centralized data, whether customer profiles, product histories, and so on?

  o Too often, employees are expected to perform as automated search machines in their companies' impossible maze of applications and patchwork information systems, installed separately and without an overall plan. In the process, they waste their own time as well as their customers', unable to focus on delivering excellent, profitable experiences. In such situations, executives apparently don't think that providing modern fast access to information is necessary to the employees' experience and satisfaction.

o This sends a deflating message to employees: "You aren't important enough for us to invest in better tools for you. Your job is just not that important. And your job is not that important because the customer is not that important." When customer service representatives waste time navigating through multiple old databases to find a simple answer for the customer, they realize that if it was important to the company, the company would have made resources available to make this information accessible and not waste the customer's time. Taking their cue from the company's lack of investment, they begin to align service level and customer care with their interpretation of the company's behavior. Employees respond to what companies do, not to what they say. They see where resources are invested and assign their priorities accordingly. Inefficiency breeds even greater inefficiency.

o If servicing the customer and creating amazing experiences are the organization's top priorities, then going to war in a 21st-century business environment with blunderbusses, Gatling guns and pointy sticks is unacceptable. This is an open invitation for the competition
to take over. Simply hoist the white flag.

o Even when companies acknowledge such deficient toolsets, they try to patch up the problem by stepping up IT system training or even changing the compensation plan hoping to force employees to master the company's maze of confusing non-coordinated systems. Stop scratching your right ear with your left hand; it just doesn't make sense.

o Instead, address the problem at the root; automate and modernize. New promising solutions are out there, such as from the Atlanta-based Jacada, that allow companies to create seamless, fast access to information and save employees, and customers, time without the traditional need to replace everything. Companies can now retain their investment in their existing systems and databases while improving significantly the employee and customer experiences.

o There's no better way to start reengineering the employee experience than by demonstrating real investment in making their work more effective, their customers happier, and their work lives much easier.

- **Apply the 3 Whys investigation.** Examine processes—particularly those you know or even suspect are standing in the way of excellence—and ask why those processes are in place. Then, ask "Why?" of the answer you receive. If a procedure doesn't make sense, you'll generally go through 3 Whys before people pause and say, "You know, it really doesn't make sense"—other than the fact that "We've always done it that way."

  - We once worked with a software company that required customers wishing to return the product to call in a request. Four employees would review that request. Within three weeks, the company would call the customer, explain that the request had been approved, and ask that the disk be returned in its original box. I asked, "Why do you use a review process? How many of the requests have been denied?"
  - "None."
  - So I said, "Why four people? Why three weeks? And why do you ask the customer to ship the disk back? What are you going to do with it?"
  - "We throw it into the garbage."
  - I said, "If customers have installed the software, can they still use the program after they send back the disk?" *Yes*, was the answer. I said, "Do you recycle the disk?" *No*. As you see, it took a few Whys before they paused and said, "This long and involved procedure doesn't make sense."

- **Reward employees for obstacle removal.** In the case of institutional hurdles, a tactic as simple as awarding $50 each time an employee identifies a process that holds an employee back from delighting customers can pay off with significant insight and resulting improvements. Mount big signs in the halls, break rooms and conference rooms so all can see. The employees know what's holding them back, and they've created ways to get around them, and to survive. A restriction on how long a complaint can be open holds them back, so they concocted the typing-sound solution to survive, and shared it amongst themselves. You think you're doing training—they're training each other about how to handle real cases. Let them teach you, so you can regain control of customer experience education and improve the employee experience.

Summing Up: The Employee Advantage

Passion is the new competitive advantage. Are you leveraging your complete employee? Are you tapping into their passion, caring and willingness to assist, or are you forcing your Barbaras and Gustavs to function robotically? Is your working environment, your employee culture and your corporate attitude toward the customer such that passionate employees would stand in line to work for you? Are you nurturing employees on a customer mission, and benefitting from the most energetic passion available? If not, return to your employee experience design, and innovate and reinvigorate just as you innovate for customer experience.

After all, to unleash the best in your people and tap commitment to excellence, you must treat employees like customers. Employees share an important attribute with customers: they are human. This attribute allows them to connect with customers like no web-based self-service or IVR ever will. Employees can create memorable, positive emotional experiences in customers that win customers over and beat the competition.

For this reason, you must bestow employees the same surprisingly amazing treatment that you deliver to customers to motivate them to excel. You might be able to force employees to process transactions, but you can't force them to smile sincerely. The sincere smile that builds a great customer experience comes from their personal reservoirs. You can't force a smile, but you can nurture it.

Treat employees well, surprise them with your care, and they will care for your business. Show them your commitment and they will reciprocate. Don't fall into the old trap of short-cuts. In today's competitive environment, you must take advantage of every edge you can get. Passionate people are that edge. Invest accordingly. After all, wouldn't you like to have Barbara and Gustav working for you? And wouldn't you like them stopping the competition from hijacking your customers?

CHAPTER 9

Readying the Organization and Developing a Culture of Change

We usually encounter one of two types of conversations when we come into a company to begin our consulting work. The first type speaks of the past, with laments that are variations of "It used to be so good here." Right then and there, we know that this organization is going nowhere. They're sitting on inertia.

The other type of conversation speaks to the future, with variations of "There's our target. That's what we want to do. And this is how we're going to do it." This organization has momentum—or, at least, the potential for it. It displays the necessary acceptance of change, and it's ready to explore how the change will impact its customers.

The first company is mired in nostalgia. The leaders aren't ready for the change necessary to build customer-centricity. They don't want to consider new ways, except if those new ways are really a means to return to the old ways in the days of yore, when product was prince and the CEO and the stockholder were king and queen.

The new kings and queens are your customers. The new princes and princesses are the employees and the value they create for your company. Is your company ready to deliver the impact performance that such a shift in perspective can—and must—bring to your business?

The Critical Need for Impact Performance

Consider that the average call center employee handles 40 calls a day and 10,000 calls annually. If that call center employs 25 service representatives, at least a quarter of a million Daily Choices will be made at that corporate touch point every year—250,000 choices that will make the difference between excellence and mediocrity. If the call center makes a quarter of a million decisions for excellence, the company's performance and reputation will be strengthened; if they're made for mediocrity, the company will be diminished.

Using an example in another setting, a bank teller may handle 30 customers a day, on average, which alone accounts for 6,500 daily decisions made each year. If we assume ten employees per branch and 1,000 branches per bank, this amounts to at least 65 million Daily Choices a year. No advertising or branding campaign can alter the results of these choices—the choices themselves will drive perception of the bank as excellent, or mediocre or worse. The strength of the bank and its customer relationships doesn't lie in the competitiveness of its interest rates, but in the performance choices its employees make, every day.

Daily Choices take place in front of external and internal customers, dominating such interactions as staff meetings, email exchanges, phone conversations, and any other situation in which an individual is in a position to help someone else. Whenever a recipient is on the other end of the action, a Daily Choice is involved, and top-down decisions from the CEO have little if any impact on these employees' Daily Choices.

The bottom line is that *a company's overall excellence is equal to the sum of the total excellence-seeking Daily Choices delivered by its people*. There's no better way to measure the strength of a company than by the quality of the choices its employees make every day. The more excellence delivered, the stronger the customer's commitment and the greater the amount of business and profits generated. The weaker its employees' commitment to excellence, the weaker its overall performance. This is a new way to view the power and strength of organizations, and it requires a different way of leading and motivating people *in order to generate Daily Choices for excellence and exceeding customer expectations*

This bottom-up organizational definition runs contrary to the way most organizations define themselves today. A top-down organization views its power, strength and brand in total as an abstract entity, loosely connected to its people. The employees are subservient to the larger organizational definition. According to this line of thinking, even if all the employees were to leave the organization, the brand will remain strong; the brand makes the people and not the other way around.

In a bottom-up organization, the organization is defined by the character and performance of its employees. The people in the company make the organization what it is. They are the ones creating the organization's assets. Although some management and marketing theories claim to have an organization based on assets other than employees, such as brand strength and reputation, those assets depend on employees and their choices for excellence. Missing one excellence-oriented employee will make the company weaker. Poor performance by just one employee will make the company weaker. The company doesn't exist without the people who, through their Daily Choices, breathe life into the company's mission statement, values, objectives, strategy, and overall definition.

The company's success isn't measured by some annual study of corporate brand strength, but by the daily performances of the individuals who *are* the company. Thus the critical need for a bottom-up view of company organization.

Most companies declare their total commitment to their employees and tout their initiatives to promote employee welfare on the pages of their glossy annual report, while relatively few companies truly understand what it means to treat employees as their most important asset.

Let me give you an example of the depth of the sea-change involved in building an impact performance platform from the bottom up. Over the past several years, I've searched for a CEO whose career began as a customer service manager. To my surprise, that search has been greeted with reactions ranging from sheer disbelief to laughter to outright dismissal. Yet, these same disbelieving CEOs had repeatedly proclaimed that customer service plays an integral role in their companies' business strategies. If that were true, I figured, then finding a CEO with customer-service roots shouldn't have been a challenge—particularly when you consider some grim statistics from our annual *Global Customer Experience Management Study*:

- Only 29% of respondents claimed that their company compensates their employees based on quality of service
- Only 34% of the respondents claimed that their employees have the tools and authority to service customers
- Only 30% claimed that their company invest in people more than in technology

Did I ever find that CEO with the customer-service roots?
More on that in a moment.

We've seen in Chapter 8 the critical importance of the passionate employee, eager and prepared to commit to making a difference in customers' lives—eager and prepare to make an impact. But if the organization is unready, unwilling or unable to facilitate that impact, the power of the passionate employee is lost. That employee will be shackled, driven toward mediocrity, and eventually lost to another company. To be fully ready for success in the arena of customer experience, an organization must prime their employees for impact productivity over functional productivity—again, converting their jobs from churning out tasks to answering a calling.

Think of employee performance as a pyramid. At the broad base of the pyramid is Functional Performance. A company that forms the foundation of its culture on functional performance treats employees as components. A workforce, in such a company's view, is interchangeable. And because functional performance is dictated by procedural manuals and policies, micromanagement is usually the pervading management style.

At the apex of this pyramid is Impact Performance. Such an environment focuses on values and the impact of the company's employees, products and services on the eventual customer. A company that flips the pyramid and makes the apex the foundation of its culture believes in a cohesive workforce, one with a common goal of providing differentiation. The pervading management style is one of empowerment.

Lurking somewhere between is Inconsistent Performance, a corporate culture mixing doses of Functional Performance and Impact Performance. Though perhaps better than a Functional Performance culture that churns out the tasks and fails to delight customers, the Inconsistent Performance culture can raise customer expectations and dash them within even a single pair of transactions. As well, the internal disconnect causes friction and conflict, with the efficacy and energy of Impact Performance being eroded by Functional Performance and the management that not only permits it but also perhaps cheers. Eventually, the company slips back into the lowest common denominator at the base of the pyramid, in which jobs are jobs and customers are merely dollar-delivery vehicles.

Introducing the Customer Impact Performance Platform

The truth of the matter is that every job has a functional purpose that can be tedious, difficult and boring if not viewed in the perspective of customer experience. If you allow employees to take that approach to their job, you'll wear them down, and grind them into parity at best and mediocrity and eventually corporate weakness at worst. *Force* them to take that approach, and you end up in even worse shape. Continued managerial focus on tasks sends a message: *Don't think. Follow the process.*

The companies mired in the "good old days" treat employees like they treat their customers, taking them for granted and expecting that the company's very existence is enough to motivate action. They hand employees a brochure like it's a generic advertisement and say, in essence, "Start working. The tasks await." At best, these companies serve as instructors—but they can't *instruct* employees to be sincere and happy. "Be happy! Smile! Now!" Process operation has a parity line, and caring, sincerity, risk-taking are extras. The employee must want to give that—you can't force it. Therefore, now you must exercise different management skills. Managers are now servants of their employees, not instructors, telling them what to do. You must flip the triangle, building a performance environment to support the employees who care, and who rise above the parity line.

Customer-centric companies turn the organization chart on its head and place the customers at the top of the pyramid. The most important employees are those who service those customers. Everyone else—including management—is there to enable the experience and provide customer-facing employees with the tools, authority and information to delight customers. In this new scheme, the higher you are in the organization chart, the more employees and managers you serve in order to better serve the customer.

Building Blocks of the Impact Performance Platform

Such a major shift in perspective involves redesigning employee understanding of their roles and responsibilities. Employees can make the transition to caring, sincerity and risk-taking—to the essentials of customer experience—only if they know that they're in charge and that there's a reason for what they do. Show them that reason. Connect them to the impact they wield on the customers and on the company. This principle is the foundation upon which the customer impact performance platform is constructed.

The components of impact performance cover these critical areas:
- Employee view into customer impact
- Employee trust in customer experience leadership
- Employee empowerment to make customer-centric decisions
- Education that stresses principles over procedures
- Performance evaluation aligned with customer experience goals
- Inspiring employee recognition and reward
- An overall culture of excellence

Examine each of these components in turn as you build toward the culture of excellence. Begin with these steps for developing employee insight into how their work impacts customers and how to successfully execute customer experience:

Begin with the basics. A simple statement sets the stage: "We are here because there's a customer who needs us." This attitude is the difference between employees going home and saying, "I helped people today," instead of, "More people bothered me with their nonsense."

Visualize impact. Instill in employees the sense that they are the critical missing piece of the puzzle customers must solve. Help them visualize accomplishments and successes beyond the tasks they have accomplished that day. In one grand example, imagine a job in which you do nothing but write upper-case letters in cursive eight hours a day, five days a week. And, in fact, it is only one letter—capital L in cursive, day after day. You don't get to write Q's or R's or even a lower-case z. Boring, right? What could possibly motivate you to write L upon L upon L day after day after day? Now, remember that this job exists. I had the pleasure of meeting Ayla, the woman who tests nibs for Montblanc pens. Her benchmark for a nib that flows properly is in writing the proper loops in a capital L. When I asked her if she found the job tedious, she told me "No." After all, she wasn't simply writing the letter L. She was testing the pen that would write the next best-selling novel, compose a momentous peace treaty, or note the formulae for a cure for a world-threatening disease. Ayla doesn't need additional motivation or more money, because she believes that every day what she does touches someone. In the evaluation terms of Virgin Atlantic discussed in Chapter 8, she's not a victim, not a cynic, not an observer. She's a player—because she understands the potential impact of her work.

Focus on customer impact over company impact. Let me ask a simple question: When you were a child, what did you want to be when you grew up? An astronaut? A doctor? President of the United States? Whenever I ask that question, I don't hear a single person chime in, "I wanted to add value to stockholders. I wanted to work for 30 years so that my stockholders' portfolios earn a lot of money." I don't know why, but I still haven't heard from this person.

Examine your corporate mission carefully—not just the stated one, but the one implied by your work environment and your actions. Read through your annual report and its long discussion of stockholder benefit and its short discussion of customer benefit. Working in this milieu, your employees have little choice but to begin to conclude that you're asking them to go above and beyond so that they can make some rich people richer.

What clues do employees detect? What do they hear from you? Do they hear that you focus on a clear mission, or that you focus on making rich people richer?

Don't get confused—the companies that execute customer experience are making a lot of money and maximizing revenue. But profits aren't the mission. Profits are the outcome of the sharp customer strategy that these companies have employed.

Provide a direct line of sight from employee to customer. Silos and job descriptions create screens that prevent many types of employees from seeing the customer and the impact their work has on that customer. As we've designed customer experience innovation, we've seen how silo myopia, territorialism, and focus on their own numbers distract employees from addressing the whole of the customer.

Many of these silos—internal services, primarily—believe they already have a superb view of their customers, and indeed they have. The problem is that they're working from an old-school vision of who their customer is: the company itself. In this top-down view, HR doesn't serve the person buying the company's products. HR serves department managers with staffing needs. Managers are their customers. And so it is with IT, serving internal customers—and the fact that those internal customers ultimately serve external customers is of no immediate concern to them. Therefore, allegiance to the internal customer creates obstacles in removing the screens between employees and customers.

When we design an organization to be customer-centric, we address such obstacles by putting into place what we call a "the martini glass" model—wide at the top and at the bottom, with a thin connector between. The wide top comprises the customers. The thin connector comprises those employees with direct external customer contact—marketing, customer service, and so on. We refer to these employees, these internal customers, as "Experience Creators." They're on the scene, speaking directly to customers, crafting the experience on the fly. The base of the martini glass comprises what we call "Experience Enablers." Without their support of the Creators, customer experience would not happen.

Train the Experience Enablers to understand their role in customer experience creation. Praise and encourage their contribution. Create a line of sight to the customer so that they see how their work affects the customers, as discussed in Chapter 2. If HR doesn't hire the right people, for example, you cannot serve the customer. That's a line of sight. In our consulting, we often map each touch point, each function in the company, to identify opportunities to delight customers rather than as performance evaluation tools.

Whatever you do, don't allow Experience Enablers to think they can exist in a vacuum, serving only their internal customers. If the external customers don't pay the bills, the Enablers will have no internal customers to serve in the first place. To be blunt, Experience Enablers who fail to understand how their work links to the external customer will be gone. The intellectual property of companies today exists in the form of customer relationships. Everything not directly affecting customer relationships will ultimately be outsourced. By not connecting with the customer experience, Experience Enablers are writing their own ticket out of the company.

In a martini-glass environment, both Creators and Enablers consider themselves to be one big office rather than a series of isolated cubicles. One U.K. company we worked with believed in this principle so strongly that when we ran its training program, the visionary managing director invited to the sessions company executives on down to the night guards to the people who cleaned the toilets. And he himself, attended, as well. That's one way to start breaking down the silos.

Put a face on the customer. This strategy is, in part, a goal of persona development and segmentation covered in Chapter 6, "Different Experiences for Different Customers." Even on such broad terms as a persona profile, employees begin to get used to the fact that customers are not case numbers, not accounts, not email addresses, not area codes. They're human beings. Allow consumers to send video over the phones so reps can see their customers. Find opportunities for Experience Enablers who are otherwise hidden in back offices to mingle with customers, perhaps at focus groups or convening customer panels.

Allow Experience Creators the same opportunities. One great example of allowing associates to meet customers directly comes from TAM, the Brazilian airline. TAM moved its call center to the airport. The first three hours of each shift, service reps work with customers face to face on the terminal floor. They then move to the phone banks for the rest of the shift. The thinking is that employees will come to understand customers better in general, with the added incentive that an agent who upsets a customer on the phone just might meet that customer downstairs the next day. The more employees see customers, the more difficult it is to treat them as if they're nothing.

This need for connection highlights the point that outsourcing call centers might have financial advantages, but outsourcing has significant experience disadvantages, as well. Distance from the customer and from the company and its overall culture of excellence can only serve to dilute the quality of service experience.

Provide a persistent face in employee-to-customer contacts. As we saw in Chapter 6, some companies have instituted systems for directing incoming calls to the appropriate agents based on segmentation. Other companies take this concept a step further and direct individual callers to the same agent each time the customers call, in order to assure continuity of relationship and a clearer employee view into impact. In fact, some companies charge extra for such premium service, or include it in a package of benefits for their top customers—for instance, customers in the upper tier of their loyalty program.

Honor your most-direct touch points. Contact centers, for instance, rarely receive the credit they deserve, despite the magnitude of their contribution to loyalty, referrals and revenue generation. Companies tend to reward marketing and sales departments while leaving their contact centers out in the cold. These front-line touch points are often perceived as an unfortunate and expensive requirement for doing business. Their budgets are often cut, their technology is frequently outdated, and employee turnover is exceedingly high. Agents are under-appreciated and under-compensated, and they operate without the tools, authority and policies needed to deliver service to increasingly demanding and often unreasonable customers. Customers expect to be treated like princes but agents are left to treat them like paupers. Invest both respect and resources in these critical functions.

Redefine roles in customer-centric terms. Go as far as designing titles with customer-centric cores. During one lengthy engagement, we arrived at the client's office each morning, waiting in a rather unpleasant reception-area atmosphere until the client took us back to the conference room. The receptionist practically ignored us, giving us the impression that she was doing us a favor by letting us in in the first place. Besides, the area wasn't particularly clean, and the magazines strewn over a coffee table were long out of date.

One morning, we presented the receptionist a stack of business cards with her name on them, and a title: "Director of First Impressions." With the title came full responsibility for the reception area. The next day, we came in to find fresh flowers and new magazines, and the entire area was sparklingly clean. All this simply by focusing the receptionist on her customer impact, not on the functions of answering the phone and making visitors sign the front-desk logbook.

Visualize team impact. Passionate employees become even more so when surrounded by passion that justifies their work and motivates them to do even better. Consider, for instance, the opposite of the tote board displayed in the Scare Factory of the classic animated film, *Monsters Inc.* Instead of the number of "Children Scared," post an electronic board at the front of the call center. Tally the number of customers who've received help: "Today, we've solved the problems of 3,000 customers. And counting." Such demonstrations turn goals from quota pressures to shared achievements and impact statements.

Place impact front and center of the agenda. As an exercise, think back on your recent staff meetings. How much time did you dedicate to understanding your impact on customers as opposed to covering the tasks and the projects you need to accomplish? Organizations often stop talking about customer impact; the subject no longer enters corporate conversations, failing to remind employees about impact, and the reason for the organization's existence.

Battle incoming negativity. What's the percentage of customers who call to say "Thank you"? Mostly, the communications coming in to those working in certain customer-facing arenas is negative, sometimes virulently so. Put yourself in the shoes of employees and see how they might think about their customers after a long day's work. To some in the call center, the company is a failure because every customer complains. To some in collection, all customers appear to be cheaters. To some in legal, all customers are liars. Sitting in one spot all day and being hammered with your company's faults can drive employees to cynicism—and eventually to new jobs. Those employees might start as players, but they lose their commitment as they absorb negativity over time, the way a ship passively collects barnacles.

The key to combating negativity is helping employees understand that the problem is not that customers dislike the company, dislike the products, or dislike the agent on the phone with them at that moment. The problem is that they have, yes, a problem. As we discuss in further detail in Chapter 11, "Deliver the Experience," those calling to complain still care. They want to rescue their relationship with you. This is not a negative; it is indeed a positive.

Most important, work with employees threatened to be beaten down by negativity to focus on the result, the resolution, the problem solved. Again, impact trumps function. Impact trumps negativity.

A Meaningful Employee Mission Statement

Company mission statements have haunted employees for decades. These grand declarations ostensibly establish corporate goals and the enthusiasm with which all associates will work to achieve them. But in a bottom-up organization, one ready to deliver customer experience through employee experience, you need a more directive, inspirational and provocative mission statement directed at a more granular level—the employees themselves, because they supply the foundation of the customer experience initiative.

In fact, a mission statement in the form of a direct rallying call helps you begin to define and establish the impact performance platform.

Over the years, we have seen some great employee mission statements—some of them so strong that they've also served as actual brand advertising slogans. Consider:

- Disney's inspirational *"Always remember, the magic starts with you."*
- USAA's personal *"Treat customers the way you would want to be treated if you were the customer."*

- Avis's competitive *"We try harder."*
- Ritz-Carlton's respectful *"Ladies and gentlemen serving ladies and gentlemen."*
- Hilton's elegant *"Be hospitable."*
- Nordstrom's empowering *"Use your good judgment in all situations."*
- Google's ethical *"Don't be evil."*
- Fairmont Hotels' memorable *"Turning moments into memories for our guests."*

Note the commonalities of these mission statements. Short, direct and demanding, they're easy to remember and easy for employees to repeat. They address employee impact, and not functional jobs. They're devoid of cynicism, and they point directly to excellence.

What's more, these mission statements ultimately apply to every employee of the organization, from the experience designers to the experience creators to the experience enablers, from the marketing strategists to the hotel desk clerks to the folks keeping reception areas sparkling clean. Adam Burke, former Senior Vice President of Customer Loyalty for Hilton, once said, "If you can't distill your core mission to something that translates easily across every part of the organization, then you won't succeed. ' Be hospitable' is the underpinning of everything we do."

When writing or revising your employee mission statement, keep these ideas in mind:
- **Write to inspire**. Meeting sales goals or besting competitors in market share isn't inspiring. Making customers' lives easier is.

- **Create a mission that truly makes a difference.** This is particularly necessary for inspiring and retaining young people, more idealistic in general through the decades, but particularly so for the current generation entering the job market.

- **Design the mission with recruitment and retention in mind.** Will it attract ideal job-seeking candidates? Would passionate people work for free to fulfill this mission?

- **Avoid the general**. Create the statement so that it is unique to the value delivered by your company. Disney properties are "The Magic Kingdom." Fairmont fuels the memory-making power of a wonderful vacation. Hilton makes a remarkably straightforward call to hospitable action in the hospitality business. Doesn't get more direct than that.

- **Don't begin with "We do."** Begin with "You will be able to do." *We do* implies function and utility—and the idea that you're already doing what needs to be done, so why change. *You will be able to do* implies continuing goals, flexibility, and empowerment.

- **Convince employees that your offer is real.** Be aware of skepticism. The question is going to come: "Is this vision going to go away, or are you actually going to measure me against the mission? Is this commitment to customer experience real, or not?"

In constructing your employee mission statement, consider adapting an exercise I conduct in my Customer Experience Management seminars to get attendees thinking about this process. Consider it a brainstorming exercise within your organization. Select a member of your customer experience design team to serve the role as a "job candidate." Solicit drafts of employee-impact mission statements from other team members, as well as from stakeholders outside the team, if appropriate. Read the contributions to the designated job candidate, and ask which job that person would take based on the mission statement alone, given the choice. Why? Use the exercise to hone the eventual statement.

The Impact Performance Leadership Challenge

When developing the impact performance platform, know that you have several hills to climb with respect to employee buy-in. They've heard it all before—the promises, the noble intentions, the alleged interest in creativity, the cheering of employee ownership of decisions and customer relationships. But employees have seen such prospects stifled again and again in the form of well-ensconced internal structures, various control mechanisms, and corporate inertia wallowing in the good old days of yore.

Now they're hearing it again. Ask yourself, why should employees trust you this time—or, for that matter, in general? We're living with a new generation of employee—one that I call "Generation Why."

Much has been written about "Generation Y" workers and their lack of commitment to their jobs. Yes, as a generation, these young people seem to possess a strongly noncommittal attitude. But these days, that attitude is pervasive within the workplace. It results from cynicism, too many disappointments, and rampant mediocrity. I call this larger, more amorphous group Generation Why because they're asking, "Why should I do it, and what's in it for me?" In defining Generation Why, we move from an age group to a lifestyle group defined by "Why should I care? Why should I try my best? Why is it worth my time?"

Managers now face a new challenge: providing an answer to "Why?" Many aren't prepared for this challenge, having long focused on the how and when, as opposed to why or what. These managers have always dispensed orders and instructions without explaining them. Times have changed.

Today, if you want to nurture excellence, you must master the why, particularly in a world where employees are increasingly entitlement-focused.

Why should employees believe that you're truly seeking impact, not tasks ticked off a checklist one by one? And why should they follow you to this forward-looking customer-centric world? Just because you're the boss? Just because, as some say, "Performance evaluations guarantee performance"? Or just because you pay them money? For money, you get them to show up. For money, you get them to answer emails and calls, attend staff meetings and go to the Christmas party—but not to give you above and beyond. If the paycheck can't do it, what will guarantee that your personnel will bring the best to you every day when they deal with your customers?

Trust.

Employees will trust you on one and only one condition. They will trust you when they understand that you add value to them. The employment arrangement is an exchange, a cyclical relationship, allowing both sides to think, "You add value to me and I'll add value to you." You must engage employees in a conversation to prove that choosing excellence is in alignment with their personal goals. Unleashing the power of *why* engages employees and results in a level of commitment that supports the Daily Choice for excellence.

"You add value to me and I'll add value to you" cannot be just a statement. Every supervisor and manager in your company must be armed with a plan to add value to their employees. You need leaders who know how to add value, not how to micromanage. From a leadership and management standpoint, you must shift to a performance infrastructure and environment built on trust in leadership.

To retain excellent employees, you must make sure that every one of your supervisors knows the dreams of their employees and how to help them achieve those dreams. What do employees aspire to be? If you don't have insight into such matters, employees will wonder why they should go above and beyond. They'll grumble, "You don't know anything about me. All you know is my identification number so you can send me a check."

In Chapter 8, we discussed the importance of hiring people whose motivation for excellence and customer service is internal. But even with these people in place, you often face problems in allowing that motivation to manifest itself in the service of excellent experience. Why are these employees not performing at the full level of their potential? What's holding them back?—as a leader within your organization, you must be able to answer this question, and to eliminate the need for the question in the first place. You must eliminate any and all obstacles to your employees fully aligning themselves with the organization's goals.

Perhaps you or others in management are holding them back because of your leadership style. Given this possibility, examine—objectively and critically—whether you are providing fear leadership or freedom leadership.

Fear leadership is driven by characteristics that ultimately ignore customers and employees, and focus on outside factors outside of a full range of control. Fear leaders:

- Focus on competition
- Are driven by fear of competition
- Need competition to define success
- Believe that customers are vehicles to success
- Define success by sales volume
- Experience constant self-doubt

Freedom leadership, on the other hand, is driven by characteristics that embrace customers and employees, and focus on factors of innovation. Freedom leaders:

- Focus on customers
- Are driven by innovation and adding value
- Believe that competition is merely "background noise"
- Believe that relationships define success
- Define success by value delivered
- Express continuous self-confidence

Freedom leadership is founded on impact, both for customers and employees. Freedom leaders understand that high performance delivers the results at the highest standards and is measured by customer actions, and that high-performance organizations are highly adaptable to change and customer needs. Freedom leaders seek to deliver superior results through shared vision, the privilege to serve, submission to customer requests, and delivering complete experiences.

And while fear leadership is based on the old ways of operating on few centralized decisions, freedom leadership embraces the new ways of multiple, decentralized decisions—the decisions made by the employees looking to you for trust.

Examine your leadership style honestly. Do you lead from a position of fear or a position of freedom? Are you truly focused on the customer, and willing to invite employees along so both they and the customer can benefit, or are you dragging them along only as means to accomplish your goals. Why, to reiterate the crucial question I posed before, should employees trust you?

In many cases, the answers lie in empowerment—granting employees permission to make decisions, and removing the fear of the consequences of making mistakes.

Empowerment—Myth and Reality

Employee empowerment is a straightforward concept, yet one that vexes organizations with misconceptions. Empowerment involves providing employees with the guidance, tools and authority to make decisions. The problem is that whenever I go to an organization, every manager swears that they have empowered their employees to do right by the customer— yet, no employee agrees.

What happened to the empowerment? My theory is that it's somewhere in the mail room, sealed up in envelopes that haven't been delivered yet. The managers have signed off on the letters, but no employees are receiving them. Still, even the executives see the problem. Our surveys reveal that less than 30% of executives say employees have the authority and tools to do their jobs.

You must give employees the power and the permission to delight employees in personalized, customized ways. Easy to say; difficult to accomplish. Once when working with a client, an executive confided in me, "Mr. Arussy, I don't believe in what you say about this empowerment business. I see nothing wrong with people following orders, because then they don't have to think. We don't need thinking. We don't need decisions." You've met this executive, though you may not have realized it, because he likely exists in your organization—and if so, you're already working toward customer experience from a deficit position.

Employees who work according to routine detract from value, and not simply because they fail to perform at superior levels. Routine employees, those who can and do operate on auto-pilot with no thinking required, add errors to the performance of your organization. In essence, they are replacing automation and its reduced likelihood of error. Empowered employees, on the other hand, with the wherewithal and the authority to make decisions and solve problems, add value to the organization, particularly in handling exceptional circumstances. And the number of those exceptions is growing daily. Customers are demanding more and more personalized relationships and treatment. If you embrace this principle, then you have by definition embraced the fact that exceptions are going to grow in your organization.

This is particularly true as business as a whole moves to self-service, from website shopping to grocery self-check-out to rental-car kiosk check-in. When customers are already asserting themselves in self-service and following the rules, it means that when they call us, they're looking for exceptions to the rules. You must design the organization with a certain level of flexibility. If the organization is too rigid, if the answer is always "No," you won't be able to deliver an acceptable level of customer experience.

Everything we've discussed about customization must now materialize in reality through the flexibility you grant to your employees. Your first job is to reconcile the conflicts, remove the obstacles that hold employees back from empowerment—including, of course, fear—and allow them to make decisions. To facilitate this endeavor:

Demonstrate that you allow mistakes. An organizational culture of excellence in customer experience begins with permission to make mistakes. People don't want to admit it, but mistakes are integral to overall performance, and messages that imply that employees aren't allowed to make mistakes will freeze the employees at the switch. They'll do only the minimum of what must be done to survive within your organization.

Here's a litmus test for whether you're ready to handle true empowerment within your organization. Ask simply, "What happened to the last person who made a mistake?" Did that person get promoted, or get booted out? The message that that latter action sends to employees is, of course, "You can't make mistakes." As an employee once told us in a focus group, "In our company, everyone is empowered . . . to make the *right* decisions." Meaning, of course, that they have no authority to make the wrong decisions. "The right decisions? Make as many as you want." This message paralyzes employees. They'll follow the rules. They'll stop thinking. And they'll become error-adds and not value-adds. You can crow all you want about the authority and the power to make on-the-spot decisions, but the crowing will be ignored if your company track record shows that mistakes lead to the exit.

Employee radar is powered up to the max here. Your personnel will watch the fate of others who have made decisions, and tailor their level of decision-making and risk-taking to the experiences of their colleagues.

Celebrate failure. At one client company, we established a special internal program, somewhat the mirror image of "Employee of the Month." Our "Mistake of the Month" program celebrated the good corporate mistakes. Managers submitted examples of employees trying. Mistake of the Month earned its honoree a special plaque, a $200 gift certificate to a restaurant, and a ticket saying, "Congratulations, you are the Mistake of July." This simple and creative initiative was like an electric shock to the company. It stated very clearly, "We will not penalize you for extending your reach but falling short. We will celebrate your personal investment and earnest effort."

There are two types of mistakes. Bad ones, and good ones. Examples of bad mistakes are when employees don't make decisions. They're afraid to take a risk, and do nothing, contributing to the company a missed opportunity at best. A good mistake is when the employee tried something different, investing themselves personally, but the outcome was not the same. Good mistakes are like the soccer player shooting for the goal and missing. They'll score eventually. Bad mistakes are like the soccer player refusing to take the field.

Specifically state permission to perform. Declare the permission openly. Put it in writing. Write it into job descriptions, evaluations, and KPOs. Be prepared to have it quoted back to you.

Quantify the range of permission granted. Such specification isn't meant to limit empowerment, fencing off how far employees can't go, but to free it, defining how far they can go. At the Ritz-Carlton, employees are free to make on-the-spot decisions costing up to $2,000 to solve a customer issue. These employees don't have any papers to fill out, they can't go to their boss and ask permission, and they can't say, "This is not my job—it's someone else's job." The message behind this is simple. The hotel chain didn't deploy this policy to waste money. The policy is based on the chain's economics of customer experience. If you consider no other factors than the fact that the average room night at Ritz-Carlton is $395, spending $2,000 to solve a customer problem wouldn't make sense. Instead, Ritz-Carlton bases the calculation on the lifetime customer value, which is a quarter of a million dollars. Now, $2,000 to protect $250,000 is a great deal.

When talking about such large sums, you'll of course have instances where employees misuse the money or make mistakes. Employees must understand that empowerment is not a privilege. Empowerment is the responsibility to make decisions and the accountability for the results of the decisions. And in fact, many employees don't want that responsibility—and if most of your employees don't want that responsibility, if they want to be told exactly what to do, and to operate with a script in front of them, you have a bigger problem than simple lack of empowerment.

Err on the side of generosity. It's better to make sure employees have more rather than less permission to act independently. The likelihood is that for every mistake employees make by overstepping their authority, they will also please and surprise 100 customers who will be amazed by your employee's ability to solve problems quickly and satisfactorily.

Empower the small decisions as well as the large. At Starbucks, every employee can provide a free cup of coffee to any customer who's dropped a freshly brewed cup. Sure, the spill isn't Starbucks' fault. But on a human level, employees can help a fellow person without penalty and with the knowledge that they have permission to do the right thing.

Don't micromanage. Constantly looking over employees' shoulders stifles needed independent action. Yes, employees must be held accountable for their results, but micromanagers often ask employees to explain their every decision. Constant questioning dilutes the sense of permission, especially when it feels like second-guessing.

Remember that you don't have a monopoly on "right" decisions. Support the right decisions, not the decisions you would have made. Support, as well, the decisions that are less than perfect but still get the job done. There's always opportunity for improvement. Cheer the effective and tweak the ineffective.

Dispense with employee process-orientation. "Process responsibility" leads to employees believing that, as just a small screw in a big machine who can neither own nor even see the big picture, they must do what they're told. Instill "self-responsibility," that allows employees not only to see the big picture, but also to understand that they *are* the big picture. They are not a screw in the machine. They *are* the machine. Proper education of the company's true business and the employees' role in that business is fully discussed in the section on education and training that follows.

Move employees across the parity line. There are two levels of empowerment. Removing customer dissatisfaction—correcting an invoice, replacing a malfunctioning unit, making a billing credit for a late delivery—is what we call "Transactional Empowerment." Such empowerment is, of course, important, in handling exceptions and solving problems efficiently and sensibly. But you must move employees above the parity line, by focusing not only on Transactional Empowerment but also on excellence creation through Experience Empowerment. By doing this, you provide employees with the ability and permission to go above and beyond, and to demonstrate not only attributes of differentiation but also attributes of excellence.

Grant not only permission, but also time. Above and beyond is not a quick fix, not a sequence that can be corralled by such measures as average handling time. Efficiency lies in solving as many issues with delight and with closure overall, not in how many issues are passed up the ladder in as short a time as possible. Give your employees the time to deliver their caring and empathy.

Remember that knowledge is power. And therefore knowledge is empowerment. The guiding principle for organizations truly wishing to empower their employees should be that grant the same knowledge and authority to front-line employees as they do to supervisors will more often than not preclude the need to escalate a problem to someone with more authority.

Trust, or move on. Virgin Atlantic, Ritz-Carlton and a number of other companies truly trust their employees to make the right decisions for customers and the company. Encourage those you trust to engage customers and try to solve their sensitive and complex challenges at the moment of truth. Those organizations that don't trust their employees would do well to not put them in front of customers in the first place.

Education—Are You Teaching Employees the Right Stuff?

One of the enemies of empowerment is the old-school approach to training, which focuses on procedures instead of delivering on customer experience. Here's an example: One company we worked with compiled an extensive internal training manual for customer service reps. That's sure to cover all the bases, right? Yet, as I read through its 137 pages, I circled the word *customer* each time it appeared. I didn't run out of ink from my Montblanc pen—because that word appeared only seven times in all 137 pages.

But there were plenty of procedures in that training manual. How to do things, when to do them, when not to do them. Again, covering all the bases—except when customers refused to run the bases the way the company expects them to. Even more puzzling, this 137-page manual that provides scant instruction on handling customer issues spends a fair number of words dictating how employees are to hold their car keys as they approach company vehicles to avoid damaging them. Apparently a scratched door latch is a greater concern than a wounded customer relationship.

The problem with today's training programs is that customers are increasingly coming to companies with problems, questions, suggestions and negotiations that don't fit into existing corporate procedures. These types of engagements are exceptions, and need exceptional solutions, as we discuss further in Chapter 11, "Deliver the Experience." The fact that they don't fit into pigeonhole A or pigeonhole B makes them more difficult to resolve in a timely manner as employees hand off or escalate customers in search of someone with the authority to handle them. That problem is aggravated because employees are being taught to not think or assume responsibility, discouraging creativity and initiative. As a result, employees perceive their role as little more than a delivery mechanism rather than as experience enablers and creators.

The Healthcare & Science Business of Thomson Reuters

As Thomson Reuters states, "We combine industry expertise with innovative technology to deliver critical information to leading decision makers in the financial, legal, tax and accounting, scientific, healthcare and media markets, powered by the world's most trusted news organization." Using databases, analytics, research and other services, the company provides healthcare business solutions for various healthcare providers suppliers (including clinicians, hospitals), employers, health plans, researchers, healthcare vendors (such as pharmaceutical companies), and government agencies, pharmaceutical companies and researchers.

THE CHALLENGE

Emphasizing the Thomson Reuters brand promise became critical to differentiating the company. In fact, though the company features an Innovation Board, this group traditionally focused on product development and not customer-service upgrades. In sum, the brand promise is: Customers are at the heart of everything the company does—for example, the company operates under a set of "Trust Principles" established in 1944. People make the difference, and performance matters. Yet, there was some evidence, gathered through customer feedback, of falling short of the brand promise. For example, there had been customer requests to "Be responsive – own the problem" and "Remove the pain of implementations."

THE STRATEGY

Barbara Graovac, Vice President and General Manager of the Employer business of Thomson Reuters, embarked on a strategy for introducing customer experience management to the company. Among her many duties with Thomson Reuters, Graovac now leads an organization-wide initiative focused on improving customer experience, and participates in cross-market initiatives to leverage business assets into new customer-focused solutions and best practices. Major thrusts of the approach included:

- **Prove the business case.** Using Return-on-Nothing analysis, Graovac established the advisability of investigating customer experience. She secured funding for a 100-day test, and assiduously measured results to prove the positive economics of customer-centricity.

- **Stress customer experience education.** Graovac conducted customer experience innovation workshops with cross-functional teams, contributing examples of customer interactions that worked. As 1to1 Magazine noted: "Employees spent time talking about how the organization presents itself as a brand and shared ideas about how to make clients heroes in their own organizations." Such work was in response to such previous customer requests to "Be responsive – own the problem" and "Remove the pain of implementations."

THE RESULTS

Customer-satisfaction and return-on-investment metrics rose significantly, leading to a companywide rollout of the strategy—including one-day customer service training for all employees and building customer experience into the DNA of the organization.

Barbara Groavac was named a 2009 Customer Champion by *1to1 Magazine* for the Customer Experience program she implemented.

After the work you've done in hiring passionate employees and innovating for customer experience and impact, you can't afford to let the power of customer experience slip from your grasp in the form of formalized This Is The Way Things Must Be.

Let's say you hire just the right employee, bringing to the position qualifications, passion, caring, energy—the entire package. On that employee's first day, she joins other new hires in an orientation session. A trainer comes in and drops his big book of policies unencumbered by the word *customer* onto the table, sending a shudder through both the table and the new employees. There it is. The employee bible—perhaps, if the onlookers are lucky, the original copy. Then the reading begins, page after page of procedures, which are followed by pages of, yes, more procedures. *Sit, fetch, roll over*—because organizations design employee training as if it is meant for dogs. They make it so that the lessons can be repeated from session to session, just as they've done over the last few decades. The underlying goal of training is to mold the employee to the training instead of the training to the employees. The same procedures are dictated to different employees in differing situations, with the goal of inducing consistent performance.

Even the most empowered employee—qualified, creative, passionate, independent—is being worn down on Day 1 with a simple and direct message: *Stop thinking. The manual does your thinking for you. Follow the rules. And the first rule you must follow is to make sure the customer follows the rules, too.*

At the end of the training, our new employee takes her first call, and encounters an exception. One of your best customers has a problem. Page 57, one of the few pages that actually does have the word *customer* on it (and perhaps the word *no* on it multiple times, too), outlines a solution that the customer doesn't accept. One complaint call upstairs later, the boss is on the phone asking who the heck this new employee is, and what the heck is going on? When challenged, the employee calmly thumbs to page 57, section 3, line 4. She points, and says, "My boss told me to do this. This is my new boss. His name is Manual." Suddenly, the training is more than just a constraint, but also a shield, and a rationale for mediocre service.

If you want to learn more about why employees are not performing, read your employee manual. Insights into employee mediocrity may actually be its most important lesson. Comb the manual, asking yourself at every page, with every procedure, "What message are we sending to our customers?" Are your training and your policies designed for predictability or for flexibility in decision-making?

Such training resembles teaching your dog to fetch. You throw the stick, and the dog brings it back, time after time. The dog has no idea why, or what else can be done with the stick. Toss, return, toss, return, all on page 57. This is the one-size-fits-all of the employees' world. Are you trying to design for Six Sigma processes with agents as machinery and customer problems as rejects, or are you trying to design for flexibility empowering employees to create enriching customer experiences?

If your goal is the latter, just as you must progress from product-centricity to customer-centricity, you must cross from training to education. There's a clear distinction between the two concepts, and an education program is one of the paving stones on the road to excellence.

The Principles of Employee Education

The customer experience revolution starts with the manual. This isn't to discount the training in the operational and functional details that a job requires—the technology, the law, the management of systems. As well, training absolutely must give employee interaction guidelines and a basic understanding of the company and the business in which it operates. But consider also how much or how little time you spend educating employees on customer life cycles, customer needs and attitudes, your customer experience promise, and your overall customer-service goals.

Training vs. education boils down to procedures vs. principles. Today, organizations focus on training employees in procedures. Training is a mechanism of tight control offering ways to address predefined problems (too bad they haven't defined those problems for the customers). Training assumes lack of employee ownership—the company owns the procedures, after all. And it grants employees minimal trust, other than trusting they will follow the procedures. Training skirts the potential of using common sense, and in fact discourages the use of common sense, which might overrule adherence to the rules the employees are being evaluated on. Training concentrates on multi-tiered resolution system, granting decision authority up the chain where resolution will be delayed and perhaps even disappear.

More effective is educating employees in principles. Education is a mechanism for providing guidelines that encourage and empower outside-the-box problem resolution—to the point of evaluating employees on how effectively they broke the rules rather than clinging to them. Education of principles allows for faster issue resolution because of a flat resolution system—a system of one, the employee empowered and entrusted to exercise responsibility and common sense.

In short, training provides rules; education provides tools. Procedures explain how, and in doing so often shut down thinking. Principles explain why, and treat employees like thinking adults.

Examples of constraining employees to think are rife, but let me give you one quick crystallization of the danger of such an approach. Let's say company procedures demand that agents attempt a cross-sell or up-sell on each customer contact. One day, an agent doesn't pitch the incremental sales to three customers, and is punished for it. Yet, company principles demand strong ROI, and the agent refused to make the three pitches because he saw that those particular customers were F.U.'s with negative engagement histories—numerous product complaints, high returns, failure to pay. The agent, educated in principles, should be praised and even rewarded.

Education as a Journey

- Companies that excel in customer experience spend far more on educating their employees than typical industry averages—in some cases double the industry average. Ritz-Carlton, the perennial customer experience vanguard among hotel chains, invests an enormous 10% of its payroll on employee training. At the Ritz-Carlton, training isn't perceived as a destination reached at the conclusion of orientation, but instead as a journey that never ends. Ritz-Carlton refreshes its employee training almost as continually as they refresh their food and flowers.

- Ritz-Carlton and other customer-centric organizations recognize that only by employing a multi-faceted and extensive training program will their employees be able to consistently deliver the highest-quality customer experiences. The multi-faceted program includes elements such as customer lifestyle analysis, emotional engagement, and communication techniques for disseminating bad news to customers.

- Key points for such training include:

Teach customer experience as a discipline. When was the last time your customer-facing associates, as examples, received customer experience training—and we're not talking about training on how the phone system works, covering which buttons to push when making transfers—but instead on the pure principles of customer experience. Some in customer-facing roles *never* receive customer-centric training. For example, it may be counterintuitive to picture collections agents as being customer-service people, yet their function must align with customer-centricity as importantly as any other individual function in order to achieve whole-company customer excellence.

Educate *everyone* in customer experience. Customer experience is on everyone's job description. Those in HR, IT, accounting, and so on must execute it—all the time. Yet, companies today typically focus customer-experience training, when they deploy it at all, only on those with the words "customer service" specifically in their titles or job descriptions. If your goal is to align the entire company with customer-centricity, then train the entire company in its tenets. Everyone must know how to speak to a customer—that's not a privilege granted only to a few employees. Someone from IT, for instance, learning the proper way to relate to customers helps them shape solutions and eventual messaging to customers even though they themselves might never find them speaking to customers face to face. Customer experience lies in principles and attitudes as much as it does in actual conversations. If you expect touch points—both the enablers and the creators—to be aligned with customer experience, educate them as to their roles and to the flexibility you are granting them within those roles.

By the same line of thinking, don't relegate education only to weak-performing employees (though they may receive additional training). Instead deliver the training to all employees irrespective of performance.

Educate continuously. Education cannot stop when initiation is complete. Incorporate regular refresher courses into the employees' routine. A growing number of companies buttress their core training programs by incorporating inspirational or motivational training to ensure that employees don't regress to "auto-pilot" mode. If your excuse is that you can't take employees away from their jobs to conduct training, you can't put them on the job in the first place.

Let's return to that calculation that the average call center agent takes 10,000 calls a year. If we assume an average spend of $300, that one agent is controlling $3 million, and potentially destroying $3 million if he or she fails to deliver at the moment of truth. I suggest that $3 million per agent is worth a couple of extra days of training. Stop thinking of employees as individuals who are paid so many dollars an hour. Start thinking of their impact their customers and on their financial impact on your company. These people are your voice. They are the face of your authenticity.

Arm employees with numbers. The numbers guide and the numbers justify. Customer experience vanguards like Virgin Atlantic Airways and Ritz-Carlton provide employees with such financial data as customer spending levels, service costs and product costs to empower them to provide appropriate, sensible resolutions that will both delight customers and profit the organization. In fact, I've personally experienced such sensibility in a way that absolutely inspired me. I was on a Virgin Atlantic flight from New York to London, working on my laptop, when the flight attendant came to me and said, "Mr. Arussy, the entertainment system is not working. Would you like 10,000 miles added to your account, or would you like £75 worth of duty-free?" I thought I was dreaming—but I quickly opted for the duty-free, what with three daughters and a wife at home and the opportunity to shop for a bunch of cosmetics I can't even pronounce.

If ever I actually saw Santa Claus in the middle of the summer handing things to people, it was that flight attendant, walking the aisles, handing people gifts. My curiosity piqued, I went to the flight purser and said, "There are really two ways that I can explain what's going on right now— either it's your last day on the airline or you are suicidal. Which one is it?" Neither, it turned out, even though the offer the flight attendant was giving was not covered by the employee manual or company policy.

The purser told me, "During our training, we were taught that every call to our customer service operation costs us £25—*before* the cost of resolution. Giving miles to settle a possible complaint on the spot costs less than that. We were also trained in the average customer margin in each cabin class, which is why we offered different levels of compensation in different classes. In tourist, we offered 3,000 miles or £25 of duty-free; if they take the duty-free, I'm still ahead because of the cost of resolution; if they take the miles, I am definitely ahead. The higher cabin classes received incrementally bigger offers, because cost of resolution for those classes is also incrementally higher."

I was impressed. She knew her numbers, she knew segmentations, and she was applying both to deliver a delightful, cost-effective resolution. She also knew she wouldn't be reprimanded because she was balancing the right numbers with doing the right thing.

To more fully empower employees, provide commercial knowledge, including such financial data as costs and margins, and customers' annual value and lifetime value.

Focus on understanding the customer. In addition to covering the financial aspects of customer relationships, stress segmentations and differentiating services based on financial drivers, customer needs, and customer characteristics as represented by the personas and customer views we developed in Chapter 6.

Demonstrate resolutions. Teach by scenario. Demonstrate how to employ principles within various situations—different ways of relating to different customers and lifestyles. Successful education programs routinely include scenario-based coaching and role-playing so that employees can visualize, practice and perfect (to the extent possible) their conduct during these interactions.

Building the Customer Experience Education Guide

Follow along with this exercise that you can conduct when innovating your system of impact performance education:

Close your eyes (well, as best you can at this moment as you read this), and imagine excellence. Envision as specific and clear a picture of excellence as you can. Picture, image, individual—it could be anything, as long as it's meaningful for you.

Now imagine a lemon.

When picturing excellence, what image did you envision? Family? Mountains? A Polynesian beach? Olympic athletes?—these are the sorts of wide-ranging answers I receive when I conduct this exercise in training and client engagements. Now, what color was the lemon? Yellow, of course. And it was slightly smaller than a closed fist, right? The pictured definitions of excellence always differ significantly. Ask about the lemon, and universal consistency reigns.

Now, go to your employees and tell them that the goal is excellence. Perhaps they'll be excited. Yes—they know what excellence is . . . and yet they don't, because individual interpretations vary so strongly. If you don't define and specify your conception of excellence, employees will operate on their own conviction of what constitutes loyalty. The customers, as well, have their differing visions of excellence. This leads to a crucial step in training for customer experience and building a culture of excellence: You must create a unified vision of the new standard, and then communicate that vision. We saw much of this process at work in Chapter 4 while discussing experience innovation and design, with your work in defining the memory you want customers to take away. And in communicating this vision, you must build a unified language of excellence.

Because experience is abstract, defining it precisely is very difficult. But there is an effective way to bring life and definition to this concept: Tell stories. The unified language of excellence exists in story-telling.

Start collecting stories of best performance, and begin sharing them through the company proactively, and frequently. Create a customer experience guide specific to your company based on customer insights, images, or anything else that can give employees insight into what excellence looks like.

Learn to tell the stories compassionately, energetically and approvingly. Bring the stories to life—these are real tales, not Aesop's fables. And they are stories that occurred and were subsequently championed within your company to drive home the relevance and the permission to deliver it. Build a repository. Launch a web portal that collects the best stories, the wins, the celebrations, the exemplary customer interactions. Whatever the touch point, make certain everyone has the same definition before them, the same stories available, the same guide to help them picture excellence and then execute it according to the standards of the stories. Include the story of the flower shop in the business of marriage maintenance.

This foundation of storytelling is an inspirational platform that everyone can stand on. This is your training manual. And, I would wager, those stories will use the word *customer* more than seven times.

With that thought in mind, let me continue my story of a search for a ;CEO who had risen from the customer service floor to the CEO's office. I did indeed find that gentleman, a very successful CEO of two major organizations. His recipe for professional success included running a contact center that was highly profitable and that visibly increased revenue and heightened brand loyalty. He achieved these goals by over-investing (if there is such a thing) in employee training, designing an incentive program, and upgrading the contact center infrastructure—everything from computers, phones, software and headsets to desks and chairs. Subsequently, turnover plummeted, while employee engagement skyrocketed. His investments yielded almost overnight improvements in cross- and up-sale revenue, customer satisfaction and operational efficiencies.

When I had the privilege of speaking to this CEO's employees, I was pleasantly surprised to discover that I was speaking before a group of MBA students. Working with a leading business school, the CEO had created a specialized MBA program for his contact center agents. He explained that their responsibility for his most important asset (his customers) necessitated that they be supremely educated. This gentleman understood that his contact center agents would need to make daily determinations regarding the type of service to deliver based on customer profitability, purchasing patterns and a variety of other financial data, and to do that, they needed the requisite level of education.

When I asked the CEO to see his training manual, he replied, "We really don't have one. But I'll tell you what—after you spend a day with my employees, you tell me what the manual is."

I sat in on a day of training, with its numerous group exercises and discussions, two words surfaced again and again. *Sense*, and *sensitivity*. I knew the manual by heart by the end of the day: "In everything you do, use common sense, and be sensitive." Financial common sense blended with caring and courtesy.

This organization didn't tell their employees how to be sensitive. It showed them examples of sensitivity at work. No script demanding "Mention the customer's name five times" was thrust in front of them. Such directives only lead to robotic repetition while the agent jots a tick mark for each time the name is said. It's not authentic.

The company showed trust in placing the responsibility for sense and sensitivity on the shoulders of their team, communicating, "You have common sense. You're intelligent. And you're human beings. Act accordingly."

Re-Evaluating Performance Evaluation

When Lou Gerstner took over as CEO of IBM in 1993, he requested to see the customer satisfaction scores for the database division. The results: 87% satisfaction. That's a decent score, until you consider that the customer attrition rate over the previous two years was about 66%. IBM was measuring the wrong things. And, we can reasonably assume that IBM was basing evaluations and employee compensation on the wrong things.

A common trap in companies is allowing silos to work from isolated metrics specific to their own function—and we'll explore this concept in detail in Chapter 12, "Measure What Matters." One impact is the downside of employees doing what you pay them to do, particularly if they are evaluated on their performance against inappropriate metrics. If you measure and compensate them on internal issues only, they will focus on internal issues only.

If you don't connect employees to customer experience in determining compensation and bonuses, you're not going to get results. Or you won't like the results that you *are* getting. You will see two-thirds of your customers that are 87% satisfied looking for greater satisfaction with a competitor. That means that you must begin holding the employees accountable for the ultimate performance of the company, and not merely for some internal measure.

We were auditing an airline service operation, and chose to concentrate on analyzing the experiences of upper-tier members of the airline's frequent-flyer program. These customers have flown at least 75,000 miles in the previous year, so they certainly represent the carrier's most loyal customers, and presumably the most profitable customers. My intent was to find the best examples of customer service given to these special customers that we could apply back to those in the lower tiers of the program. During the audit, I noticed something very interesting. Watching the monitors that tracked incoming call traffic, I saw that the call system would cut off customers who were on hold for more than 59 minutes. You read that correctly—not *59 seconds*, but *59 minutes*. I was stunned to learn that the cut-off was exercised on 400 customers a week. Each week, 400 of the airline's best customers were subjected to ridiculously long hold times, and then simply dropped from the system.

When I talked to the VP of customer care—who, by the way, began the conversation asking if I'd learned about any "quick wins" they could deploy immediately—I told him that a configuration error seems to have crept into the system, cutting off the most- profitable customers. He said, "That's not a configuration error. That's how I manage the system. It's very simple. I'm being measured on average handling time, which consists of wait time and talk time. If we answer 400 people within 59 minutes or more of wait time, I'm not going to make my numbers. My kids are not going to make it to college." He paused, then said, "By the way you caught me on a good week. Sometimes I cut them off after 25 minutes."

"What about the CEO's number?" I ventured. "The one in the memo from the top office that declares, *The customer is absolutely number-one.*"

The VP said, "I have no idea what you're talking about. I manage a single number: average handling time." The VP was leveraging a little-known customer service secret. Customers who drop off voluntarily—"abandoned from hold," in the jargon—aren't calculated into average handling time. If customers refuse to listen to the generic music and the persistent announcement that "Your time is truly valuable to us" over and over, that's the customers' problem. They're not patient enough. And as my smart-aleck VP of customer care told me, "I just turned it from a reactive situation from to a proactive one. I didn't want customers to wait so long until they finally decided to hang up themselves—I was just trying to help them out."

If you want to start a revolution and change, re-evaluate the components of performance evaluation. And a revolution it is indeed, because productivity-based or efficiency-based evaluation and compensation conflict with a customer-centric strategy.

Install customer-centric goals related to each component of performance evaluation, including:
- **Job descriptions.** Do Key Performance Objectives stress functions or results? Have you formalized customer-centric objectives formalized, or have you presented them as just "good ideas"? People do what they are being paid for, not what they are told.

- **Metrics.** Are employees' numeric goals function-centric or customer-centric? If you don't hold them accountable to ultimate customer spending, they won't care about that and won't work to impact it.
- **Compensation.** Employees do what you pay them to do. You pay them to engage in fragmented activities, they'll be happily fragmented all day long. If an insignificant portion of their pay depends on customer results, customer results will get insignificant attention.

The more-advanced companies today use performance evaluations as a coaching mechanism and not as a compensation benchmark. The coaches present the criteria that all employees should be evaluated against, and design coaching based on performance against those criteria. These companies don't measure purely on how many servers IT fixes, but also on how many customers benefited and how the company's bottom line benefited from fast, uninterrupted server performance.

Instead of traditional task-list evaluation criteria, install job descriptions, metrics and compensation that reflect performance against these criteria:
- Decrease in customer complaints
- Improved customer's perception of and attitude toward the brand/organization
- Increase in customer "Thank You" letters
- Increase in customer ideas and insight
- Decreased customer attrition rate
- Increase in customer referrals
- Increase in overall customer base
- Decreased cost of new customer acquisition
- Increase in customer interactions with the organization
- Increase in customer and prospect purchase consideration
- Increase in customer acceptance
- Increase in customer upgrades
- Increase in sales of accessories
- Increase in cross-selling results
- Increase in customer overall wallet share
- Overall growth in business per customer
- Increased annual customer value
- Increased lifetime customer value

Customer-centric factors must be included in all departments in the organization. Customer experience attributes, combined with touch point analysis, will assist in implementing an organization-wide customer focused plan, as we'll see in Chapter 12.

On top of this, look to clarifying standards for performance recognition and Moment of Truth recognition (which we'll discuss in a moment), as well as change recognition and incentives. By "change recognition," I refer to incentives to facilitate the change management needed as you put the customer experience program into place, to be effective over a stated period of time during the change. You want to reward those employees and departments that adopt the new program quickly and willingly to send a message to the organization as a whole. We cover this topic in greater detail in Chapter 13, "Leadership and Change Management."

As a general rule, base 30-35% on the sorts of joint goals listed above—nothing less than that. I've seen plans that tie only 2% of compensation to customer satisfaction and customer performance. Who's going to sweat for 2%? Who's going to slow down their rush to happy hour for such a slim incentive? The remaining 65-70% is then tied to the employee's specific function.

American Express, for example, ties 70% of call center personnel compensation to an annual customer-satisfaction survey that asks customers to rate not the department or the organization, but the specific agent the customer interacted with. Amex employs this system to manage 15,000 agents in the U.S.—1.5 million complete surveys that they can attribute directly to employees.

Scores are used as benchmarking not only for compensation, but also for coaching. Employees are informed that their supervisors are there to coach, and their supervisors are on their side. And indeed they are, because supervisor compensation is also linked to customer satisfaction, in increasing percentages at higher levels of management.

The survey is based on Net Promoter Score metrics, measuring customer willingness to recommend the agent based on the customer's experience. The survey measures how the employee handled the call, and recognizes that the problem that motivated the call might not allow the agent to achieve first-call resolution. Therefore, the measurement focuses on call handling and not issue resolution, seeking to understand if the agent has handled the customer with such tact and service that the customer comes away with a memory of a great customer experience with that particular touch point.

In fact, one of the best tests of your readiness for customer experience lies in your employee compensation. If you pay people based on productivity, you get productivity. If you pay them based on quality, you get quality. In our *Customer Experience Management Benchmark Study,* just 31.3% of executives say their compensation directly reflects the company's commitment to customer experience, meaning that in well over two-thirds of the cases, employees are ultimately getting paid to do little more than execute processes.

Just 40% of executives say that their employees have the tools and authority to solve customer problems and to do what they need to do for the customer; 38% report that employees are well-versed in how to delight customers; 31% say that current compensation reflects their company's commitment to the customer experience. Understand what these numbers are telling us: Most employees show up to work with nothing more than a pathetic smile to serve the customer with.

And note, as well, the conflict that these numbers show. The number of executives confident that their companies deserve employee loyalty is rising, while the number who provide adequate tools to those employees is shrinking.

Recognition and Reward—Do You Inspire?

Though employee motivation and incentive programs are very popular, they present problems. The traditional thinking with such programs is that they incent employees to accomplish certain goals.

The sad fact is that companies assume that incentive programs can change behavior, to make employees do something they don't want to do on their own, and so behavioral change becomes the programs' only goal. If the employee doesn't want to perform certain tasks or achieve certain goals, the thinking goes, then certainly throwing some more money or perks their way will get the job done. But any incentivized behavioral change will not be driven by authenticity. The change will simply become a matter of continuing to go through the motions by adjusting to a different set of motions.

That sort of change is not sustainable. Once the reward has been achieved, or if the goal is taken away, new behaviors evaporate and going through the old motions takes over again. These problems are exacerbated when rewards and incentives are built into the employees' overall compensation package as a supplement, usually with no incremental result. Above and beyond is a difficult height to achieve if the employee is not inherently passionate about the goal.

The true purpose of incentive and motivation initiatives lies in recognizing those employees who have achieved above and beyond, and to be certain that their accomplishments are not taken for granted. By rewarding and inspiring excellence, such a shift in thinking sustains better performance over the long term. It fuels internal motivations and, consequently, the sincerity of the employee effort, which translates to greater authenticity. On the other hand, not recognizing achievement will condition failure.

Incentive mechanisms must be in place to encourage taking responsibility and the risks that come with it. "Greater risk, greater reward," goes the saying, and it applies here. In shifting to customer experience, you are asking employees to take responsibilities on a moment-by-moment basis that they've never exercised before. The payoff for such a shift must be apparent—and appealing. The employee is thinking, "I'm going to break the rules, go above and beyond, take a risk, and what do I get? Two tickets to the movies?" Such penurious thinking only fuels cynicism. Instead, reward with style and panache—and a big splash doesn't hurt, either.

Here's an example from one of our clients, a 500-seat organization with very specific goals we wanted to achieve. Number-centricity was very heavily ingrained with the employees. It was a nose-to-the-grindstone group, staring at their computers and almost mumbling a mantra: *Get the end-end-of-quarter numbers, that's it, move on*. The notion of customer-centricity made these employees very skeptical, and movie tickets weren't going to impress them.

To demonstrate the seriousness of our intent, we leased a Porsche, and parked it in front of the office right next to the CEO's parking space for all to see. We announced that the employee who met both productivity and quality numbers during the week would get to drive the Porsche for a week and park in the premium parking spot—where we dispatched a cleaning crew to wash and detail the Porsche daily. Our message was—"You're going to inspire our customers, so we're going to inspire you. You're going to give them an experience, so we're going to give you an experience."

We let it be known that the Porsche was leased for a year to further indicate our seriousness, and we pumped up the "splash" factor with a mailing to employees' spouses notifying them that their spouses could win a Porsche for a week.

The success of this incentive surpassed our vision. We found that when employees drove the Porsche home, neighbors would come up and say, "Very nice. Are you dealing drugs now?" The recipients crow with pride about how they earned such recognition—and they've told stories about the neighbors stopping by to get their pictures taken with the recipients. We anticipated what we call "the departure moment." The employee is enjoying the prestige for a week, then come Friday morning, it's time to return the Porsche—and nobody's believing the story about losing the keys. "Keep the key—we have plenty to that car. We'll put that key on a plaque for you if you manage to find it." Come Friday afternoon, and the employee's friend in the next office gets the keys. How does that make the employee feel? "This is personal now. He's driving my Porsche. I want to get it back."

That latter reaction is one key to effective recognition incentives. If someone is going to win, someone must lose. Sending an employee to the Bahamas doesn't help you if other employees don't see that *they* aren't going to the Bahamas. If someone is going to be driving the Porsche, the others must realize that they aren't driving the Porsche. You can take this too far, however. I've seen a reverse version of this that I don't endorse—though it does use a large dose of that "there must be a loser" aspect. In one European company, all the salespeople drive company cars—Audis. Beautiful shiny black Audis. Except for one salesperson—the worst salesperson of the month drives the company's old Russian Vlada.

Be sure to properly showcase the winners. Even the way the rewards are presented will signal to employees if you're taking the hard work and the employee seriously. Make reward and recognition presentations in front of all employees, not just in front of management. Doing so helps you to both inspire and educate. Stage the celebration. One company holds an annual gala dinner for the company's top performers, and the ceremony has as much pomp and fun as the Oscars. If you simply hand over a bit of paper recognition in a gift card, you miss the entire point.

Staging celebrations is one way of "writing" the stories that appear in your new employee handbook. Involve the employees in general by giving them input into who is selected, through a ranking or voting system. In this way, employees become authors of the stories, as well.

You can accomplish such grand gestures without incurring grand expenses. Recognition is a state of mind, a signal that hard effort is not taken for granted, and it doesn't have to be expensive. But it does have to be inspirational. A typical program might invest, say, $2,000 a month on a prize. Each of the monthly winners are honored at a gala event, where a $10,000 prize trip to anywhere in the world is awarded to one winner. Keep in mind one rule: Dollars don't work as well as merchandise which doesn't work as well as experiences. Imagine the incentive value in courtside tickets to a pro basketball game, VIP seats at a premiere fashion show, or a visit to a NASCAR pit—during the race?

And you may find that many delightful experiences are sitting in a drawer in the desk of the CMO's administrative assistant or elsewhere in the company, lying idle and offering you low-cost rewards. Through sponsorships, company ownership of sports or fine arts season tickets or box seats, and other corporate connections, you may have access to a wealth of unspent experiences intended for customers and executives that would absolutely delight your employees. For no additional cost to you, you can deliver amazing experiences to your top performers.

One Virgin Atlantic experiential reward, which I speak of elsewhere in this book, involves nothing more than a few extra minutes and a trip down the hall. When a call center agent books a million pounds of business, CEO Sir Richard Branson stops by, gets on his knees, and personally thanks the agent. Other types of such low-cost/high-impact rewards might include lunch for a week in the executive suite, handwritten letters from senior executives, a company-wide broadcast thanking a particular employee for exceptional. Apply your customer-experience innovation internally.

The Porsche initiative I described did not increase the incentive program budget. Instead of dividing the budget into small, ineffectual pieces that we could pass around to almost everyone, we consolidated the budget into something visible, eye-opening and aspirational. You give out small gifts, you receive small effort. Put your employees in a Porsche, and they'll put your customers in a Porsche.

Are you inspiring employees with incentives and recognition, or are you just tossing ten or twenty bucks into the paycheck? To receive above and beyond, you must inspire. You can't buy above and beyond. Look for whatever you can find to give your employees an experience to help them visualize how far you want them to take this, and how serious you are about the initiative. Don't settle for handing out $25 supermarket gift certificates. You'll get what you pay for. Eschew the traditional. If you want a culture of excellence, inspire with excellence.

Summing Up: The Power of 10

Is your organization ready for customer experience and letting a culture of excellence flower within your walls? To evaluate, answer these milestone questions:

- Do your employees understand what you stand for?
- Do your employees share your values?
- Do your employees know how to translate those values into actions?
- What empowerment do your employees need to get the job done?
- How do you measure their performance? At parity or above and beyond?
- What informal messages do they hear about your culture? How do these messages shape their performance?
- What do employees say about you when managers are not around?

- What happens to risk-takers in your organization?
- How do you deliver recognition and rewards to employees who make an impact?
- What is the inspiring reason for employees to go above and beyond?
- What obstacles stand between your employees and empowerment?
- What authority do they need to do get the job done?
- What information do they need to get the job done?
- What can you do to provide them with more power to get their job done?
- What accountability do you need to put in place with the required empowerment?
- What tools do they need to get their jobs done?
- What education do they need to make the right decisions?
- How do informal rules affect their ability to get the job done?
- How would you recognize and reward Impact performance?

Can you manage excellence that has employee choice at its core? The answer is, yes, but not in the traditional ways, directed from above. It can be institutionalized by creating fertile ground for superior performance to flourish. Just as a basketball coach cannot mandate success on the court, neither can the new excellence manager.

Excellence is the opposite of top-down management, and executives must recognize this in the way they interact with their employees. The role of managers must transform from one of keeping employees focused on mechanical tasks to one of creating environments that bring the best out of their employees naturally.

Persuading your employees that excellence is good for them is a primary dimension of your new role. This persuasion starts with an inspiring mission. Employees need to see how their work can make a difference. Focusing on the positive impact their actions have on customers often presents the most compelling mission. To illustrate that point, I'll leave you with a story of impact experience that I encountered on a business trip:

Checking into a Doubletree Hotel in Madison, Wisconsin, I first met Moria, the hotel's assistant front desk manager. I knew her name, of course, because of her name tag. But she also wore a button imprinted with nothing more than a number: 10.

It was the same button worn by the cheerful, smiling driver who had met me at the airport when I arrived from a client meeting in Ann Arbor, Michigan. As we rode in from the airport, he asked me about my flight, and about the reason for my stay. When I explained that I was spending the day at the University of Wisconsin the next morning, he said, "There's a free shuttle from the hotel to UW. You should sign up for it."

I nodded. I was tired, and frustrated by my stay in Ann Arbor. I'd been up early, going downstairs at about a quarter of 6 hoping to catch a swim at the hotel pool—which, it turned out, officially opened at 6. When I asked the gentleman at the reception desk if I might sneak in early so I wouldn't have to rush quite so much to catch my flight, he didn't bother to look up from the computer monitor that was more important to him than me. His words were cold and formal. "You have to wait until 6 a.m."

The Madison shuttle driver wasn't satisfied with my tired response to his suggestion. He accompanied me into the hotel lobby, where he personally made arrangements for the morning shuttle as I checked in, receiving one of Doubletree's signature chocolate-chip cookies and meeting Moira and some of the rest of the staff—each of them welcoming and cheerful, and each of them wearing a button proclaiming "10."

"I have to get up early," I said, "probably before your pool opens, but I'd like to be able to take a swim."

"Just give us a shout," Moria said. "We'll take care of it."

I smiled—ironically, the Ann Arbor hotel had also encouraged me to shout, though not in such a direct or positive manner.

The next morning, when I carried my luggage into the lobby on my way to meet the shuttle, Shannon with the hotel staff suggested that I leave my bags. "We'll bring them to you when we pick you up to return you to the airport." And, of course, she offered me another signature cookie. Because I'm in the business of testing customer-centricity, I declined the cookie and asked if they could bring one to me when they picked me up later that day. True to Shannon's promise, that afternoon that delicious cookie was delivered, along with my luggage, by another personable driver. The promise was fulfilled even though Shannon and the afternoon driver were on different shifts.

All in all, a simple yet incredible experience, one that wasn't fueled by huge budgets, nor by demanding concessions from a senior manager. Instead, it was enabled by people on the front line. I still clearly recall the names of the individuals with whom I interacted—Carl, Nick, Liz, Shannon and Moria—more names remembered from this one hotel than from the last 50 hotels I stayed at combined.

Think back on your most recent employee interactions. Do you remember the names of the people you dealt with? Did they do anything that made you want to remember their names?

Did they exhibit any of the key elements that made my experience (and I suspect the experience of their other guests) so great?

- **Moria's team anticipated my needs.** I needed transportation to the university and they delivered it.
- **They were proactive,** reserving a spot on the shuttle at my preferred time.
- **They were flexible,** opening the pool before regular hours. And cheerful in doing so.
- **They paid attention to the smallest detail.** Who needs to tote luggage around all day when it isn't necessary?
- **They offered an extra touch**—in this case, the signature chocolate chip cookie. This is a Doubletree touch, but the employees never failed to deliver it.
- **They kept their promises,** even delivering a continuity of great experience across shifts by transferring responsibility for the commitments made by the previous shift
- **They consistently performed with excellence,** every step of the way.

Earlier in my stay, I had a chance to tell Moria how impressed I was with the service and overall experience. She smiled, then said, simply and powerfully, "Customers— without them, we are nothing."

Sometimes the truth hits you so sharply and strongly that it becomes impossible to ignore. Excellence . . . or nothing. Yet, this simple truth all too often escapes too many companies and their employees. Somehow they forget why they're in business.

"Customers—without them, we are nothing."

This attitude was reflected in the button that had puzzled me when I first met the shuttle driver, and then encountered others on the Doubletree staff: That mysterious number "10." When I got to my room, however, I discovered the button's meaning. A note on my bed made it clear, saying that should I feel I couldn't rank employees "10" in performance, I should immediately notify a manager.

As simple as that. 10. My Ann Arbor experience involved the same digits. One and zero. Clearly, the Ann Arbor staff considered themselves #1 and considered me . . . a zero.

In stark contrast, the Madison Doubletree raised the bar of performance and expects that each employee achieve this level every day. They visibly communicate to guests and employees alike that they expect nothing less than excellence. This hotel is simply unwilling to compromise on their high standards and expect their employees to perform accordingly.

How high is your bar? Is this bar visible and clear to your employees and customers?

In the case of the Madison Doubletree, the bar was worn proudly on a button pinned to each associate's shirt. I'm reminded of another such display, confirming to employees the goals and the standards expected of them each and every day. Above the employee's entrance at the Makati Shangri-La hotel in Manila, Philippines, hangs this bold sign: "Through this pathway pass the most respectful, courteous and sincere hotel employees in the world." But not all of them. Just ask Moria.

CHAPTER 10

Performance Platform: The Tools to Deliver

Imagine this scene: As the regular customer enters the restaurant, the maître d' addresses her by name and asks about her recent trip to Greece. She shares a few details before being escorted to her regular table. There, a server is waiting with her favorite drink, which he places before her as the maître d' seats her.

"Would you prefer your usual?" the waiter asks.

"Yes, but with mashed potatoes instead of salad today. And, if I may, I'm in a bit in rush."

The waiter goes to the kitchen, places the order, and asks the cooks to reprioritize their preparation to ensure quick delivery to his customer.

After the customer finishes her meal, which has clearly met her expectations because of the kind words she has for the chef, the waiter suggests that the bill will be settled directly to her usual credit card so she can depart quickly. On her way out, the dessert chef hands her a small, elegant paper bag. "Your favorite dessert," he says, smiling, "for your sweet tooth."

What a touch, she thinks as she leaves—*and that's why I dine here more than at any other restaurant in town.*

At a restaurant with few regulars, such delightful customer experiences are entirely possible. The limited number of customers enables the staff to remember personal data and preferences. And operating only one location, with a regular staff and a predictable clientele, the restaurateurs can reprioritize seating, stock unusual but often-requested items, and generally be prepared to go the extra mile—by knowing what the extra mile is in the first place.

But how do you provide this level of service for millions of customers spread across the globe?

Before I answer that, let's consider the elements critical to our story of the regular customer's personalized dining experience:

- Understanding her value.
- Maintaining records of previous engagements, and reacting to them.
- Engaging her on an emotional level, in a small but meaningful gesture of chatting about a recent vacation.
- Aligning the best resources—the best waiter and the finest food—with her value.
- Prioritizing effort and resources with her needs.
- Knowing her preferences and needs, and making proactive offers based on those preferences.
- Utilizing stored data—in this case, credit card information—to streamline service.
- Coordinating multiple touch points, such as the dessert chef capping the experience with an unexpected gift.

These elements fall into five broad categories of gathering and leveraging information, a performance platform, as it were. These categories are Information, Channel Delivery, Insight, Measurement, and Customization. On a small scale, such as a single-location restaurant with an established clientele, these categories are deployed with good memories and careful note-taking. And back to answering our original question, achieving that level of performance on corporate, even global scales is also entirely possible, enabled by technology and software tools that can enhance and support the experience and empower tens of thousands of employees to personalize the experience for millions of customers.

In this chapter we'll identify these tools in broad terms and examine how they fit into an overall customer experience technology infrastructure. Each can deliver a value on its own specific to one or more of the five categories we've identified here, and together they move the organization closer to the promise of customer-centricity.

In describing the need to evolve the customer experience tools to deliver exceptional experiences we will examine two stages of evolution toward customer-centricity:

- **Customer Experience 1.0.** This first stage takes place in the present, and examines already-available tools deployed across different disciplines to make the work of the customer experience professionals more effective.

- **Customer Experience 2.0.** This second stage takes place in the future, and assumes constant, rapid innovation that will only serve to solidify and empower customer relationships through personalization and customization. All functions of the organization will be aligning their resources to match customer value with the level and availability of talent and resources.

Customer Experience 1.0

Our first goal is effective management of the customer experience through technology and the performance platform.

The diagram below illustrates the Customer Experience Tools Framework, depicting the variety of the types of tools available to the customer experience professional and the role they play in improving and delivering overall customer experience.

Information. The goal of Information customer experience tools is to provide a relevant, updated single view of the customer. Various tools are available to unify the different customer databases within the organization. They enable organizations to then analyze the unified databases and segment them into relevant, meaningful data sets that enable organizations to create products, special offers and promotions to develop better purchasing response from customers.

Some of these tools may propose to start from scratch and build a brand-new customer information hub, such as the SAP CRM. Such an approach provides a fresh start, free of the constraints of the organization's legacy tools and assumptions. These tools deliver such new capabilities as linking Twitter and Facebook interactions into a single repository of customer information.

Another major advantage of SAP CRM and similar tools lies in linkage to such backend operations as inventory and process management. Such linkage enables organizations to move more quickly to Customer Experience 2.0 and its enterprise-wide customer-centricity.

Other tools in the Information category seek to leverage existing infrastructure. Information can be integrated within an organization without necessarily investing in an entire CRM architecture. You can layer service-oriented architecture on top of existing data structures, and create a unified customer vision across all organizational touch points. Such consistent, related information forms the foundation of your customer relationship.

In either case, your customer information must be integrated and shared across all functions. In most organizations, this information is still scattered and not managed centrally. Such fragmentation and disorganization leads to confusing views of customers and conflicting offers and treatments. No one silo can own knowledge that's unavailable to other silos. Some silos are hoarding information for self-serving purposes, without regard to how that information could be applied to enrich the customer experience. This is, as we've discussed, the danger of organization-centricity.

One point: if you outsource technology, your third-party vendor must have access to the same data that you would apply had you kept the technology internal. For example, if outsourcers see only the customer service database but not the accounting database, they have no way to link the information, which ties their hands.

Channel Delivery. Channel relevance depends on two factors: customer preference and communication relevance. Different customers prefer different channels of interactions, and certain types of interactions are appropriate only within specific channels. I may prefer to examine the product at a retail store then place the order on the web. I may purchase the product through a channel partner, then call the help desk for support. I may conduct business on my iPhone, while receiving customer service tips via Twitter.

Companies must provide both channel choice, and exceptional quality of experience within each channel.

A variety of companies provide multi-channel solutions that help organizations unify their channel strategy. In advanced cases, we've seen tools that allow customer service employees to see exactly where customers got stuck on a web session, so they can take over the session and lead the customers to their destination. One of my favorite features in channels is "last employee," where customers can opt to speak to the specific associate who served them most recently to ensure continuity and efficiency of service. Many innovations are evolving in the channel space as new channels of communication evolve via the web.

Insight. Business analytics tools are critical to best understand customer trends and customer personas, and to subsequently understand how to tailor solutions and offers to each customer segment. A wide variety of tools are available in this area, and many of them are even more tightly integrated with the customer information hubs than the tools I described under the "Information" category above.

Complementing these analytics capabilities are customer feedback management tools, such as customer survey systems, which provide additional layers of insight into customers' preferences and overall perception of value. These applications range from low-end do-it-yourself survey tools to robust enterprise feedback tools. The beauty of the robust tools is the ability to tie customer survey responses into the customer information hub to ensure that the next person who interacts with this customer knows the up-to-the-minute status of any given customer relationship. For example, if a customer expressed dissatisfaction with the resolution of his or her complaint, the accounting team engaging with the customer knows to not instigate collection for non-payment until the issue is resolved. The more you know about your customers, and the more you analyze your customer information and behavior, the more intelligently—and emotionally—you're able to personalize experiences.

Developments in this area include using speech analytics to better assess customer preferences, perceptions and challenges. For example, by analyzing in-coming customer service calls, you can track how customers respond to certain issues and how they prefer to speak about your products. This capability is critical both for designing marketing campaigns and for product development, and for crafting sales and customer service campaigns, as well. Speech analytics can also help support employee coaching efforts by providing additional guidance as to how to improve the overall performance.

Measurement. In this category are two types of tools, both of which are important in order to track progress and to set clear goals for all involved:
- Those designed to measure the interactions between customer and company—for example, assessing performance metrics in a call center.
- Those designed to measure employees' performance—following the call center example, enabling organizations to track employees' performance by either recording the calls or monitoring web sessions and email exchange.

It's critical to balance the measurements game and not get stuck on making and analyzing the wrong metrics. For example, we often see companies focusing on numbers related to call completions or web sessions, while paying very little attention to the quality of the interaction or the level of satisfaction that results. Remember, measurement tools are just that—tools—and simply using them is not an end in itself. What's measured—and how the resulting measurements are analyzed, interpreted and coordinated throughout the organization—is your operational and strategic challenge. You must establish standards for interpreting and applying measurements with the goal of increasing overall performance from their use. Chapter 12, "Measure What Matters," goes into detail on how to establish those standards and maximizing metrics.

Customization. Loyalty-program tools and marketing-customization tools are now increasingly stepping into the customer experience realm. They support the key function of tailoring the experience to each customer, responding to stated preferences and to segmentation based on transactional and other behavior. Loyalty tools allow companies to customize offers and rewards to each customer based on their track record and preferences. The marketing-customization tools allow marketers to create customized solutions to each customer, such as print-on-demand customized books and customized campaigns.

Customization tools usually fall within the marketing domain, with its goals of personalizing communications, offers and experience. However, customization is not placing the customer's name in the first line of a mass-produced letter. Customization is tailoring and shaping entire programs, all the way down to the individual employee's level of performance.

Customer Experience 1.0 Already at Hand

As you review the Customer Experience Tools Framework, you may find that some of these tools are already in your organizational arsenal, though they may not yet be fully utilized. Examine your needs for additional tools in light of the complete picture. Many companies succeed while still in the process of adapting to the new tools, because the tools are not the goals, but rather the vehicles to accelerate success. Approach them with clear goals and a clear strategy for achieving those goals. And prepare yourself with full understanding of the organizational and operational changes required to maximize each tool's value.

Customer Experience 2.0

Now we enter the future of the Customer-Centric Organization—total alignment around the customer, powered by the convergence of technology platforms in the five critical categories.

In customer-centric organizations, all functions operate on the priority established by customer value. This value is quantified, specified, and shared with all employees across all touch points. Customer-centric organizations embed the centrality of the customer across the organization and disseminate critical information associated with specific customer value to all employees, regardless of level or tenure. This knowledge guides customer engagements and improves the quality of experiences that customers receive, as well as allows employees to align the level of resources allocated to those customers.

In this fashion, each function can run its operations, allocate resources, and set priorities appropriately. Only by ensuring transparency around customer value can each touch point allocate resources according to customer value, align its operations with that of the overall business, and ultimately fulfill the organization's lofty customer-centric promises.

The graphic below illustrates a typical enterprise with customer-facing functions highlighted in light blue and back-office functions highlighted in dark blue. Adopting a customer-centric business model requires that all functions work in unison to provide consistent and high-quality experience to customers.

To illustrate how such a customer-centric business model can be deployed, let's take the preparation of a customer quote as an example. The moment of truth comes when the salesperson delivers a price quote to a customer. Leveraging the embedded centrality of information and enterprise accessibility to it, the salesperson can consult the customer's value and status (e.g., prior adherence to terms and conditions, payment history, and so on). Such information guides the salesperson in tailoring the amount quoted, terms of payment, allowance of previously agreed-upon terms, and so on. Additionally, the salesperson can view such operational elements as real-time inventory status to provide accurate delivery estimates. Providing this type of information-enriched quote not only ensures a proper fit between company and customer, but also establishes trust with customers by empowering each employee with the ability to deliver a customized experience.

The Pinnacle of Customer-Centricity

Whether working within Customer Experience 1.0 or 2.0, customer experience practitioners seek to align the right resources with the right customers. Highly customer-centric organizations can deliver different types of experiences to various types of customers because they allocate resources according to customer value. Higher-value customers receive service from the organization's best employees and have access to the most-effective interaction channels, which are also likely the most expensive to the company. In contrast, low-value customers are directed to low-cost channels such as web self-service, or are serviced by less-skilled employees. These customer-centric organizations ensure an ideal fit between resources (both human and technological) and customers to ensure a desirable and profitable experience that benefits both customer and company. These companies have an almost innate ability to respond to a customer request with the right offer without either compromising on price or value. This flexibility allows organizations to treat customers as unique individuals while maintaining the profitability of the relationship.

The graph on page 215 illustrates the alignment between customers and resources (human and technological). The horizontal x-axis represents customers' business value from low to high, left to right. The vertical y-axis represents talent and resource value based on performance from low to high, bottom to top. The green boxes reflect the optimization line, which begins when low-level resources are committed to low-value customers, and builds as better resources and talent are matched to higher-value customers, ending with the best resources and highest commitment being devoted to the best overall customers. On the graph, the optimization line is depicted in shades of green, lighter shades reflecting the intersection of lower-value resources and customers and darker shades reflecting higher-value resources and customers. Matching resource allocation with customer value along this line will produce the most efficient ROI.

Ideally, companies should assign their top resources to the highest value and highest potential customers. As this graph illustrates, top resources (#10 on the y-axis) should be assigned to the highest-value customers (#10 on the x-axis). However, many product-focused companies will assign higher-quality resources to lower value customers to meet pre-defined delivery dates or service level agreements (SLAs).

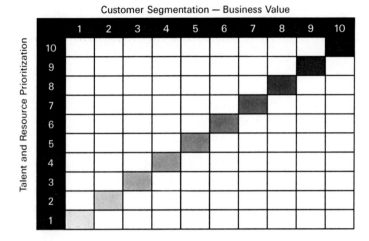

Customer Segmentation — Business Value

Following this model allows organizations to utilize and allocate talent and resources effectively to minimize waste. Customer-resource alignment above or below the line mismatches the power of the resource with the power of the customer, and represents areas of diminished effectiveness.

The model, you will note, is particularly effective when viewing customers that fall within the inefficiency zones in the context of our Financial Segmentation and Lifestyle Segmentation models established in Chapter 6. Each of the four Financial Segmentation Groups—the Moneymakers, the Misunderstood, the Lost Souls and the F.U.'s need to be handled at levels appropriate to their value—or lack thereof.

Building the Pinnacle

When working toward this effective alignment, be wary of falling into the common trap of utilizing only traditional customer data from customer-relationship management (CRM) systems. Excluding other sources of data limits the effectiveness of a variety of business functions, particularly those in the back office.

Numerous information sources must be tapped to develop understanding and profiles of talent and resource performance on the one hand, and customer value on the other. These sources include CRM, enterprise resource planning (ERP) and the related tracking of key performance indicators, finance, sales force automation (SFA), and inventory management, along with talent and workforce management, and business analytics tools. This aggregated data allows organizations to calculate customer value and assign resources accordingly. They will minimize the waste that's inevitably associated with servicing low-value customers with top talent and via expensive channels, and vice versa.

Now, let's look at examples of the underside of the pinnacle, the dysfunctions that can occur when companies don't employ a unified view of the customer in order to guide their work and create the appropriate customer experiences.

1. Customer service has no view of inventory, and must answer incoming questions about stock vaguely, or not at all—forcing them to hand off the customer and deflate the customer eperience.

2. Field service can't coordinate parts availability, so is unable to work with customers closely to update them on status.

3. Legal has no view into customer business value in order to prioritize their work

4. Finance attempts to collect from customers with a dispute over quality, interfering with dispute resolution.

5. Manufacturing can't forecast production needs based on the quantity and size of orders in the sales pipeline, so risks coming up short when deals are signed.

6. Product management can't see customer-service challenges and proactively react to them.

7. Human resources fails to track performance based on customer results

8. Marketing launches a campaign without coordinating with distribution to assure delivery to customers responding to the campaign.

9. Advertising is launched without readiness of service operation.

10. Customers are serviced based on arrival, not value priority.

As noted, each is an example of how one touch point can misfire when lacking information already within the company. You can extrapolate other points of dysfunctional misfire, from IT not knowing of a big ecommerce promotion potentially generating server-straining traffic, to sales selling big contracts to customers who have failed to pay, to R&D developing concepts that marketing research has proven to be risky.

This cross-functional visibility, as you can see, becomes one of the core drivers of "Different Experiences for Different Customers," as well as for a number of other elements critical to delivering customer experience, including:
- Employee empowerment.
- Measuring what matters.

- Alignment with CRM and branding.
- Performance impact management.
- Complaint and idea management.
- Voice of the customer.

Summing Up: Small on a Global Scale

The answer to our original question—*Can we provide small-restaurant levels of service on massive scales?*—is most definitely *yes*. Using the tools in the Customer Experience Tools Framework, every one of your employees can be that maître d' serving that valued regular patron, no matter what location she chooses—perhaps one of your bistros on her next vacation to Greece.

CHAPTER 11

Deliver the Experience

Strategic Steps: Deliver

A stressed-out customer calls into a flower shop, demanding, "I need you to ship a dozen roses right now to this address." He rattles off an address and his credit card number.

The customer service rep pauses, then says, "Sir, would you tell me why you are stressed."

"Ma'am, it's none of your business—please don't ask me questions. Just ship the roses."

"Sir, I promise to do that right away. But can you please tell me why you're upset? I can sense it in your voice." She continues to prod for an answer, gently and quietly, extending the call without a single thought to average handling time.

Finally, the customer blurts, "I forgot my anniversary yesterday. My wife isn't talking to me, so I'm sending roses to see if she'll forgive me. Are you happy now?"

The agent says, "I'm truly sorry about what happened. Here's what I'd like to do. With your permission, when we send the roses, I'll write a note saying that we apologize for shipping the flowers to the wrong address yesterday. And I'll add a small box of chocolates. Will that work for you?"

After a moment of quiet, the once-agitated customer says, "You're going to do that for me?"

Now, picture that customer from where he's calling. He's sitting back in his chair, relaxed once again because one savvy customer-service agent made his problem go away. And, in fact, it is that very situation—and that very chair—that reveals the secret of what customers really want. Many studies show that customers have one primary desire: They want a chair—a comfortable chair in the middle of a peaceful green meadow. They want to sit in that chair, in quiet surroundings, completely relaxed. Metaphorically, of course, unless you happen to be selling chairs and/or real estate. Customers want to sit in that chair after dealing with your company. They had a problem, they came to you, you took away the problem. Now they can sit in the chair and bask in the peace of the meadow.

These customers didn't turn to you for a link to your web site so they can turn into a human Google. They came to you for solutions—and they came to you for memory. The first question asked when designing your customer experience strategies was "What memory do you want to leave behind?" When customers finish filling out a form, click out of the website, finish reading a direct-mail piece, walk out of your retail store, what memory do they take with them?

All of us are a collection of memories. We hold onto our recollections, good or bad. We don't hold onto products, research or documents—we hold onto memories. Customer experience is based on and influenced by memories, and not necessarily memories of your company. When customers experience your product or service, your people, and your entire organization, will they find themselves sitting in that chair, enjoying the memory, or are they going to be overwhelmed, with bad memories crowding out the good?

Let's look at the progression we've made in our quest for customer experience so far. In Chapter 4, we designed memories; in 5, we invited the customer to create and participate in their own memories; in 6 and 7, we honed those memories; in 8, we deployed the employees to facilitate the memories; in 9, we evaluated overall organization readiness for delivering the memory; in 10, we outlined the platforms for execution.

Now it's time to deliver. We're at the moment of truth, the moment of memory creation. Have you succeeded?

Companies face millions of moments of truth each day with your customers. The moment of truth is when you and your customers get together. It always boils down to an experience. It could be at the call center, at the point of sale, in mailings you send, or at the website. What experience will be created at that moment of engagement? What happens during that experience will determine the memory, the profitability and everything else. How great that experience will be depends on us.

In some ways, your organization is the sum total of your moments of truth. In other ways, your organization will be summed up by a single moment of truth. Your customers are demanding more than ever before. We live in a world where every call to your call center can be on YouTube tomorrow. Every call. All it takes is one. When employees face customers, they have two and a half minutes to create greatness or to destroy loyalty. According to Gallup, a single bad experience will reduce customer loyalty by 66%. While you're reading this, your employees, those face-to-face with customers and those operating the background mechanisms that enable customer experience, are determining the level of loyalty you will get from individual customers.

As we saw in our discussion of empowerment in Chapter 9, "Readying the Organization and Developing a Culture of Change," the average call center agent takes 10,000 calls a year. Multiply that by the average customer spend, and you'll understand how much revenue that single agent is responsible for. If we assume an average spend of $300, that one agent is controlling $3 million, and potentially destroying $3 million if he or she fails to deliver at the moment of truth.

Establishing memories is about fulfilling aspirations, and about fulfilling promises. Today, marketing messages promise that "We'll do everything for you. You're number one. You're the reason we're here." Hallmark would do well to have a special section of "We love you, customer" greeting cards. At the moment of truth, customers will apply four litmus tests to these messages to gauge your sincerity and the delivery of your promise:

1. Emotional engagement. Are you treating your customers as human beings? Are you delivering memory?
2. Complaint resolution. How do you handle complaints? *Do* you handle complaints?
3. Idea management. How do you handle customer ideas? *Do* you handle customer ideas?

4. Customer rewards. How are you saying "Thank you" to customers that bring added value to you?

In sum, these tests revolve around what we call a "center of exceptions," and viewing exceptions as a positive. In this view, exceptions exist as differentiating advantages instead of as interruptions of your busy workday. The center of exceptions is geared to providing customers with the sense of uniqueness, individualism and caring for their one-of-a-kind interaction with you. It possesses the capability to solve complex, outside-the-box issues at the first point of contact by the first person they speak to. Its staff is informed and empowered to solve the problems and can adapt the rules to delight customers.

In a center of exceptions, the guiding principle is that every request is recognized as unique and is treated as such—to allow for immediate resolution. All interactions, human or otherwise, should incorporate this principle so that employees are willing and able to deliver on the promise of delivering a personalized customer experience.

Moreover, the center of exceptions recognizes that human interactions offer customers (and the company) unique value. The true test of the success of such value delivery is whether service personnel were able to surprise customers by exceeding their expectations. As we saw in Chapter 5, self-service is in the process of being redefined and expanded, into Self-Service 2.0, which brings engagement and co-creation into the self-service scheme of things. But even in Self-Service 2.0, non-human mechanisms have limitations and rules to abide by. An airline website that allows you to select your own seat when booking a flight can't necessarily help with special needs—or complaints if you encountered seating problems on a previous flight. Such self-service is pragmatic, and puts the consumer in control, yet when problems arise—when exceptions arise—that self-service can't solve, consumers demand even higher level of service, and an experience personalized in contrast with the less-personal self-service mechanism.

In sum, exceptions demand exceptional performance. The center of exceptions gathers exceptions, and it delivers them in exceptional, differentiating experience.

The characteristics for successful centers of exceptions include:
- Every interaction is recognized as different and requires unique resolution.
- Any interaction that isn't or can't be resolved through self-service is seen as an exception and is treated accordingly.
- Employees are empowered and are expected to solve any issue without the need for escalation.

- Resolution is always personalized for the customer.
- Employees ensure that each experience is exceptional by consistently demonstrating knowledge, urgency and caring during every customer interaction.
- Unique customer requests and challenges represent an opportunity for innovation.
- Primary objectives should be to surprise and please customers during every interaction.

During live customer interactions, companies can highlight competitive differentiators through the quality and service they provide. A center of exceptions should consistently demonstrate to customers its ability to address exceptions, resolve unique issues and combine them with emotionally engaging service.

Honeywell Aerospace

Honeywell Aerospace is a global leader in aircraft parts manufacturing, with $12 billion in annual sales at the time of undertaking a customer experience transformation. Honeywell provides integrated avionics, engines, systems and service solutions for aircraft manufacturers, airlines, business and general aviation, airport operations, the military, and space operations.

THE CHALLENGE

In 2005, Honeywell was a fragmented company with 12 business units. Customers seeking product information, technical support or other services were forced to wade through a maze of contact points and information sources. This lead to service/experience inconsistency, and ultimately to decreased customer satisfaction and increased customer complaints. Honeywell sought to improve customer satisfaction, reduce costs, and move from a purely engineering- and product-centric approach to a customer service-centric approach.

THE STRATEGY

Transform customer experience as part of an overall restructuring of Honeywell Aerospace. The larger corporate changes allowed deployment of customer-related changes, using these tactics among others:

- **Leverage executive buy-in.** "We never faced a problem of executive buy-in," says Honeywell Aerospace VP of Product and Customer Support Adrian Paull. "Our new CEO was focused on customer-centricity from Day One." Day One was in January 2005 when Robert Gillette took the CEO reins.

- **Work with a sense of urgency.** The customers feel the urgency. In fact, in designing customer experience innovation, Honeywell included this customer survey question: "Do we demonstrate a sense of urgency when you have something of a great deal of importance?"

- **Identify the problem areas.** In conducting a complete experience diagnostic, Honeywell analyzed the gap between customer perception and employee perception of performance at various touch points. For instance, the above question about urgency, posed to both groups, showed that customers answered positively less often than employees.

- **Remove obstacles to WOW performance.** Honeywell consolidated more than the business units. It reduced the number of published contact phone numbers from 270 to one. And because customers regularly called for technical and product information, Honeywell expanded its only knowledge base and product catalog, created a Tech Op Center that reps could consult 24/7 when asked tech questions.

- **Personalize the engagements.** Access to newly centralized information allows intelligent call routing, so that incoming calls are routed to the most appropriate rep based on the caller's job and position in the company, and view the customer's previous contact history. "I think this is a complete game-changer," says Paull.

THE RESULTS

As a result of these initiatives—bolstered by a new education program, wow-performance incentives and a bold and persistent employee communications campaign—within 12 months of deployment, Honeywell enjoyed a 20% increase in customer satisfaction. And, writes *Customer Relationship Management,* "The makeover also helped the company land a $16-billion deal with Airbus for the company's forthcoming A350 airliner, a deal that one Jefferies & Co. analyst said is a direct result of Honeywell's restructuring."

As you work to deliver the experience, to create exceptional service, let's examine each of the customers' four litmus tests—emotional engagement, complaint resolution, idea management and customer rewards—in turn:

Litmus Test #1: Emotional Engagement

Every business works against a larger background of emotional issues that underlie all business engagements. Think about the emotional engagement associated with, for example, a cell phone. For a teenager, that's an identity question, not a handset question. Customers are trying to achieve larger solutions than purchasing a product or service. Every vertical conducts the business of the functional and the business of the emotional, the business of the Bigger Picture. Without emotional engagement, you are a functional commodity, and you're back to pricing.

Let's return to the problem-plagued flower customer and the solution-savvy customer-service agent. The interaction between the two exercised two major customer-experience principles:

1) **Different experiences for different customers.** This customer's need was different from that of someone sending flowers for Mother's Day or for a funeral. In fact, thinking back to the principles of persona management we discussed in Chapter 6, the caller certainly fell into a lifestyle segment we might call The Romantically Forgetful. Do you think that's he was the first absent-minded husband she'd encountered—even that day? In fact, about three forgetful types call in each and every day. The flower shop may not have thought about their response to The Romantically Forgetful in official segmentation terms, but certainly they knew their clientele well enough to design experience, and to define their true business, specific to that group.

2) **Emotional engagement.** The caller didn't have a problem as much as he had emotional issues—stress, frustration, desperation. The rep dealt with those emotions by delivering emotional value in return—relief, relaxation, confidence. And, of course, a memory.

Certainly, none of this happened by chance. The secret is that because the rep faces that situation about three times a day, she has everything set up to respond—a well-oiled machine. This rep will call our Forgetful Romantic a couple of days later and say, "Sir, I'm calling to see how your anniversary went, and while I have you on the line, let's be a bit proactive so it doesn't happen again. How about you giving me all the dates and anniversaries and birthdays of your friends and family so I can put them in my reminder system? I'll call you two days before each event to remind you and we will decide what to send them." The total experience she has delivered turns a $29.95 single sale to a customer relationship worth over $5,000 over a five-year period on average.

That's the power behind great experience. Truly successful customer experiences employ emotional engagement to solve the real problem behind stated requests. You don't exercise emotional engagement for its own sake. Understanding interactions from a perspective of emotions gives you clues about the complete challenge customers face. From those clues, and from an understanding of the issues behind stated request or traditional transactions, you derive ideas on how to best address those challenges.

Yet, the concept of emotion makes the corporate world very uncomfortable. Companies believe that emotions can neither be managed well nor fit cleanly into a pie chart, so therefore must be ignored. The efficiency-oriented operations companies so pride themselves on are full of logic and predictability, and they tend to treat the customer accordingly.

The bean-counters have no clue how to factor emotions into their financial models, and so emotions are treated as the type of irrational behavior that must shied away from.

That thought process is fundamentally flawed. Businesses that build themselves on logic alone will be very expensive to operate. Purely logical customers shop for the lowest price on every purchase, demonstrating no loyalty at all, and forcing the businesses to invest in "acquiring" those specific customers again and again, through expensive incentives.

You want emotions in your relationships with customers. You need them. Emotionally-loaded terms like *relationships, loyalty* and *experiences* were borrowed from personal relationships where individuals prefer a deeper commitment to a single individual over the shallow relationships with many. *Relationship* means making an emotional selection and sticking with it. The stronger the relationship, the longer it lasts, and the deeper the commitment. This is exactly what you want from your customers—a deeper, longer commitment to your products and services even if they aren't the cheapest on the market.

Best of all, emotional engagement needn't be cost-intensive. What did the flower sale cost the company, other than a little extra handling time? They didn't have to redesign the entire experience—just the thrust of the specific interaction. The rep reacted to the emotion, and to the real need. Rule #1 in customer experience management is that the problem you are solving and the value you are delivering is not in fulfilling on the transaction at hand. Companies keep answering the flower question when the real issue is saving marriages. That's when they lose the memory, and that's when they lose the business. That customer will remember the transaction for years, and turn to this flower shop first during those years. The flower shop doesn't need to advertise or send direct mail. This customer is now connected to somebody who understands the real problem, not the functional problem.

Again, look back to the Lifestyle Segmentation established in Chapter 6, "Different Experiences for Different Customers." You can often view Lifestyle Segmentation as Emotion Segmentation—such as when the Business Traveler segment in our hotel example seeks a place of serenity in which to prepare for a hectic business day.

The Basics of Emotional Engagement

To retain the memories, to engage emotionally, and to deliver to customers the pleasure and the honor of basking in relaxation in that quiet meadow, consider these guidelines:

Listen. Our flower shop rep used a very powerful tool for handling emotion: a ready ear. Yes, in this case, she was listening for cues that would allow her to choose the proper business experience for that customer. But listening in and of itself establishes human connection and demonstrates caring. For example, our group once conducted a trial with a large insurance company. The company advertised a stated policy cancellation procedure—no hassles, and no questions asked. When customers called to cancel, the agent handled the requests efficiently—no arguing, no counter-offers. We decided to buck the no-questions-asked policy in one small way, with one simple query: "Why?" During the trial, customer-service reps politely asked the reason for the cancellation and simply listened to the reply. The results: during that cancellation call, 17% of callers decided to stay with the company. They'd been heard out. They'd gotten a complaint off their chest, or unburdened a personal problem, or maybe just talked themselves into recognizing the value they were receiving.

Now, imagine the impact you'll have if you take listening to the next step by designing experience based on what you hear.

Stop thinking "average handling time." Take *time* to listen. Emotions have no average life cycle. Delivering emotional engagement will of course increase average handling time, but it will also increase the two metrics you're really interested in—"average revenue time," and what we call "average nurturing time"—simply by asking a worthwhile question.

Return emotions. The problem with emotions is that they're usually expressed only in a nurturing environment of emotions. They demand mutual commitment in order to deliver commitment. In the long, uncomfortable affair companies have with emotions, they tend to exploit the customer's emotions but not deliver any emotions in return. That's probably why there are very few companies who will put emotions in their name—as Southwest Airlines did with the symbol LUV. Understand that relationships and loyalty require reciprocity. Loyalty is about emotions. "I'm willing to give you emotions," the customer is saying, "but you must give me emotions back."

Give employees permission to engage with customers on emotional levels. Few companies succeed in emotionally engaging their customers through direct or indirect company customer interactions because their employees simply adhere to corporate policies and follow the process. This sends a clear message to customers—"we care more about our policy than we do about you."

During human interactions, customers reveal cues. They bring up personal matters such as vacations, funerals, investments, and other issues at home. When customers supply such cues, employees must recognize the opportunity to make a human connection. If a parent's child is graduating school and is applying for his or her first credit card—recognize this achievement. If someone is requesting a change of address because she's moving from an apartment to a house—celebrate this milestone.

Simply following processes and adhering to policies might get the job done, but will rarely, if ever, establish an emotional connection that customers will remember and cherish. At the most basic level, all that employees need to do is listen, pay attention and react in a manner similar to when their family and friends share news with them.

Train employees on matters of experiential emotion. Too many companies leave it to their individual employees to define emotional engagement. Lack of corporate definitions and guidelines leads to personal definitions and varying outcomes of employee performance—some with absolutely no emotional engagement at all.

Employees must recognize and accept the opportunity to make human contact as a personal opportunity to help someone. As discussed in Chapter 8, to do this successfully requires hiring and retaining right people, those able to establish an emotional connection with customers. To that end, companies must adapt their hiring criteria so that they select individuals with a strong service orientation and who see serving people as a personal and inspirational mission.

Emotional engagement cannot be considered a chore and cannot be mandated from above. Employees must internalize the beauty of having the ability to help another human being through good and bad times.

Converse. Avoid the concept of "following a script." Provide touch point employees with inspirational and tangible guidelines that demonstrate the general principles that they should adopt when delivering the experience. These guidelines should describe the different customer personas as well as their lifestyles, challenges, aspirations and frame of reference as they relate to your products and services.

Celebrate the celebrations. Illustrate your commitment to emotional engagement by publicizing stories and examples that showcase how employees have emotionally engaged customers.

Share customer emotions with relevant company touch points. Use the cues picked up from customer interactions as more than conversation starters or as leverage points for constructing the experience for a particular engagement. Gather and record emotional cues as you do other more traditional customer data points. For instance, pass information about needs and requests to sales for cross-sell and up-sell opportunities. If milestones are linked to recurring dates, file the information for generating future congratulatory messages. All such information can also be used for targeted marketing campaigns, custom offers and other tailored communications.

On a larger scale, perhaps a chance customer comment might be enough to assign that customer to a particular lifestyle persona. Or, if the emotion the customer expresses is part of an emerging pattern from other customers, perhaps a new lifestyle persona is forming in front of you—just as it likely did for the owners of our example flower shop.

And a Rose for You . . .

Face emotions and understand that emotional interaction is a strength and not a weakness. Just because you can't place it in a pie chart doesn't mean it doesn't exist. Allow your people to add their emotional touch to the overall customer experience and to create positive experiences and memories in your customers' hearts. Demonstrate your sincerity and authenticity so customers will willingly forgo the next price cut from the competition. Emotional customers aren't problematic customers. These are customers who care. Customers who share their views with the world. Customers who pay you premium and stay for the long run. So unleash the power of emotions.

Litmus Test #2: Complaint Management

All companies boast of their dedication to resolving complaints. "We need to listen to our customers." In reality, no one wants to talk to an upset customer.

What is a complaint to you? A nuisance? A baseless accusation? A little problem blown out of proportion? An interruption from someone looking for excuses or freebies, or who simply likes being annoying? Discard those notions. You *want* to talk to upset customers. Their anger—their *caring*—is an opportunity for you. A University of Pennsylvania study shows that about 4% of upset customers voice their complaints. The rest of them don't bother. What does that tell you about what they think about you? "I don't believe in your product. I don't believe in your company. I don't believe you're capable of fixing the problem. And even more than that, I don't believe our relationship is worth saving." The silent message from uncomplaining customers is that they're about to jump to the competition, or return to you—loudly this time—and press you on price.

In contrast, the 2% who do bother to complain are saying, "I still believe in this relationship, and that it's worth saving. Therefore, consider complaints as a *second chance and an* opportunity to rectify a broken relationship to preclude defection. Complaints are customer declarations that they're not giving up on the relationship yet. In fact, research shows that disgruntled customers who were treated well ultimately became more loyal to the company than customers who didn't experience problems, because when the relationship was tested, the companies proved themselves willing, caring and customer-loyal. And, importantly, devoting resources to delightful complain resolution is still a cheaper way to capture a customer relationship than acquiring a new customer.

What's more, complaining customers aren't simply grousing about their problems. They are exposing processes and products that don't work. You must compensate the complainers, of course, and fix their problems, but these are payments in exchange not only for those particular customers' continued business, but also for the continued business of all the customers they represent—those in similar situations who are *not* complaining. Hiring a consulting firm would cost tens of thousands of dollars to find out what that one customer is seeking you out to tell you—for free. If you look at customer complaints as a nuisance or an annoyance, you'll never learn anything from them. One of the strongest business moves you can make is to abolish the word *complaint*. Replace it with *idea*.

Simply said, complaints are great. They're good for business. Welcome them.

Certainly, the conditions that lead to complaints are bad for business, which is why I stress that you must meet expectations before you can expect to exceed them. Still, problems and errors are part of the game. Organizations must learn to not treat these problems as exceptions to the rule, but rather to embrace these exceptions and create special processes to deal with them and still delight the customers. An ideal problem-resolution process will delight customers to such an extent that they will look forward to sharing their problems with the organization in the future.

The Basics of Complaint Management

Designing an ideal problem resolution process should include the following steps:

Approach the complaint with a sense of urgency. The first rule of every complaint resolution: *One and done*. Emphasize speed to resolution in complaint management. A clear sense of urgency demonstrates to customers that their issues matter to you. It also demonstrates a true sense of responsibility. When customers call in, whoever touches those customers must have the power to resolve the issue. If you don't believe that an employee should have that power, don't put that employee in front of the customer.

As I've noted, the one-and-done rule is particularly important when fielding contacts from customers who are coming from a self-help experience, whether trying to place an order on the web or questioning the details of a kiosk transaction. Even in a world increasingly dominated by self-service media, customers expect that when they exhaust the self-service option, companies will step up and deliver exceptional and personalized "live" service.

Once again, this means that customers coming to you from self-service experiences are moving from Tier One problem resolution and expecting Tier Two—while your call center agents are thinking that they're about to deliver Tier One. This is a major shift. Assume automatically that customers using the web are calling looking for exceptions. They're looking for ways to break out of the box. They tried the box, and it didn't work.

If you can't deliver one-and-done, or if the agreed resolution is immediate but the fulfillment of the resolution takes some time, keep the customers informed. Communicate anticipated delays and time frames for resolution.

Assume that the customer complaint is valid. My consultancy often identifies an unspoken belief among customer-service professionals that customer disappointments and frustrations aren't warranted. Accept that even great companies make mistakes that inconvenience their customers. Understand those areas where mistakes or exceptions might occur and educate your service staff to recognize them and act accordingly.

Respect the complainant. Customers who experience exceptions are still good customers. Treat them with respect and not as outcasts who abuse your products and services. Identify customers by name, which personalizes the experience for both the customer and the employee, who can now see the complainant as a person.

Employ the customers in complaint resolution. Provide customers with options—put them in the driver's seat by providing alternatives. Or, as appropriate, ask them directly for their preferred resolution. Give employees permission to accept, or to negotiate solutions based on the importance of the customer to the company.

Take responsibility. Take full ownership of the problem. The common apologetic response doesn't resonate with customers or compensate for taking full responsibility. Acting evasively and not providing clear problem resolution demonstrates lack of commitment toward the customer relationship. On the other hand, a company that takes ownership of the problem and provides a decisive and clear response demonstrates a long-term commitment to the customer.

Consider assuming responsibility even if it is not your responsibility. A major New York department store built a portion of its customer-service reputation on the fact that it would go the extra mile with their customers by such actions as accepting returns for products not purchased at their store—and even for products in categories their store never carried in the first place.

Don't just apologize. Compensate. Customers expect more than mere apologies and expect you to take additional responsibility for their problems. Design an apology kit that allows your employees to send some form of compensation, preferably something visual, so that they can *see* that you're taking ownership. The compensation needn't be expensive, but it does have to be tangible—a magazine subscription, a music CD—it must be something that the complaining customers can associate with the fact that you took ownership. Design the kit to be multi-level, so that the compensation can be proportionate to the seriousness of the complaint and to the overall value of the customer making the complaint. In apologies as in experience, one size does not fit all.

Clarify the definition of resolution. There are two types of complaints: Solvable and unsolvable. An example of a solvable complaint is an incorrect invoice. Fix it, end of complaint. An example of an unsolvable complaint is a traveler's disastrous trip, from the people partying in the next room all night to the obnoxious seatmate on the plane home. You can't fix an already-completed excursion; you can't return the sleepless night to the customer. You can't design a process to address unsolvable problems.

The traditional thinking is that people who call with unsolvable complaints are looking for an apology. In focus groups we've conducted for clients, these customers have told us, "I don't want your apology. If I want pity, I call Mom." Customers with unsolvable complaints are seeking psychological balance. They're saying, "I'm left with the consequences of something you've done, and we need to rebalance it."

Saying "sorry" doesn't return balance, because doing only that doesn't demonstrate that you're taking ownership and responsibility. Here in particular you need to deploy an apology kit. This serves to rebalance the customer, and establishes positive memories.

Solve what can be solved—compensate for what can't.

Inform relevant personnel. Install mechanisms for collecting data from the complaints and for acting on that data to dissipate the source of the complaints. Measure complaint repetition. Ensure that all relevant stakeholders in the organization are informed about the problem and suggest remedies to prevent negative incidents from happening again.

This is part of the official role of the Customer Council that we will discuss in detail in Chapter 14, "Reinvent the Experience: The Governance Model." Complaints and exceptions play a significant role in the Voice of the Customer, which helps drive continuing innovation in the customer experience strategy.

Similarly, Personal Portfolio Managers, as discussed in Chapter 6, must be kept apprised of complaints and problems—either directly or through the Customer Council—so that they can maintain a close view into their particular customer segments.

Arm employees with enterprise-wide information. When customers call with questions or complaints, front-line associates can't intelligently answer questions or solve problems if they're kept in the dark on matters affecting the company. All organizational functions—including marketing, sales, R&D, product development, field service, finance and legal—must proactively inform front-line associates about such matters as advertising campaigns and defective products, so those associates can intelligently and confidently interact with customers. Treat your customer-facing departments like you treat your media relations department. Media relations works to handle communications with the mainstream press to get word out about corporate policy, corporate decisions, product recalls and the like to people on a broad basis. In a sense, the call center serves the same role on a one-to-one basis, spreading the word perhaps as powerfully as the media relations people do. After all, front-line associates, from the desk clerks to the call center agents, form the public face of a company, and no company wants to look ignorant and foolish.

Follow up. Make sure that the customer is satisfied with the service and remedy. An ideal follow-up demonstrates that the company is interested in the customers' issue, not getting them off the phone as soon as possible. Companies should also inform customers about any remedies you've taken to prevent their issues from recurring. Beyond resolving the original problem, this action demonstrates to customers that their problems will lead to better future performance. It also further demonstrates that you're taking both the problems and the customers seriously, and gives the customers a sense of ownership in the solution and in the company itself.

Put the complaint in customer perspective. Through the fog of complaints, long wait times, product defects, and difficulties reaching customer service agents, customers easily forget the immense value that they receive from the companies they routinely do business with. This is a particular problem with reliability-based services such as utilities, cable, telecommunications and insurance. Only when problems occur do customers take notice and gauge these companies on response times, ease of operator access and duration of outage. Train your employees to identify opportunities to remind complainants about the overall value they receive, without appearing annoying and artificial.

Complaining customers are focusing on the problem at hand and not the larger level of service. For example, when we worked with FedEx, we asked their customers what reliability level would be acceptable to them. Their answer—90-95%. Then we asked them to estimate FedEx's current reliability level. The average answer—54%. Yet, not one of the customers we surveyed had experienced a reliability level below 95%.

Stress overall value with such information as percentages of on-time deliveries, the number of problem-free purchases, the length of service without a complaint, and, as appropriate, overall up-time of service. This information helps complainants understand the value provided and fosters a sense of understanding and tolerance when problems do occur.

Recognize the next time a customer does business with you. Record the details of the complaint and of its resolution in the customer record. Make sure that employees who serve customers for a second time demonstrate extra sensitivity and knowledge of past history.

Complaint Management at Work

How you handle customer problems and complaints reflects the type of relationship you want with your customers. Customer loyalty and the willingness to provide repeat business is determined by the manner in which organizations behave during contentious moments.

Customers will forgive companies' mistakes as long as the companies demonstrate responsibility, ownership and commitment. Ensuring a delightful problem-resolution process is a major testing point for every company and determines the future of their customer relationships. So stop over-processing your rules and start creating delightful exceptions to that rules.

Let me give you a personal example of complaint management at its finest. My youngest daughter loves American Girl dolls, and she once convinced her grandmother to order an impressive set of American Girl doll furniture—my daughter is very skilled at convincing. Opening the package when it arrived, my daughter discovered that the doll bed was damaged. My wife called the company, expecting the typical corporate game of shifting blame onto the shipping company.

The customer-service agent apologized, and said, "But there's a problem. First, is it safe to use the furniture?"

"Yes."

"Unfortunately, we don't have a new bed in inventory. We expect a shipment in May. Ask your daughter to play with the furniture until we can replace it, and then we'll collect the damaged one."

All was good. My daughter happily played with the furniture. But in May, a package arrived, with a note saying that the promised shipment of replacement beds hadn't yet come in. In compensation, the company was sending some new doll clothing—a line specifically for the doll my daughter owned. Of course, my daughter wanted more delays so she could get more accessories.

American Girl created a memory—and the memory they did *not* want to create was disappointment. Ask American Girl what their business is, and they will tell you they aren't in the doll business. They're in the business of celebrating girls. Celebrating girls is an emotional memory. It is a commitment. And you build the commitment into the price.

Answering the call for help

Complaints, in their purest form, you see, are customers' personal pleas for help. Remember that customer experience practitioners are in the business of memories. You have a customer who's hurt. You must design your responses to complaining customers with the memory in mind. How will you make the memory of your complaint resolution so powerful that customers will be sorry they don't have more complaints? Not that we're trying to encourage complaints, of course . . .

Litmus Test #3: Idea Management

Complaints are viewed in business jargon as "exceptions"—variances from the day-to-day business operation, requiring special handling. It seems that customer ideas are dropped into the same bucket of exceptions—interruptions of the business day that must be dealt with begrudgingly, or ignored altogether. But remember that we have established that complaints are ideas, and ideas—oddly enough—are ideas, too. Customers can be your richest source of ideas and incremental innovation. Just as you need set procedures that deliver efficient and even delightful problem resolution, you must establish mechanisms to hear and respond to customer ideas so you know exactly what they need and how to make them loyal.

Again, I pose the questions from earlier in this chapter: How do you handle customer ideas? *Do* you handle customer ideas? As an experiment, call your own contact center or your receptionist, and say, "I have an idea for you." More than likely, you'll be asked, "What's the problem that we can help you with?"

"I don't have a problem. I have an idea."

"What can we do to help?"

"I don't have a problem. I'm very happy with your company. I just have an idea that might help you."

The associate, not knowing what to do, will at best ask to hear the idea and then pretend to be listening. At the end, the associate will say, "Good idea—thanks for the call."

"What are you going to do with the idea?"

"Nothing. But it was a good conversation."

Imagine the danger in telling your spouse that, in essence, you're not listening, but thanks for the input. So why is such an attitude dangerous on a personal level but acceptable on a professional level with your customer? If you aspire to emotional engagement with your customers, be prepared for ideas. Ideas are personal, and therefore they are emotional statements. If you shrug off ideas, you risk the customer thinking, "You're not listening to me."

If you consider a complaint an opportunity, how can you possibly not say the same when customers approach with positive communications? Suppose you did more than nod and say "Uh-huh" and sign off with "Thanks for calling." Suppose you set into place mechanisms that would eventually enable you to declare in emails, in advertisements or as a footer at the bottom of your web page, "This year we've collected 7,000 ideas from customers, and implemented 372 of them. Customers, we thank you."

The Basics of Idea Management

In addition to soliciting ideas through such Voice of the Customer mechanisms that I'll describe in Chapter 13, "Leadership and Change Management" and to customer-fueled innovation techniques described in Chapter 4, consider these, yes, unsolicited ideas to help you reach the point where customers join your unofficial R&D team:

Listen for ideas at all touch points. Call center, web site, notes on paid invoices—customers will take the opportunity to speak their minds. Alert these touch points that they're now part of the overall corporate listening mechanism, and train them in procedures for delivering the ideas and related pertinent information to the proper stakeholder. Ideally, as mentioned before, that stakeholder is the Customer Council in charge of monitoring the success of the customer experience initiative. Much of idea management involves passive collection of unsolicited ideas—the proactive element is being alert for incoming brainstorms.

Dig for hidden ideas. Customers can also deliver ideas without specifically stating them, or knowing that they are presenting ideas. As we saw in Chapter 4, requests for services or concessions out of the ordinary can signal overall customer need. Stop trying to get your customers to do what you've predesigned them to do, and start opening up to the possibility that there is more out there that you can do. Recognize that each one of those diverse requests represents another opportunity. In fact, here is another avenue for developing segmentation. Adapt yourself to the exceptions, to the specific customer needs, and then charge for fulfilling those needs. Grow your business by finding other customers with the same "exceptional" needs. That is the essence of the Self-Service 2.0 principles discussed in Chapter 5. Watching consumer activity—ideas that they implement themselves but don't tell you about—can be very instructive.

Don't evaluate ideas at the touch points. Collect all ideas and move them through the system. Don't be like our sample associate, pooh-poohing the idea and then hanging up. An idea that seems ridiculous to the front line may actually be genius, or combinable with another idea. And an idea that seems ridiculous may indeed be ridiculous, but passing it on allows for response and feedback returned to the customer—especially if it's a highly profitable customer. As well, the "idea" may indeed represent a customer problem, indirectly stated, that must be solved.

Acknowledge and follow up with idea contributors. As is the case with complaint resolutions, customers must be informed about idea progress and/or implementation. Again, this is part of building customer dialogue, and about respecting the customer's role in the business relationship.

Prepare for full management of incoming customer ideas. If you have not yet created a Customer Council within your organization, allocate staff someone to specifically manage the key steps in the idea-management process. The idea-management team will follow through on the ideas, from evaluation to resolution. These steps include:
- Centralizing the gathering and recording of ideas.
- Assigning idea evaluation to appropriate personnel and touch points.
- Centralizing the evaluations for go/no-go decisions, and prioritizing the go decisions for order of implementation.
- Coordinating the budgeting of staff and monetary resources to idea implementation.

- Monitoring the idea's impact, based on such metrics as cost savings, additional transactions generated, incremental size of transactions, touch point efficiencies, and so on.

- Updating all stakeholders of the impact, not just for the purposes of reporting but also of justifying the investment in idea capture, and of motivating increased idea-capture activity.

- Publicizing successful ideas to various constituencies—from front-line employees to department heads to the public at large—with the goal of emphasizing the differentiation idea management brings to your organization.

- Rewarding the customers who brought you the ideas, including those who may have offered valuable evaluation and suggestions.

Establish idea-capture nets. Companies set up various sorts of "listening posts" to solicit customer input, from customer panels to call-center monitoring systems to combinations of surveys, focus groups and the like. Available to you today are web-based communities, which are in a sense huge global suggestion boxes where customers can propose ideas, and other customers can evaluate, build upon and even vote on those ideas.

A great example of such an idea-capture net comes from Dell Computer, a company that learned the hard way to take customer complaints seriously, and responded admirably. Dell's once-superb reputation in the marketplace had taken a hit. Customers complained about the company's product quality and about its lack of innovation. Dell was losing its close brand connection with its customers, and sought a mechanism to facilitate reconnection.

That mechanism took the form of IdeaStorm.com. The combination of features on this community website told customers, in essence, "Tell us what to do. Don't tell us what's bad. Share with us how to fix what's bad and make it good again." IdeaStorm.com served as a platform to promote products and services, but its true purpose and its true impact extended far beyond that product-centric goal. In demonstrating true commitment to listen to the voice of the customer, Dell not only reestablished personal, emotionally engaging relationships with its customers but also created a participative mechanism by which solid ideas—ones relevant and important to overall customer needs—were identified and fast-tracked.

IdeaStorm.com made customers a part of Dell's R&D effort. The site gave Dell's customers a platform to exchange ideas with other Dell users and with Dell itself. The site allowed customers to posting of new ideas, and to discuss them. A ranking mechanism then turned the ideas back over to other customers, who voted on which ideas they liked. And then Dell focused on the top ideas. When Dell itself developed new ideas, it could run them by its customers first through the website before launching them to the marketplace.

By the end of 2007 – 8,150 ideas provided, 568,562 promotions were conducted, 57,592 comments and suggestions on the original ideas submitted—and more than half a million customer votes were recorded.

Dell employed the power and the wisdom of all their customers to identify the most important issues. More recently, Starbucks is doing the same. With MyStarbucksIdea.com, the coffee vendor uses web technology to reach out to millions of customers at any time, inviting positive suggestions and then allowing others to vote on them.

You don't extra personnel to engender such participation and such response. Simply provide a means for conversation. You can put such customer-communication mechanisms in place without a huge tech investment. Including time for planning and setting up the customer dialogue, within two months you can deliver a very powerful message to the customer: "We're listening. Don't come with a complaint; come with an idea." You can hire this sort of conversational idea net as a service, as such corporate veterans as Godiva, Home Depot and Hasbro have done. Experiment for a month, a year, however long it takes to establish the initiative's impact.

Such tools are available today, but they require you to rethink how you go about gathering customer input, and to reevaluate your perception of your presence on the web. Remember the point that I stressed so hard in Chapter 5: The web is not a channel. The web is a conversation. You must decide whether or not you want to participate in this conversation.

If you want to create a quick win that shows the customer that you're serious about this, Idea management is a perfect way to create engagement. Imagine the power of over half a million customers believing that they impacted the roadmap of the products and the service available to them. Such beliefs are more than emotionally engaging—they're emotionally satisfying.

Litmus Test #4: Customer Rewards

In many ways, the customer relationship can be viewed from the perspective of "hiring" customers to perform a certain job for you, and you pay them with the products, services and experiences that solve their problems, help them achieve their goals, and enrich their lives.

As with any employment agreement, you must also provide bonuses and special recognition for those customers that serve you above and beyond the call of duty. Positive customer actions are often taken for granted, when in reality customers should be rewarded for their contribution to the relationship.

When I talk about customer rewards, I'm not talking about bribery. Nor am I talking specifically about loyalty programs, such as airline frequent-flyer programs, although such initiatives are certainly a part of an overall rewards discussion, as we'll see in a moment.

I'm talking about basic, simple things to recognize the customers who are giving you their best business. Do you have a way to celebrate what they bring to you? Even in tough economic times and while facing smarter, more aggressive competition, you have customers who have doubled their business with you this year. How are you going to honor that devotion? You have customers who will reach their tenth anniversary with you. How do you celebrate such milestones?

Customers deserve "bonus pay" for any number of special contributions they make to your brand and to your bottom line—and to the benefit and experience of other customers, as well. Therefore, deploy a structured program that recognizes and rewards based on the milestones that you have determined impact your business most positively.

Despite the analogy of "bonus pay" that I've used here, rewards certainly don't take the form of financial compensation, or of extravagant, costly gifts. Celebrations, congratulations, expressions of gratitude, special access or privileges, and other gestures can incur very little cost and deliver big impact. This is particularly important within a B2B environment, where corporations impose often-strict guidelines as to the types of gifts employees can accept. Again, simple and celebratory are effective key components within the concept of rewards.

The Basics of Customer Rewards

The first rule of utilizing rewards as a customer experience tool is understanding that rewards are not carrots, and they are not bribes. They reward behavior not to condition behavior, but instead to reinforce the value companies see in the customers' actions, and to encourage repeat behavior. And, ultimately rewards are mechanisms of recognition, of experience, and of delight.

To make rewards an integral part of delivering experience, consider these steps:

Specify what will be rewarded. Set triggers for recognition. Benchmark what types of customer activity brings value and ROI beyond simple transactions. For instance, reward customers for reducing your costs.

When working to move customers to more-efficient self-service mechanisms, are you willing to reward them for taking on some of your job? Are you willing to share in the savings? Reward any increase in the customer's level of loyalty, by whatever measure you assign to define an increase—greater frequency of purchase, greater spend, greater value to the brand and desirable behaviors of any sort. Design a customer scorecard to determine the most profitable customers.

Such loyalty indicators can include:

- Providing referrals and recommendations.
- Providing meaningful insight and feedback, including survey participation, idea suggestions and even a complaint that alerted you to a broader problem.
- Longevity of relationship, and attendant milestones.
- Stage of the business relationship lifecycle.
- Engaging in cost-reductions, as seen in the example about self-service.

Here's a test. What customer actions, if performed right in front of you, would make you beam and say "Thank you!" more than once? Now take it the next step. Innovate how to say "Thank you" as loud and clear as you would if you were able to say the words in person.

Then again, say those exact words in person. Segmentation as established in Chapter 6 and diligent maintenance of customer records allow you to know the value of specific customers when they interact with you. Say thank you on the spot. Present a reward independent of the engagement at hand, whether that engagement is a transaction, a complaint, or even something as simple as the customer responding to a survey.

Be spontaneous. Some companies, particularly in the hospitality business, have been engaging in what has been termed "stealth loyalty." Hyatt Hotels, for instance, employs an official program called Random Acts of Generosity. Personnel on Hyatt properties are free to grant perks, upgrades and complimentary services to customers on the spot, and are even supplied with an official card on which staffers can write personal notes when presenting the gratuity. Hyatt has but one rule for issuing Random Acts of Generosity. They can't be extended to make up for a problem or a service failure—that's something quite different. The Random Acts must indeed be random.

Design "addictive" customer rewards. If customers leave you in the middle of the relationship, they stand to lose special treatment or a level of thank-you. This addictiveness is one component of loyalty programs. If customers leave with thousands of unused points or miles in their accounts, they're discarding not only the worth of the balance, but also the potential achievable by building on that balance with future activity.

Don't confuse rewards with incentives. The best rewards are delivered in gratitude, not dangled as enticements. After all, you're working toward delightful experiences. A critical element of delight is surprise. Achieving something you've worked hard for is gratifying and fulfilling, certainly, but it is hardly surprising, nor is it necessarily delightful.

Leverage your loyalty program. Loyalty programs come in a variety of flavors and structures—you likely know them best as frequent-flyer miles programs or credit-card points programs. Rewards in the overall context of compensation and in the specific marketing context of loyalty marketing are ultimately the same concept, one simply more formal than the other.

Note that I said "leverage" your loyalty program—don't depend on it. Today, such programs are not differentiators; they're table stakes. If you don't have one, you can't play the game. And many programs work only as incentiv-izers (see my point directly above) instead of as experience differentiators. Every company must attend to the critical question of the core experience and its quality and value in the eyes of the customers before they rush to depend on a loyalty program to spur repeat business. As I discussed in the context of rewards in general, a loyalty program is not a mechanism for conditioning behavior, as many companies think.

In fact, some companies rush to loyalty programs in order to cover a harsh reality: their products and services are not that exciting. They seek redemp-tion by giving away freebies to mask the boredom their products or ser-vices evoke. If your experience is not great, a loyalty program won't com-pensate for it. Worse yet, some companies make the mistake of choosing lipstick-on-the-pig shortcuts that increase the cost of doing business without addressing the overall value provided to customers.

A great example of such a problem comes from the pioneers of loyalty mar-keting itself: the airlines. Since 1982 when American Airlines established its AAdvantage frequent-flyer program, the airline industry can hardly demon-strate any visible impact such as increased loyalty or improved margins as a result of the loyalty program. As a form of compensation for ever-depreciat-ing values to customers, customers took full advantage of the program, but the additional value to the airlines, business was marginal. The struggle the airlines have had with limiting bonus tickets, increasing the miles required for each ticket, and other tricks demonstrate how the loyalty program sim-ply did not build loyalty because the service was not authentically exciting. The airlines' loyalty programs prove that you cannot fool customers. They will not come back to a lower-quality value or boring experiences subject to ongoing value reduction efficiency efforts. Simply put, loyalty programs will not save you from the truth.

However, in and of themselves, loyalty programs can add to your repertoire of experience-building and experience-execution tools, particularly when offering rewards and gratitude. But, some will ask, isn't a loyalty program a mere incentive that drives the customer forward like the mule slogging after a carrot at the end of a stick? No—that's like hiring an employee who only wants a paycheck. Isn't it, they will ask, a mere conditioned signal, a few points thrown the customers' way so they drool a bit as they picture a big-screen TV like Pavlov's dog salivating at the ring of a bell? Not when executed with the proper care, innovation and customer focus.

Granted, there are dozens of carrot-and-stick loyalty programs on the market today, failing to exercise the ability that such programs have to not only reward desirable behavior and delight customers, but also to gather data that you can use to tailor products and experiences to individual customers, to segments, and to your customer base as a whole. A solid loyalty program is an exercise in customer interaction and exchange. It is a device that— much like the idea-capture net embodied in IdeaStorm.com and MyStarbucksIdea.com—brings the customers into the inner circle and allows them to experience the brand and develop a level of brand ownership. Loyalty programs provide:

- Transaction and preference data.
- Customer self-identification—loyalty program members are raising their hands, and their program membership allows you to easily relate activities to specific customers.
- Efficient communications and engagement streams.
- Opportunities to test rewards.
- Platforms for recognition and appreciation of exceptional loyalty.
- Straightforward communication to customers that you're not taking them for granted.

At its best, a loyalty program is formalized emotional engagement. And just as loyalty in general is about a reciprocal exchange of emotional engagement, a loyalty program as a specific marketing tool is about a reciprocal exchange of value. The customer delivers value to you in such forms as greater depths of information.

Just as you do with any other corporate touch point, design your loyalty-program experience to delight and to engage emotionally. Innovate the rewards and recognition in such programs with the same customer focus and the same innovation that you apply to your customer experience program in general. In fact, you can look at a loyalty program in terms of the overall concepts we've established throughout this book. For instance, loyalty program tiers are in a broad sense persona management. Redemptions are rewards for going above and beyond in the form of problem-solving merchandise or emotionally engaging recognition and aspirational experiences tailored to customer dreams and interests. Points accumulation is another system of establishing milestones.

Again, how do you differentiate your loyalty program from all the others out there? How is the experience in belonging to your loyalty program surprising and delightful. How does your loyalty program feed emotion back to your best customers, recognizing them, making them feel appreciated, and inviting them to participate in the brand with their ideas and their constructive criticism? Finally, how does your loyalty program go about solving the customers' real problems, while making that chair in the quiet meadow comfy and relaxing?

Thank you for listening . . .

Believe me, customers are watching for and expecting something in return when they deliver value to you. They're thinking, "I'm giving you loyalty, I'm giving you business—are you taking my loyalty for granted? Or are you going to recognize and appreciate my loyalty and my value?" If the appreciation you display is generic, you're going to get generic loyalty—which is choosing to make transactions based on price. If the appreciation is customized, personalized and rewarding, you will regain loyalty and emotional engagement.

Summing Up: Delivering Exceptional Experience

Between growing customer demands for great experiences and the availability of multiple interaction channels, the traditional definition of the human interaction for customer service is gradually becoming obsolete. The future definition will focus on delivering exceptional customer experiences for all types of challenges, but particularly those that can't be resolved through self-service. All customer experience practitioners must set higher standards and aspire to handle all interactions, particularly exceptions.

Adapt business strategies, empower employees, enhance technology and information infrastructure, create extensive training programs and deploy relevant incentive and recognition programs to meet and exceed heightened customer expectations. Doing so will increase employee satisfaction and improve employee performance, reduce customer attrition, and increase revenue and profit. Ultimately, the most successful companies will transform traditional customer service functions into a unified center of exceptions that will deliver great experiences and command customer loyalty.

Business today operates in a new world where the usual and reliable fail to meet the ever-heightened expectations of those we conduct business with. In this world, you must excite and delight your prospects and customers to gain and maintain a competitive edge in this hyper-competitive environment.

Welcome to the center of exceptions, where you deliver exceptional and personalized solutions for the most complex of issues, where you set the new standard of excellence. And isn't it a lovely coincidence that this center is in the middle of a quiet meadow, where a comfortable chair awaits your customers?

CHAPTER 12

Measure What Matters

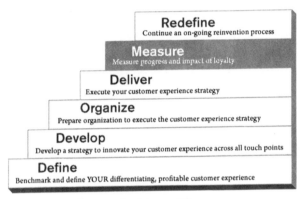

Strategic Steps: Measure

A client once told me, "Lior, we just improved customer experience by 90%!" Great news. When I asked how he accomplished such a remarkable upgrade, he showed me the results of market research conducted to identify loyalty factors and to map the customer experience. The company conducting the survey identified specific loyalty factors that my client should focus on to build stronger customer relationships. For greater accuracy, the results were divided to 8 geographic regions, reporting measured loyalty factors specific to each region. As I reviewed the results, I was shocked to discover that in 5 out of the 8 regions, the number one loyalty factor was . . . invoicing. The message was simple: "Excel in invoicing and customers will be loyal to you."

"We upgraded our invoicing process," my client crowed, "and now our invoices are 90% accurate."

Yes, clear and accurate invoicing is an important touch point in the total experience, but believing that such a basic function can be a source of differentiation and loyalty results from misunderstanding differentiation or, at worst, self-deception.

I've observed more and more of those questionable results coming from reputable sources. One source is easy to define: Applying the wrong metrics to customer experience. As customer experience began to hit the radar screens of corporations worldwide, market research companies jumped at this new opportunity to offer their services. Unfortunately, these researchers often don't extend beyond applying old-school methods of measuring satisfaction to a decidedly new discipline. In doing so, they measure processes, not experiences—invoice accuracy, not differentiating delight. They fail to capture the level of emotional engagement of the complete experience—and as we've established in our discussions of innovation and design, emotional engagement matters. Because old-school methods ultimately measure how to fix processes and eliminate dissatisfaction, they can't measure how to create differentiation.

Measuring what matters is hardly a new concept for companies seeking to engage in customer experience. *Knowing* what matters in customer experience is entirely new territory, and calls for a shift from old-school metrics to the metrics of delight. Delight *can* be measured, and here I will show you how to build an effective, actionable Customer Experience Map. This map provides a view into where your company stands in terms of current delivery of customer experience, current potential of that delivery, and consumer perceptions of your performance against areas they consider important.

To build the Index, you must first pull your organization out of the mire of self-defeating metrics, the ones that promote unproductive activity. Within call centers, for instance, employees are often evaluated on average handling time. The shorter the call, the more efficient the department, the lower the cost of call-handling. Two minutes and thirty seconds and goodbye. So what if the customer feels rushed, even if the question or complaint was resolved? So what if the customer feels compelled to call back because the complaint wasn't resolved, or the quickness of the call made the customer forget a second question? If that second call is handled in under 150 seconds, it's within the stated acceptable guidelines, and, oddly, can show up as a *positive* in a report. And if you don't believe that it's happening, reflect back on the story I told in Chapter 1 about call-center washroom-time metrics.

Then, contrast that with an American Express revamp of its call-center metrics that I described earlier. Realizing that their traditional measures for employee effectiveness and company effectiveness limited in their ability to forecast future spending, they launched a customer-based survey that followed the Net Promoter Score model. Each employee is held accountable to 100 completed surveys evaluating their performance each year; 50% of the employee's compensation is tied to the results of the hundred surveys. Now the he-said-she-saids and the rationales and excuses don't matter.

In fact, Amex saw a resulting change: when the agents didn't make their numbers in terms of the surveys, the employees turned to the supervisors for help in solving customer issues. As employees became accountable for delivering great customer experience, they held each other accountable for improving the customer experience.

This organization moved away from operational numbers like average handling time—which fails to measure how well the call was handled, or if the issue was resolved—to focus on the ultimate number: the employee and the customer, one-to-one. When you're willing to build the business by focusing on the numbers that ultimately matter to the company, you will begin to achieve real performance.

And if you don't follow a rigorous, detailed evaluation process, you can't identify and quantify actual moves of the customer-experience-performance needle. Therein lies the importance of the Customer Experience Map.

Beyond Satisfaction

Another mistake companies make is assuming that satisfaction metrics suffice as customer experience metrics. Satisfaction is important, but in itself it's an insufficient measurement. "Are you satisfied? Are we good? We are? Thankyouverymuchgoodbye." You need to know if your brand and your customer are connected emotionally and if your experience has nestled comfortably into your customer's lifestyle as part of that connection. You need to know if you lived up to your brand promise, and if (and how) customers will act differently.

Ultimately, you must evaluate on behavior: the question isn't whether customers are happy or are willing to recommend you to friends, but whether they're also willing to spend more. If the experience you deliver doesn't lead to improved behavior, you didn't impress the customer; you didn't rise above parity. You want to learn how each customer engagement—from transaction to call-center conversation to website visit—will affect future behavior. Will customers:

- Stay the same
- Spend more
- Spend less
- Buy more
- Rush to a competitor

If you can identify customer issues and behaviors and calibrate them against subsequent behaviors, you can predict future activity in the areas you've identified, and you can justify investment in those areas. Many companies have a wealth of customer satisfaction data but are unable to create The Number that will compel upper management to specific action based on that data. Management sees that customers are saying they're satisfied, and that they're going to act in a certain way. This satisfies the boss, even though the customers aren't actually taking those actions.

We as customer experience practitioners must demand more from our metrics by rejecting traditional, generic statements. Asking customers generic questions to gauge the quality of the customer experience will generate generic responses and help you build a generic experience. "Were the agents you dealt with courteous?" The customer says, "Yes." Now, what do you do with that answer? The customer says, "No." Oops. Now, what do you do with that answer? And in fact, the likely response you'll get will indeed be in the affirmative. "Yes, your employees were courteous." Now you can nod, satisfied, but you have little actionable insight into how the customer perceived the experience overall. If the employee was courteous but unhelpful, for instance, that "Yes" answer fails to identify a poor customer experience.

Some companies base satisfaction standards on the popular Net Promoter Score (NPS). This metric, created by consultancy Bain & Co. and Bain consultant Fred Reichheld, asks customers to rate a company on their willingness to recommend the company after a transaction, on a 1-10 scale. The number of customers rating the engagement as 6 or below is subtracted from the number rating the engagement as 8 or above. The resulting figure is the NPS. Such a system has its use, but the answer it delivers is somewhat like how Douglas Adams, in his *Hitchhiker's Guide to the Galaxy*, answered the Ultimate Question of Life, the Universe, and Everything: 42. Adams explained that he chose that answer because "42 is a nice number that you can take home and introduce to your family." But it's not an actionable answer. Knowing your customers' willingness to recommend is useful, but your metrics must ultimately measure how well you delivered against brand promise, where you failed in delivery, and how you can reinvent the experience to eliminate such failures.

Net Promoter is a good system as long as you can use it to determine delivery against brand promise, correlate it with revenue performance and not just satisfaction, and use it as a foundation for improving and reinventing the customer experience as needed.

Customer-centric brands measure themselves against their unique value and not against generic measurements. They identify the questions that most closely correlate to what customers expect from them and correlate these expectations closely to future purchases and greater loyalty. Ritz-Carlton asks its customers a defining question that correlated closely to their promised value: "providing a sense of well being." The hotel chain was able to calibrate answers to this question against future activity, and found that strong scores from responses demonstrated the highest likelihood of repeat business and customer loyalty.

Asking questions that yield insightful and actionable answers might not get the glowing responses you crave, but they will identify opportunities for growth and improvement. At the top of the list of questions to ask customers is whether the organization delivered an exceptional experience. While the response may not always be the desired "Yes," a low score should push your organization to discover and rectify the reasons for the failure so that you can meet, and even exceed, the high standards that your customers have set.

Total Experience Metrics

The ultimate goal of the Customer Experience Map is to assess and present a holistic view of the experience. And by holistic, I also mean companywide. Organizations are often unified in name and logo only. Brands that design and deliver customer delight are unified in measurements, as well. They hold every employee in the organization accountable to the same customer-centric metrics. Product-centric brands, on the other hand, have different functions operating according to their own sets of objectives and measurements. The inconsistency of measurements and standards in siloed environments ultimately leads to several problems:

- **Unfulfilled brand promises.** Customers seek fulfillment of brand promises across all organizational touch points, and are confused by disparate attempts to deliver varying degrees of value.

- **Unproductive, independent actions.** In doing benchmarking work for a credit card company, customers we surveyed clearly told us that they viewed the company's ads so negatively that many stopped using the card after seeing the ads. When we reported this to marketing, to our absolute amazement, they told us that they had no intention of changing the ads. "We need to meet our numbers for brand recollection. We're meeting our numbers."To worsen matters, the marketing department had such sway in the company that we were asked from above to not share the negative numbers with the rest of the company to protect that department.

- **Lack of ownership.** When I ask clients "Who's responsible for the customer in your company?", perhaps the most honest answers I get are "It depends" or "A bunch of nobodies." I don't get those answers that often. The CEO often gives the typical response. "Everyone is responsible for the customer." To that I respond, "OK, if your number-one customer goes to a competitor, who gets fired?" The shrugs that I receive in response are very loud. If employees have responsibility with no consequences, they have no responsibility, and no motivation to deliver delightful experience. It makes for an interesting demotivational poster: "Everybody's responsible for the customers, but don't worry, we aren't measuring, and we don't care."

- **Failure to deliver delight or to identify and correct experience miscues.** Take, for instance, quality-monitoring metrics applied to how the call center handles complaints. In such cases, the complaint's root cause is likely not customer service. The root cause likely surfaced somewhere else—perhaps in legal, in accounting, in field service. Yet, quality monitoring is designed to evaluate just the call and the person who took it, not the situation that prompted the call in the first place.

- **Failure to encourage cooperation across silos.** The purchasing department, for instance, doesn't care about call-center metrics. They just want to achieve the lowest cost. But if you can demonstrate that more-expensive and higher-quality purchases lead to fewer dissatisfied customers, reduced call-center load, and increased profits overall, the purchasing department will begin to care about those call-center metrics.

- **Employee frustration.** Continuing the example of selective measurement, employees wonder why the concentration is only on them, and why other departments are not also being held accountable. Imagine a call-center employee's reaction: "I just took the call. I did my best, but I didn't cause the problem. Are you also talking to the people who did? Maybe I should have taken a washroom break instead of answering the phone."

The consistent delivery of customer experiences that reflect the brand promise is predicated on unifying and aligning departmental and corporate objectives. When all departments or functions are thusly unified, they will ultimately deliver the desired experience. The Customer Experience Map helps you unify disconnected organizational functions with a common set of objectives and measurements. In the absence of unifying measures, the customer experience directive will be perceived as a suggestion, not as a corporate imperative. Most employees will simply ignore it. Thus the importance of conducting measurements in the context of the complete experience and not within silos.

Mapping the Customer Experience

Begin by mapping a holistic view of the customer experience within your organization. Such mapping centers around accountability. As we all know, you can manage what you measure. You're about to map the complete customer journey from three standpoints:

- **Assessment.** Evaluating the quality and priority of experience.

- **Alignment**. Evaluating how the experience fits your customers' lives.

- **Action**. Evaluating the results of your experience.

Assessment: The Quality and Priority of Experience

Begin with customer surveys to establish two critical metrics:

- The level of importance customers place on individual touch points.

- The level of customer perception of how well those touch points deliver on their functions.

Within that second metric, customer experience is measurable on two critical factors: *attributes* and *attitudes*. I'll give you an example to better define these components. Imagine you're in a restaurant. Tonight's entrée d'jour for you: "Steak," you order. "Medium rare, please, and I'm starved. Please bring it in 15 minutes." The steak arrives in 14 minutes, and it's cooked to perfection. But when the scowling server delivers it, he grunts at you indignantly, plunks the plate down, and says, "Here. Eat this, you carnivore." Your appetite disappears. The *attributes* were fine. The *attitude* was off-brand. Customer experience entails not only what you do it but also how you do it, encompassing the personality of your associates, the language of your documents and statements, and even the way you answer the phone.

Measuring attributes is typical and fairly easy within a commoditized environment, but you must also measure attitudes in order to create and maintain differentiation. Companies in good times and tough times keep customers because they have established an emotional bond with customers. Without that bond, the relationship is based only on pricing.

You must measure and understand the depth of your emotional relationship. Rational satisfaction—"You shipped it on time, thank you"—is insufficient in preventing customers from migrating to your competition. As I've noted, studies show that 83% of satisfied customers will talk to the competition.

When measuring customer perception of your organization's emotional attitudes, ask specifically about:

- **Customer knowledge.** Do employees know what the customer needs? Do they readily have answers to questions? Do they have the tools to perform their jobs?

- **Willingness to serve.** Are employees passionate about what they do? Do they take extra steps to satisfy customers?

- **Emotional engagement.** Do employees treat customers with caring and compassion? Do they fulfill emotional as well as functional needs?

When performing assessment, be thorough in covering the touch points you survey against—the number of touch points may surprise you. In one B2B engagement, we helped the client map 50 different touch points. This exercise will help you identify all potential interaction points where you might be losing loyalty. A starter list could include (in alphabetical order):

- Advertising
- Agreements
- Brochures and collateral
- Collections
- Conferences
- Cross-selling
- Customer service
- Dealers
- Delivery
- Direct marketing
- Distribution
- Invoicing
- Manuals
- Manufacturing
- Operations
- Packaging
- Pilot / Trial
- Post-sales service
- Pricing
- Problem-solving
- Product design

- Products
- Proposals
- Reception
- Retail
- Sales
- Samples
- Service
- Technical expertise
- Upgrade
- Website

As you approach this assessment, remember that you're working with the understanding that not every touch point is equally important in delivering the results we seek. This is because we aren't seeking overall satisfaction but instead are working to drive satisfaction and experience at the points most critical to your customers. Therefore, don't assume that any given touch point is unimportant. You might not think that vending machine placement in your hotel's hallway isn't a critical issue—but maybe it is. If you don't measure all touch points, you'll lose a true perspective on the balance of touch point importance, and might overlook a touch point whose importance to customers isn't something you've considered.

Alignment: How the Experience Fits Your Customers' Lives

Closely related to the important element of emotional attitude within customer experience is the way the experience and the brand align with the true customer needs that we've identified and designed experience for in Chapter 4, "Innovate the Experience." Customer experience must align with two significant components:

- **Brand Promise.** What total solutions does your brand pledge to customers? How important are those promises—are you making the right ones? Does customer experience live up to the promise? This isn't a matter of only falling short of promise. Execution of experience might be superb, but if that excellence in areas that the brand doesn't communicate to customers, customer experience will be out of alignment with brand promise. In this case, it is essential that you measure the linkage to *your unique* brand promise, and not to generic standards of performance.

- **Lifestyle Fit.** Do your organization's values mesh with your customers' values? Does customer experience allow customers to engage with you in ways relevant to how they perceive life and how they live it?

Action: The Results of Your Experience

Once more, you must ultimately evaluate the success of customer experience on consumer behavior. As a result of your experience, do customers spend more, encourage their friends to deal with you, come to you with suggestions—in other words, do experiences motivate positive action? Do they make customers more loyal?

Important here is that we measure future customer actions and not just perceptions. Don't measure what customers *think*; measure what they intend to *do*—and subsequently follow through in doing.

The loyalty you seek to measure takes two forms:

- **Personal Loyalty.** This is expressed in actions that customers take directly with your organization. Do they repeat purchases? If they already repeat, do they increase repeat frequency? Do they spend more with each transaction? Are they willing to stay with you longer—are you retaining their business and therefore their loyalty?

- **Network Loyalty.** This is expressed in actions that customers take outside your walls. As we discovered in Chapter 5, "Customer Experience in the Virtual World," social networking and word-of-mouth (both traditional face-to-face conversations and electronic information-sharing) wield tremendous power. Do your experiences surprise and delight customers so much that they can't wait to tell their friends about it? Are experiences so interesting and relevant that they make a good story to tell? Are your products, services and execution so good that customers will be willing to recommend you to their network?

All these factors must be considered in developing the holistic view of your customers' perception of the experience at each of your touch points, and, therefore the experience with your organization as a whole.

The Continuing Assessment

Remember that customer experience mapping, assessment and evaluation are not static, one-time projects. Such assessment must be repeated at regular intervals to gauge the success of your efforts and guide future action. This cycle of assessment, therefore, becomes an integral component of Change Management as I'll discuss in detail in Chapter 13, and continually refreshing and reinvigorating your customer experience, as I'll discuss in detail in Chapter 14. At intervals determined by your customer experience execution team, measure again and again the brand's alignment with customer lifestyles and values, research again and again the impact customer experience has on loyalty. In rolling cycles, benchmark and improve, and rebenchmark and improve.

Such continuing measurement implies to customers and employees alike that you will take action on within the areas that are the subject of your surveys. As you'll see when we discuss the mechanics and strategies of survey-taking, you must follow through on that implication, first by taking action, and second by demonstrating to consumers and employees alike that the voice of the customer is being heeded. More on that in sections to follow.

Leading Indicators Measurements

There are two types of measurements:
- Measurements that explain what has already happened.

- Measurements that can point you toward what's about to happen. This measurement is a leading indicator.

Often, the measurement category is related to timing—when you make the measurement. Analyzing the results of an annual customer survey, for instance, is usually too late. When you conduct a transactional survey right after a customer interaction, you can act on it immediately and individually, before the relationship begins to deteriorate. And because other customers might have similar experiences, what you learn from the survey can be a leading indicator of future problems that you can solve promptly.

Here's a system we often use with our clients: When customers interact with the company—contacting the call center, visiting a website or visiting a retail location—we ask them to rank the experience on a 10-point scale, 10 being Excellent. If they rank us 5 or below, a dedicated team immediately receives a message identifying the dissatisfied customer. Within minutes, a team member emails or calls the customer, saying, "We just saw that you are not satisfied. What's going on? What can we do to rectify the situation?"

Such immediate surveying moves from tabulating delayed results and finding problems that should have been fixed months ago to a process that delivers leading indications into what it is likely to be of concern so problems can be dealt with promptly. This conversion can take multiple forms. Customer behaviors and characteristics, for instance, can deliver leading indicators. For example, speech analytics provides an effective tool for identifying what might happen. Using speech analytics, you analyze on a daily basis the calls that came into your call center, review the language customers used, gauge the stress they was exhibited, and classify and enumerate the top issues they brought up. In a sense, the customers are telling you directly about the health of the situation so you can address it before it blows up into something much bigger.

Leading indicators usually take the form of patterns, but can also take the form of outliers—fringe responses. For example, let's say a call comes into the customer service center asking for a replacement part on your primary product. The product's been in-market for many months now, and no one else has complained about that particular part before. Right now, that complaint is statistically insignificant—it's one complaint. It's an outlier, and as with statistical analysis, outliers are often disregarded. All other customer-service calls are complaints and questions about other issues. However, if you measure and pay attention to the fringe complaint, you can identify issues that might become something much bigger over time. Perhaps that usually reliable part is wearing out, and others will need replacement, too. Perhaps your supplier delivered a batch of bad parts, and a recall is in order. View such fringe complaints as leading indicators and address them as appropriate before a much larger population will be affected.

The important point here is that by measuring in real time and not waiting until the end of the year or the end of the quarter to find out if people are happy, you can act now to make sure those quarterly and annual reports are reflecting more customer satisfaction than you would have had otherwise.

The Unanswered Call:
The Current State of Customer Surveys

The deployment of customer satisfaction studies has grown over the last several years as customers are routinely bombarded with requests to rank products, services and overall customer experiences. At face value, offering customer satisfaction surveys may seem like a good idea, as it signals a company's willingness to expose itself to the scrutiny of its customers and listen to those people who keep it in business. The long list of companies offering these surveys attests that companies are finally embracing the need to establish reciprocal and mutually respectful relationships with their customers. Or does it? While the number of offered customer surveys is long, the manner in which they're being designed and delivered is filled with holes and faces a long road toward even minimal improvement.

Despite reams of reports that are sliced and diced according to customer segmentations, organizational functions, geographies and every other criterion earnest analysts can devise, this information generally sits on a shelf collecting dust. Then the companies shamelessly approach their customers the following quarter or year with yet another request to sacrifice even more time to provide their feedback and insight so that this time, companies can (but rarely do) improve. Why do companies continue to bother their customers with more and more customer satisfaction surveys that will inevitably be placed with their predecessors on the same shelf, ignored by the same people in the company? The simple reason is ego.

Companies love measurements and like nothing more than to see these measurements validate how great they think they are—so they can display that statistic on their website for all to see. In some cases, executives may deploy surveys for the more practical reason of compensation (bonuses are sometimes tied to customer satisfaction metrics). More often than not, surveys serve to reinforce what companies already think about themselves. Companies seek customer approval and validation while customers seek improvement in the form of the recommendations and feedback they provided. Companies routinely fail to comprehend that if customers truly wanted to validate and thank them for policies, processes and service, they would have already done so.

At the heart of the gap between corporate and customer expectations lies a difference in needs. Corporations desire feedback, appreciation and validation while customers demand action, change and improvement. Even in cases where the intent to improve products, services and experiences exists—companies often don't know where to start and how to implement a customer-centric survey. Lacking guidance, companies often design and execute surveys with limited possibility of turning results into concrete actions.

The 10 Deadly Sins of Customer Surveys, Plus One

Over the years, executives have asked us, "What can we do to improve the effectiveness of customer surveys?" We've replied, "Don't ask if you can't act."

"Oh, you mean that our surveys should seek actionable information." They nod contemplatively.

"Yes, we mean that. But we also mean, 'Don't ask us to help you improve your surveys if you can't act on improving your surveys.'"

"We can act on them."

"But will you?" And here's where these executives are stumped. Perhaps the better initial responses are "Don't ask if you won't act," or "Don't ask if you act frivolously."
Asking questions and then doing nothing other than nodding contemplatively is one of the deadly sins committed by corporate survey takers. When we at Strativity Group conducted our "Discovering the Real Answers: Customer Surveys—The New Realities" survey of *corporate executives* (not customers), we found some disturbing statistics:

- 71% of respondents claim that there was little survey follow-up to change behavior in their organizations.

- 77% of the participants find it difficult to get buy-in for change within their organization.

- 71% of the participants state that there was very little survey follow-up internally to change behavior in the organization.

- 54.6% of the survey respondents highlighted the difficulty with linking the survey results into action.

- 52.3% of survey participants design surveys to validate current performance.

Survey takers might approach their jobs with noble intent. "We're listening. We're creating a customer dialogue." But who really is doing the talking? Perhaps the companies conducting the surveys. And who's doing the listening? Only the customers, and they aren't hearing anything. Surveys too often fail to translate into meaningful follow-up that leads to measurable improvement. And customers, listening for the follow-up, begin to resent the silence.

So, then, I have an effective survey you can immediately adapt and profit from. It is a survey that I give my clients, and that I ask you to take right now. How many of the following 10 Deadly Sins of Customer Surveys do you commit? Answer honestly, and, as with any survey you're involved with, listen and act upon to the responses.

1. Surveys With an Attitude. The most common sin is designing a questionnaire geared toward reaffirming and validating the greatness and behavior of a company, not toward conducting a true customer dialogue. Many customers realize this deception and either choose to not respond or to respond in the exact manner requested by the company, thereby precluding the chance of learning customers' true feelings and limiting the opportunities for improvement. In short, "You get what you ask for." By committing this deadly sin, companies guarantee that they receive the scores they ask for—while ignoring and alienating their customers and encouraging repeat behavior that desperately needs improvement.

2. Failure to Capture Information About Employee Emotions. Many companies measure the attributes of their products and services but routinely fail to capture the emotional element of the total experience—the emotions of their employees. Inappropriately known as "soft skills," positive attitudes deliver positive results. Failing to capture and measure the emotions and attitudes associated with your experience is a combination of not recognizing their importance and the inability to measure them. Customer survey results that lack emotion-based measurements are incomplete and present a distorted view of the customer experience.

3. Statistical Myopia. Surveys are often designed by people with PhDs in statistics rather than by people who truly understand customers and how companies operate. Typically, statistics-based surveys aren't designed with follow-up actions in mind, but rather as an exercise to qualify a thesis in statistical analysis. These surveys' results will be statistically valid but the gap between the results and required actions will be too difficult to bridge. Although all studies must be statistically valid, there is a tendency to go overboard with means and distributions and rejection regions and nuisance parameters and other statistical elements of the study's design. Such concentration on the statistical art can blind managers to actionable insight. Managers who use these statistical studies may enjoy doing so as an intellectual exercise, but will fail to connect it to real life and follow up with concrete actions.

4. Searching for Data, Not Strategy. Customer surveys are often treated as just another spreadsheet full of numbers. The decision to launch these surveys is not made as part of a customer-centric strategy, but rather as a non-committal data-gathering process that must take place for some stated (or often unstated) reason. Companies rarely establish a strategic intent for the study prior to deployment, leading them to create surveys in search of numbers, not answers. As such, managers view the information as FYI or as yet another set of numbers they need to calibrate against other daily data sources, from analyst reports to news articles. When launched as a data-gathering activity, customer surveys receive little attention, to say nothing of follow-up actions. Lacking strategic intent at the study's onset results in limited strategic impact at its conclusion.

5. Challenging the Results. When customer opinions are finally analyzed, correlated and reported, a typical manager response is to challenge the validity of the results often citing other sources of data from internal databases or external reports to contradict the survey's findings. They may also cite personal encounters with customers who said "exactly the opposite" of the survey's findings. This deadly sin will lead companies to challenge their customers' feedback rather than internalize it. Behind this deadly sin lies the attempt to avoid any change, even necessary change, and maintain the status quo.

6. Spinning the Results. Survey goals can't be defined after the fact. Define specifically and realistically what constitutes success or acceptability, before you conduct the survey to prevent defensive stakeholders from interpreting the results their way. The bar that you set as the threshold of acceptability establishes whether you seek parity or excellence. Considering 6 on a 10-point scale as a victory will make you feel good, but won't accurately reflect the voice of the customer, and won't allow you to trend that number upward in the future. One of our customers was very proud of its 85% satisfaction rate, and I was pleased with such sterling customer appraisal until I discovered that the company considered an answer of 4 as expressing satisfaction—that's 4 on a 1-10 scale, not a 1-4 scale. Here's an opportunity to communicate to your colleagues the high standards you're setting. Raise the numerical goals to broadcast specifically the importance of excellence and the company's expectation of delivering it.

7. Analysis Paralysis. "Can we segment the data by zip codes in southern Alaska?" Endless analysis often leads to postponing necessary changes and actions. Rather than facing the results head on, some managers dig deeper into the numbers, creating endless ways of slicing and dicing the data in the hope of finding a better picture than the one painted by the report. The search for more data generally lacks any actionable purpose and is often nothing more than the pursuit of numbers for numbers' sake. The common threat is the same—the more people engage in data analysis, the more they delay execution. Managers trying to digest the resulting piles of reports about every possible scenario will be unable to take any substantive action.

8. Lack of Prioritization. Customer surveys provide a wide variety of ideas for follow-up action. To make use of these ideas, they must be prioritized. Attempting to fix everything, although admirable, is simply not feasible. Design surveys to identify and prioritize areas of importance, or managers won't be able to move from gathering data to taking action. For example, a customer satisfaction survey may deliver low scores related to a company's website, failing to reveal that customers see more importance in improving customer-service department response times. Prioritization is predicated on importance and satisfaction, not on satisfaction alone. In the absence of prioritization, companies may find themselves addressing the wrong issues or assigning resources to areas that aren't very important to their customers. Worse yet, a company may end up debating endlessly on where to get started and delay urgently required actions—disappointing customers in the process.

9. Lack of Cross-Functional Leadership. Responsibility for addressing customer survey results mustn't fall on only a single function in the organization. Ensuring that all touch points are addressed and the overall experience is being improved requires cross-functional coordination. *Any* cross-functional effort faces challenges, as each function operates according to its own agenda and metrics. However, with customer surveys, the challenges are magnified because they reveal people's faults and problems. Customer insights are subsequently treated as hot potatoes and tossed from one function to the other. No one wants to assume responsibility for such failures as faulty service or poor-quality products. Customer survey results can often lead to finger-pointing and only a fully mandated cross-functional leadership can mobilize an organization's functions, agendas and personal opinions toward the required results. Most companies commit this deadly sin by not assigning such leadership in advance and, by extension, not allowing real attention to execution to take place.

10. Lack of Change Management. The single purpose of customer surveys should be improvement through change and survey designers must account for this when preparing the survey. Customers view surveys not as their opportunity to praise the company but rather as the company's promise that the time spent responding will be honored with changes to policies, processes and the overall customer experience. Because the corporate view of the purposes of these surveys stands in stark contrast to the view of customers expecting results from their feedback, companies take limited or no proactive action to ensure that when customers demand changes to policies or processes, they can take immediate and corrective action. The tendency of demonstrating reactive rather than proactive behavior as it relates to change will fracture a relationship that needs healing.

+ Plus One. Lack of Customer Follow-up: Customer surveys raise customer expectations. When customers are told that their opinions matter, they take it seriously and expect to see changes, particularly when they have committed time and effort to provide feedback. When companies do in fact act and change policies, alter processes and add services to reflect customer feedback, they seldom communicate these changes back to the customers who provided guidance in the first place. The customers' next opportunity to learn of these changes is when they're making their next complaint (when it may not matter). During this time, the customer has likely harbored ill feelings toward the company, possibly communicated these feelings to others, refrained from purchasing additional products or services, looked at competitive offerings, or even purchased from competitors. The lack of follow-up can render necessary and highly desirable changes useless. Avoid this problem by communicating these changes to the customer, improving your brand's image. In our client engagements, we request commitment to reporting back to survey-takers within 90 days of the survey's completion, detailing actions taken based on survey results.

Planning an Actionable Survey

These deadly sins are often committed unintentionally. At the heart of the problem is the rush to conduct customer surveys because companies have to, not because they truly want to. Whatever the motivation, by committing these deadly sins, companies not only fail to reach any meaningful achievements with their surveys but also often alienate the customers they care so deeply about. These companies also encourage existing bad behavior by demonstrating to their employees a total lack of caring about their customers. Employees take this message to heart and reflect it in an attitude unbecoming those who work to serve customers and strengthen customer relationships.

To avoid this pitfall, companies must create survey programs as a strategy for listening, prioritizing and executing on their customers' feedback and insight. Any company not ready to act on customer opinions shouldn't ask for them. Listening entails more than letting your customers speak. Unlike speeches, dialogue entails equal participation. These ten-plus deadly sins represent anything but respect for customers, treating them as objects and not as partners.

Companies that conduct true dialogue with their customers do so knowing that customer benefit and organizational change lie at the heart of this two-way communication. These companies plan extensively before a survey takes place and set a series of actions in motion following the survey's conclusion. We call these actions "Dialogue to Delivery," which features these critical elements:

1. Serious approach. Design your survey and the survey request to clearly indicate that you value the input and will put it to use. The survey that American Express uses to, in part, determine employee compensation specifically reveals that fact to customers. When consumers understand that their voices will be heard, response rates go up. We've seen surveys—long ones, with up to 65 questions—averaging 14-15% response rates. That figure is astounding. And higher response rates reflect greater customer motivation to tell you what's really on their minds, rather than going through the motions and slapping down some answers just to have answers in place.

2. Strategic intent. What do you want to achieve by obtaining customer insight? What do you plan to do with the results? Establish your goals and the hypotheses you're trying to validate, and the actions you seek to substantiate. Lacking a strategic context, conducting a relationship study for the sake of conducting a relationship study provides no value to you or to your customer. Conducting transaction analysis for functional and not strategic purpose—to establish corporate bonuses, for instance—does nothing to further the excellence of your customer experience. As we've noted, conducting studies and inviting the voice of the customer without actionable response is a breach of customer trust. Only after you detail your strategy and define your expectations can you move on to designing the questions that reflect your strategic intent. Such intent establishes the starting point that dictates the fate and effectiveness of every survey. As with any dialogue, what you're seeking to achieve dictates the tone and quality of discussion.

3. Actionable questions. Ask questions whose answers can guide execution. Think about how you would execute in the event that you receive certain feedback. Yes or no questions usually get you nowhere. They may affirm or invalidate certain assumptions, but will generally not lead to change.

Even when questions are geared to validate behavior, you must seek answers that explain "how" rather than "what." And always leave room for customers to provide ideas on how to achieve the change that they want.

4. Meaningful response mechanisms. Make certain customers have opportunity to say what they really want to say. Open-ended questions help, certainly, but even on something as straightforward as a ratings scale, you can make the mistake of shorting feedback opportunities by offering too limited a range of choices. Take, for example, a typical 1-4 scale:

- Strongly disagree
- Somewhat disagree
- Somewhat agree
- Strongly agree.

Such limited choice gives the customer no latitude for truly expressing an opinion, and delivers you skewed information at best. Most dissatisfied customers won't give you a 1 or a 2 unless they have an exceptionally poor perception about the area the question addresses, so you perceive a level of satisfaction with their answer of 3. In fact, some cynical survey designers purposely use such a system—with seemingly harsh choices on the lower range and no opportunity for a neither-good-nor-bad rating or specific "no opinion" or "does not apply" options—to elevate the results from customers. Ask the same question on a 10-point scale, and you can clearly see how choice limitation lifts scores overall. As well, such limited scale ranges—even a 5-point scale with a middle shrug-of-the-shoulders answer—are very difficult to trend. The 10-point scale, with more increments and greater opportunity to gauge incremental shift from survey to survey, is far easier to base trend reports on.

5. Foundation for dialogue. Design for customer feedback. Seek insight that helps you improve your performance, not ensure the status quo. Avoid questions that validate existing behavior and ask questions that may give you answers that hurt. Tough questions will produce valuable information to help you innovate and improve. Allow customers to voice their own opinions instead of forcing them to confirm yours by leading them with questions that only you care about. Ultimately, survey success depends on the questions you ask. Ask irrelevant questions and you get irrelevant answers. Ask tough questions and you get brutally honest answers that help you achieve your strategic intentions.

6. Change and communication: Be ready for change. Change management is critical, and it's predicated on asking the correct questions and on maintaining ongoing communication with those people who will carry out those changes—your employees. Involve employees early and update them on proposed and actual changes. Maintain a dialogue (email, by the way, has *not* proven to be an effective dialogue mechanism) so employees will more readily embrace these changes and be able to provide feedback about the program. I've noted the role of change communication to customers in demonstrating your willingness to adapt to their needs. Such communication also demonstrates that willingness to employees.

We'll examine change management in detail in Chapter 13, "Leadership and Change Management," and the role of the Voice of the Customer in experience reshaping in Chapter 14, "Reinvent the Experience: A Governance Model."

7. Prioritization and execution: Avoid over-analyzing the results and prioritize what matters most. Review the data to identifying a few meaningful areas you can actually do something about. Consolidate the data with three to six objectives for change. Obtain executive commitment and allocate resources appropriately. With proper resources, you should be able to move quickly to execution and deliver the results your customers are asking for.

Ultimately, consumer dialogue and response are mechanism for differentiating your business through greater customer intimacy. The success of any survey, as seen from customers' perspective, depends on your willingness and ability to plan the survey as part of a strategy, to design the survey with the intent to drive change, and to execute and communicate change to customers. Allowing customers to see that you've acted on their insight, and haven't taken their feedback for granted, closes the circle and leverages your customer surveys not only to make internal improvements, but also to strengthen customer relationships. Nothing drives loyalty more strongly than a company listening and executing on its customers' insight, sending a message that the relationship is built on mutual respect.

Loyalty Through Listening and Acting

Customer dialogue is a promise, not a sales pitch. Companies that understand this refrain from copying others and design surveys as part of a customer-centric strategy. These companies wish to leverage customer insight for innovation and change, and ultimately to reach competitive advantage. They wish to infuse their employees with a customer-centric mentality that will be reflected in their attitude and behavior; and that ultimately will strengthen customer relationships. These companies base customer dialogue on mutual respect and can therefore strengthen customer loyalty by demonstrating that they act on their customers' insight. The payback is significant not only in creating better products, services and experiences, but also in creating a differentiating relationship with customers. It is this commitment to listening and acting that creates loyalty.

Anything less than full commitment to execution and follow-up actions will damage the customer relationship. If you don't intend to follow up and change in a meaningful way, don't conduct a survey. On the other hand, turning insight into action is a powerful method to establish an authentic and loyal relationship with customers. To achieve such a relationship, customer surveys must evolve into a strategic dialogue with full commitment to execution. When establishing this evolution, companies will effect both change and differentiation that customers will notice and respond to in an extremely profitable way.

Summing Up: Right Questions, Right Answers

When people ask me, "What questions should we ask?", I have a simple but demanding answer. "What expectations are you trying to create and fulfill?"

Just as your customer experience metrics tell your employees, your management and the company as a whole how strongly you value customer experience delivery, your customer survey questions tell your customers how high you've set your standards, and the level of quality you're trying to achieve.

Are you creating scores in order to *justify* people's performances or are you creating them to *improve* performance? Are your metrics designed to say, "Hey, Mr. Customer, you forgot to send me a thank you letter so here's your chance?" Or are they designed to say, "We know we can do better; please tell us how. Two different designs, two different goals, two different tracks of dialogue, two different types of insight-gathering. And customers will call your bluff very quickly on the former. Customers are sick and tired of the "Am I great or what?" surveys, and they're far more willing to cooperate with an honest dialogue about what else can be done.

Surveys that communicate an invitation for insight and innovation are, in a sense, a part of co-creation. The attitude of such communications brings customers into the process, saying, "We want you to contribute. Tell us what's missing. We value your insight."

To encourage such insight, weave the core elements of customer experience into the dialogue. In addition to the questions related to attributes, attitudes and perception gaps that form the foundation of the Customer Experience Map, again consider questions around these other rarely explored but often-enlightening topics:

- **Alignment.** The way the experience fits the customers' lives.

- **Brand Promise.** Value and brand fulfillment. The customer originally bought into a promise that differentiated you from your competitors. Now determine if you are living up to that promise. Evaluating general performance level is not a measure of differentiation.

- **Value Fit.** The customers' values vs. the company's values. This is where the emotional bond is beginning to form. Ask at least one question that explores the customer's lifestyle and how the brand plays a role within that lifestyle

- **Action.** The results of the experience. Will it affect loyalty–both on a personal level (intent to repeat purchase, intent to increase purchase, intent to stay longer) and on a network level (intent to recommend)?

And what would I myself ask? An easy but equally demanding question that reveals standards and sets high expectations is "Did we pleasantly surprise you today?" Directly and succinctly that question asks, "Did we cross the parity line? Did we exceed your expectations?"

Some organizations aren't willing to submit themselves to that level of expectation, because it's too high a bar to jump. Yet, as we saw in the example of Ritz-Carlton correlating future transactions with high scores to its question, "Did we give you a sense of well-being?", the higher the bar that you set, the more chances you have to actually get there.

CHAPTER 13

Leadership and Change Management

Consider the transition to customer experience management as a move from the Planet of the Product to the Planet of the Customer. This transition is not incremental change; it is transformational change. Just as you must be innovative and dedicated in designing for customer experience, you must be creative and disciplined in managing the change required to achieve that design.

The transformation to customer experience management also requires a strong element of evangelism. Customer experience evangelism escapes the old tools to institute change within an organization—facts, as if information alone will instill the need for change, and fear and force when only the facts fail to inspire. Such traditional methods bring the traditional responses to change, including such means of resisting as rationalizing previous failures, projecting blame on others for those failures, and—far more dangerous for those who understand the need for change as we'll see later in this chapter—outright denial that change is in any way necessary, or that any given employee or department bears responsibility for change.

Evangelism, on the other hand, manages change by laying the groundwork for opportunity for the company as a whole and the stakeholders within it. This energetic approach to change management showcases new hope within the organization, invigorates employees with new skills that can enrich employees and the employee experience, and sets the vision for a new future for the company.

Evangelism is not cheerleading. It is leadership. Executive evangelism begins with communicating a clear vision, not proclaiming empty phrases in meetings and memos. Establishing vision is the crux of our exercise in building actionable, meaningful mission statements in Chapter 9, "Readying the Organization and Developing a Culture of Change." The customer experience vision outlines the current state of customer-centricity within the company today, the specific goals for the future, and the gap that separates present and future. The vision communicates the specific efforts that will be taken, the resources that will be required, and the metrics that will be used to evaluate results. It specifies specific roles—what is expected of whom—for each activity and function within the company, thereby creating a clear line of sight to the customer. And the vision establishes a timeframe in which its goals will be realized.

Here's a classic example of the power of vision and the danger of ignoring it. In the 1855, the Bessemer process for mass production of steel was patented, followed by the steel-frame construction that allowed buildings to reach higher than the then-current limit of about ten stories forced by the physical limitations of concrete construction. Skyscrapers began appearing around the world.

The varying reactions to this innovation are educational. In Chicago, doctors and architects argued that skyscrapers would lead to illnesses when the skyscrapers' shadows forced "eternal midnight" on the masses. This was a serious claim, so much so that in 1893, Chicago banned building structures higher than 130 feet, or ten to twelve floors. London and Paris instituted similar bans. (In fact, when the Eiffel Tower was erected in Paris, the respected French national newspaper *Le Monde* reported that the tower's magnetic properties would draw neighborhood houses toward it, causing them to tilt.)

New York responded differently. They embraced the technology, knowing it could lead them to becoming the most important business center in the world. With that vision, they broke the rules, and issued an ordinance specifically approving such construction. New York promoted the concept of consolidating all corporate operations in a single building, a concept that led to New York's stature as a center of commerce.

People will resist change. They can also resist vision, but vision facilitates cooperation, dedication and the willing pursuit of innovations, procedural changes and new goals. Thus the importance of change management and change evangelism. In painting a clear, detailed vision of customer experience within your brand, the evangelist must make a clear, public commitment to that vision.

In addition to creating and sharing vision, the customer experience evangelist is responsible for:
- **Assigning resources**, not merely shifting some existing resources or throwing just a few dollars at the problem.

- **Setting priorities and making trade-off decisions**, and not trying to layer this customer-experience thing over existing efforts. Customer experience is not an addition to the to-do list. It is an overall shift and expansion of focus.

- **Measuring progress with hard numbers**, rather than best guesses, anecdotal evidence or no measurement at all. Nothing breeds success like proof of success.

- **Resolving cross-functional conflicts**, and not allowing silos to continue clanging against each other. Such conflicts must be resolved in the context of the customer experience vision and established priorities. The evangelist can also gather and charter a cross-functional steering committee, formed of representatives from all touch points.

- **Commitment to the long term, not a one-time event.** Customer experience, after all, is a matter of "Repeat, repeat, repeat," and not a matter of "Next?" The truth behind unsuccessful customer experience initiatives is usually lies within the inability to implement long-term customer strategies in rush to implement quick fixes and shortcuts.

- **Enthusiasm and leadership by action.** An organization's leadership is expected to serve as a role model for its employees. This element is critical, so let's spend a little time with it.

Leadership by Action

If the CEO and senior organizational members don't act in ways that reflect brand values and promises, employee behavior will remain unchanged in most corporate arenas, including that of customer experience. Some senior leaders believe that announcing a new customer perk or adding bonuses based on customer satisfaction metrics proves that they take the customer experience initiative seriously. They're wrong.

In fact, customer experience management, to succeed, requires a detailed plan for what the leadership role model is all about and how it should manifest itself in everyday behavior. An organization's executives must be front and center and rally the entire organization behind the new brand promise so that it can live up to, and possibly even exceed, customer expectations. They must understand the manner in which they are expected to visibly change their own behavior. They are the ones who must communicate brand messages internally as well as to external parties such as shareholders, analysts and the press.

Serious commitment to the brand entails making substantive changes to personal schedules and allocating more time to brand and customer experience initiatives. If calendars remain unchanged after the launch, executive support will dissipate quickly. Unlike a CRM implementation, brand initiatives require the active involvement of senior leaders because the brand is an expression of the organization's value proposition and represents a promise to customers. Senior leaders demonstrate the importance the organization attaches to the value proposition.

Senior leadership commitment often boils down to small actions. At Nordstrom, a recognized WOW brand, the CEO answers all his calls. He doesn't shy away from picking up a piece of trash and placing it in the nearest trash bin. As I've noted, at Virgin Atlantic Airways, when a salesperson tops 1 million pounds of sales, CEO Sir Richard Branson goes to the salesperson's office, gets down on his knees, and says, "Thank you."

The leadership role starts with small actions that demonstrate that what matters is not keeping the organizational hierarchy, but making sure customers receive the best experience.

Ask of your company these questions:
- Do senior executives know how to change their behavior appropriately?
- Do you have a personal commitment from each executive to act in alignment with the new brand?
- How do you ensure that all employees see the change in action by senior leadership?

Vision and reaffirmation of that vision through everyday commitment to customer experience principles from senior management is not a matter of dictating by fiat what must be done. Senior leadership cannot act as the customer experience police, enforcing behavior by demand, threat or intimidation. Not only must they espouse the new values, but also they must personify them.

The customer experience evangelist must assume a set of roles and responsibilities that, in total, bring clarity and a sense of commitment to the quest for customer experience. This includes incorporating customer experience into staff meetings regularly; learning about and understanding the challenges impeding delivery, perhaps through town hall meetings; connecting with customers to collect further insight by listening and not selling; aligning the organization and addressing address cross-functional conflicts; and maintaining alignment by enforcing adherence to customer-experience metrics and to rewarding employee achievement of customer-centric goals.

Remember, however, that customer experience evangelism can't be forced onto CEOs. It can be suggested, developed and instilled, as we'll see later in this chapter, but when it comes to effective change management in the quest for customer experience, you must listen to the CEO.

A customer experience management study by Aberdeen Group demonstrates that a key success factor of best-in-class organizations is their high level of customer-experience-sponsored initiatives: 40% of all best-in-class organizations reported CEO sponsorship of CEM initiatives, while only 11%

of the other organizations reported similar CEO sponsorship. In fact, the study found that CEM initiatives undertaken by most non-best-in-class organizations are sponsored by a VP of Customer Service rather than the CEO.

In my customer engagements and in our CEM Certification program sessions I often hear comments along the lines of "My CEO doesn't want to sponsor or be involved—he wants me to make this thing go away." While such comments are disappointing, they reveal a basic truth. CEOs generally don't perceive a CEM strategy and related initiatives as strategic drivers of success. These CEOs view CEM as a solution to address broken processes and outdated technology without requiring their direct involvement. Other CEOs also fail to view customer experience management as strategic to their organizations but do so out of a perception that CEM is all about smiling and acting cheerfully. CEO reluctance to directly sponsor and be an active advocate for the customer experience sends a powerful message: CEM is not strategic and won't affect your ability to meet your top- and bottom-line targets.

If your CEO doesn't place a premium on the customer experience, your planning should be focused on fixing broken processes, delivering customer experience training to employees, and increasing customer satisfaction scores. You will be expected to address the customer experience while keeping a low profile and keeping organizational disruptions to the bare minimum. Without a mandate from the CEO, you can't drive true customer experience innovation, such as breaking down silos or designing experience-centric products and services. However, if you're fortunate enough to be led by a CEO who values customer experience initiatives and recognizes their importance to the organization, your charter will be radically different. You'll be expected to drive organizational change or, at the very least, to create competitively differentiating products and services that will increase your customer base or increase the amount of business that existing customers currently give your organization.

During the course of numerous research and consulting engagements, I've encountered many customer experience professionals who refused to internalize the CEO's mandate. As a result, these professionals failed to understand their expectations, utilized resources inefficiently, and ultimately had little to show for their efforts.

Building the Case for Executive Evangelism

How do you help your executives be champions of this type of activity within the organization? How do you build the case for evangelism in the first place? The following key tactics will help you design and execute a strategy that softens the ground for evangelism and for an overall environment conducive to change. We'll cover these in detail throughout this chapter, but first the 30,000-foot view:

- **Build the business case**, as you've done in our Return on Nothing evaluation in Chapter 3, "Economics of Customer Experience." In building the case, identify the key measurements of the organization. Tie these measurements to the business case your proposition is founded upon. Once again, deploy The Number as motivation.

- **Sound an anecdotal "wake-up call."** Bring the business case to flesh-and-blood life with anecdotal views into current customer needs and the experiences they receive. Some companies require executives to listen to recorded customer calls to get a sense of what's going on "out there." Other companies post customer complaints and comments on internal intranets to further sharpen the wake-up call.

- **Identify key challenges the organization faces to meet its targets.** Link customer experience to addressing the challenges. As examples, if the organization seeks to build employee morale, demonstrate how customer experience can reduce pressures, create a more rewarding environment, and encourage personal passions. If the organization faces heavy competition, demonstrate how focus on the customer gives you competitive advantage. If the organization is stumbling in the area of innovation, demonstrate how customer experience facilitates consumer input, better understanding of customer need, and overall deeper insight. Later in this chapter, we'll apply specific methods of making these connections throughout the organization.

- **Invoke upper management's perception of excellence.** Ask executives to build their own story of exceptionally great or bad experience to connect personally with the changes that must be made from the organization's current situation in order to visualize and execute their personal vision of excellence.

- **Assess the organization's appetite for change.** And then whet that appetite. Systematically overcome individual points of resistance to adapting new procedures and philosophies.

- **Align stakeholders with the benefits of customer experience.** Bring everyone to the table, making it easier for the evangelist to take the message to the organization as a whole.

Sometimes executives—even those truly committed to CEM—will set you on the path to customer experience, and then disappear. They tell you how important the focus on the customer is, but then you can't find them. They don't respond to emails. Their calendars are jam-packed. Perhaps they don't yet understand the importance of the initiative; they don't have that burning number before them. Or they may simply not understand what's expected of them in providing customer service evangelism. When they say,

"You have my full support," they may not realize what "full support" means.

Stress the specifics of the executive role as often as possible. Make it an agenda item in every meeting discussing the strategy. Point out that the executive role includes:

- Frequent verbal communications that set the path and establish support for the initiative. Be prepared with the exact messages you need them to communicate—in other words, write the messages yourself. And, as ` previously, Executive Evangelism is commitment to the long term, not a one-time event. It is a matter of "Repeat, repeat, repeat," and not a matter of "Next?"

- Cross-functional conflict resolution. Don't overplay the CEO card—doing so will cause resentment and may actually suppress function cooperation. Yet, don't hesitate to use to call the CEO in to resolve conflicts.

- Prioritization of customer experience vs. other agendas. Prioritization can be direct but it need not always be so. For example, when the CEO asks, "What do you need from me?", ask for a mandate. Ask the CEO to require that everyone in the company from director level and up listen to customer calls. At Honeywell, everyone at that level receives a weekly recording of representative calls from the call center, including those from customers with the biggest problems. Each staff meeting starts with a discussion of that week's recording, so executives can't avoid fulfilling the mandate. This view into what's happening on the front lines helps shape positive attitudes toward improving the customer experience.

- Instilling urgency and resolve, and setting the attainment of The Number as an overall goal.

THE CUSTOMER EXPERIENCE EVANGELIST'S TOOL KIT

- Economics of Customer Experience, as we discussed in Chapter 12.
- Customer validation—again, from Chapter 12
- Ecosystem Mapping, as we discussed in Chapter 2
- Leader's agenda mapping, and linkage to leader's current agenda (as we discussed within this chapter)
- Ongoing communication and feed of stories
- Tangible examples / guidelines

- A Celebration / Launch Plan, as we'll discuss in Chapter 15
- A long-term momentum growth plan—again, to be covered in Chapter 15

Whetting the Appetite for Change

The success of any customer strategy is predicated on the organization's capacity for change. Many strategies have failed because the strategies' owners didn't understand their organizations' capacity and reluctance to consider all things new. There are numerous motivations for such reluctance, including stubbornness, short-sightedness, self-denial, fear and even pride. We'll consider these and other motivations in greater detail in a moment, but let's pause to consider that matter of pride—a very powerful human emotion. Proposed change can be perceived from two different perspectives:

- We've failed. We've not done our job, and now we have to get our act together.

- We've done well, but now we're going to take our successes to the next level.

Remember that those affected by the change are human, with sensitivities and feelings. No matter how much logic you use in presenting change, if you hurt those affected, you will have incredible difficulty in establishing buy-in on the short term and in reversing hurt feelings on the long term. A core strategy in change management, therefore, is invoking the second of the two possible perspectives about change by recognizing and appreciating past achievements, even if you won't be retaining all of their principles moving forward. This will build a bridge of good will among employees called upon to execute the new initiative.

Even with this foundation, however, and even though transformation is not optional in this rapidly evolving world, not everyone will understand, accept, and/or cooperate with this challenge. In business, one thing never changes: Everyone loves change as long as they aren't the ones that have to change.

During a client engagement, I worked with an organization operating in a commoditized market and facing intense competition, heightened pricing pressures, and threats to its core value proposition. Given this environment, we expected at least a moderate sense urgency and cooperation. What we met instead were challenges and obstacles at every turn. Meetings were constantly delayed or canceled, and approvals were routed through a seemingly endless list of decision-makers. In one instance, a single customer questionnaire was subjected to more scrutiny than any document that I've ever seen in my entire career. Overnight, executives became linguists obsessed with ensuring that every word was reviewed and reviewed and reviewed again. The purpose of the survey—to engage customers and identify their challenges—was ignored in favor of grammatical niceties, to the pleasure of English professors worldwide but not to the executives staring at the bottom line. One executive even "cleverly" announced that he didn't have the time to review the questionnaire—enabling him to question the validity of the results later on (since he never had "the time" to review the questions before the survey was deployed).

That executive aside, most of the executives who resist change will posit that their seemingly endless list of excuses and delays results only from their strong interest to "get things right." I will argue that these executives simply don't want to face their predicament of having to face change.

As I said, some things never change.

If you're responsible for implementing a customer strategy, you must identify and then overcome such resistance to allow the strategy to be internalized and adopted throughout your organization.

The resistance you receive often takes the form of what we call the 7 Great "Escapes"
1. "I don't believe in it."
2. "Interesting idea, but I need to see another analysis and then design a series of focus groups before we revisit the concept."
3. "Emotional engagement? You're kidding, right?"
4. "It's not my job. Focus on the customer-facing people."
5. "I don't know how to do it."
6. "So you think I've been messing up the way I've always handled things?"
7. The most common and dangerous "Escape"—"I'm already doing it."

Your responses:
1. "I don't believe in it." *Belief has nothing to do with it. It is about a business strategy to maximize revenues and profits.*
2. "Interesting idea, but I need to see another analysis and then design a series of focus groups before we revisit the concept." *Delays lead to lost revenue.*
3. "Emotional engagement? You're kidding, right?" *Customers are emotional. Branding is about emotions. We need to connect emotionally to create loyalty.*

4. "It's not my job. Focus on the customer-facing people." *It is your job. Everyone is in the customer business. Your leadership sets the tone for the whole organization.*

5. "I don't know how to do it." *That's a legitimate concern. We'll provide the support you need to succeed.*

6. "So you think I've been messing up the way I've always handled things?" *Not at all, but now we have some exciting new opportunities to explore.*

7. The most common and dangerous "Escape"—"I'm already doing it." Your response to this assertion must be considerably more detailed. It's a problem you usually encounter when all indicators point to vigorous, companywide support for introducing customer experience strategies.

The Most Dangerous "Escape"

I'm confident that you've heard or seen the exact words I've listed below, or perhaps more eloquent variations thereof, more than once and perhaps dozens of times:

- "By becoming a customer-centric organization, we will be more profitable."
- "We must focus on the customers."
- "The customer is the reason we're all here."
- "We must remember who pays the bills."
- "We need to strive to delight customers, not just to satisfy them."
- "The customer experience is the way to differentiate ourselves in the future."
- "Everyone in our organization owns the customers."
- "The customer is job Number-One."
- "Do whatever it takes to satisfy our customers."
- "The customers drive our business."
- "Customer relationships are the cornerstone of our existence."

The speaker is perhaps the CEO, and perhaps some other senior executive. The venue is a strategy meeting or an annual employee meeting or an earnings call or a companywide memo. These messages support the commitment to customer relationships/experience/strategy/all-of-the-above. All around you—and all the way up to the executive suites and down to the front-line personnel—people nod, and their agreement is sincere. It seems as if everyone is finally on the same page when it comes to improve customer relationships.

So why does your organization rarely make serious progress on the matter? Why, 12 months after such pronouncements, can few employees agree that you've become a customer-centric organization? Why has customer turnover remained flat, or has continued to rise? Why does price pressure continue to rule your business? Why have you failed to capture a larger portion of budget from customers? Where did all the lofty commitments go wrong?

Welcome to the biggest enemy of customer strategies, the greatest of the 7 Great Escapes: "We're already doing it." Every function in the organization attending that experience proposal meeting agrees wholeheartedly to support the initiative and the concept behind it because they're convinced that they're already executing it. At the end of the meeting, representatives of each silo are likely glancing at the others about them while thinking, "So you guys get *your* act together."

This strong belief among many executives that their employees are already fully engaged in customer-centric activities blinds them to the truth. The resistance to changing and transforming the business to become customer-centric often results simply from conviction that "We're already there" or that any required changes are merely incremental and not an order of magnitude.

Besides, these executives believe that already-made organizational changes, such as adopting a service-oriented compensation plan, support a customer-centric strategy, when in reality those changes, like the rest of the company, remain very much efficiency- and cost-reduction-centric.

Surrounded by T-shirts and inspirational posters all claiming commitment to customers, it's easy to fall into this trap. This is denial by T-shirt, entrapment by inspirational poster. It's precisely the lack of admission that the organization is more process- and efficiency-centric than customer-centric that will strip it of the opportunities to grow the business through better customer relationships.

The biggest enemy of customer strategies, therefore, is not the lack of funds or resources. It's not lack of ability or expertise. It's refusal to admit current reality. Executives must fully understand what's wrong with the way they currently run their operation and what customer-centricity is all about. Before devising any sort of strategy, you must confront the "We're already doing it" attitude head on. Organizations must fully understand how their current way of doing business differs from interacting with customers in a customer-centric way.

This denial is so pervasive in organizations that it's difficult to detect. At one time, I appreciated organizations that approached me and my colleagues with a clear, fully articulated explanation of their customer-strategy problems. It took me time to realize the superficiality of their understanding and the severity of their denial. Now, whenever I meet with a new client who rushes to agree that they need to improve their customer relationships, I confront the client with the reality first. They are often seeking a panacea, a pill they can swallow and make the whole problem go away. They want to quickly check this little customer-centricity item off their to-do list. It's tempting to agree with them and take their business. But without clients fully recognizing what's at stake and how far they are from being a truly customer-centric organization, doing so would be a serious mistake and a recipe for disaster. Without this clear understanding of the gap between the current and the desired, the customer strategy will not be implemented to its fullest potential and will fail to deliver the desired results.

It's easy and quite tempting to fall into the trap of the quick agreement. Executives don't easily accept requirements for change and transformation. Like any other initiative, the magnitude of the transformation and the results are proportionately linked to the magnitude of efforts and debates. If it's easy to agree with, and easy to base a mug slogan on, it's not a transformational strategy, but rather an acceptance of a small incremental project. In fact, when presenting a customer strategy, don't just expect push-back. Hope for it. If you receive none, you're not reaching the right people or the "right people" aren't taking you seriously. To achieve a truly differentiating customer strategy that results in growth and profitable loyalty, organizations must overcome their own biggest enemy: Self-denial of the truth.

Blocking the Escape Routes

The other listed "Escapes," from "I don't believe in it" to "I don't know how to do it," can sometimes be entirely sincere. Despite this possibility, never take the Escapes at face value. This isn't a matter of trust; it's a matter of establishing an across-the-board approach to combating resistance to change. Similarly, other sources of resistance can be and often are at work. For some, the idea of change—what many see as disrupting the status quo—is simply frightening. Better the devil they know than the devil they don't. Or pure ego may be involved. Executives often believe that they know what works and what doesn't, and are subsequently unwilling to take any real measures to change what needs changing. But you can overcome these factors and any others by working systematically with your customer experience mapping and analyzing the motivations, pain points and resistance factors of all stakeholders in the sea change you are proposing.

This mapping is based on one primary assumption about those who look for the Escape clause: You are a threat. Assume first and immediately that in the eyes of those who resist, customer experience threatens their position, their workload, their compensation, and even their very jobs. The map identifies those threats, and gives you tools for demonstrating that you are really proposing opportunity. You can build a case for why resisters should cooperate.

For an example of stakeholders resisting an empowerment tool directed right at the customer because they see that tool as a threat, consider an instance in which a company installs a CRM system without putting a change-management strategy in place. Six months after the system is up and running, no salespeople are using it. The system is not the concern. Consider a consistent behavior among salespeople. Ask them why they lost a deal, and they'll point to the product, the price, the conditions, the CEO—*everything.* When you ask why they landed a deal, they'll answer something to the effect of "It's *my* connection. It's *my* relationship with the customer. It's *my* golfing skills with the customer. The customer doesn't want our product. I perform magic to make the customer buy."

From that viewpoint, it's easy to see that salespeople don't place information into the CRM system because doing so threatens them with transparency. Using the system exposes their processes, gives away their secrets, and reveals their magic. With the secrets revealed, they feel the threat of replacement if anyone can step in and steal the magic. The salesperson is saying, "Pay no attention to the man behind the curtain."

This example demonstrates the criticality of establishing a change-management strategy early in the customer-experience process so that you can understand potential conflicts, the likely sources of resistance, and the scope of potentially conflicting agendas of all the silos within the organization. Lay out this strategy in a structured, point-by-point plan of action. In assuming that whoever you speak with will oppose your strategy, such mapping allows you to ask the questions and devise the answers you must consider to prepare for the conversations you must have with each silo.

Such preparation prepares you for worst-case scenarios, informing you of the potential points of resistance. What is IT's agenda? HR's agenda? Marketing's agenda? Knowing the answers to these questions, you can connect your agenda to their agenda. You can help stakeholders achieve what they need to achieve, using your agenda, and bringing all disparate goals into alignment.

Do *not* assume that people understand what you want to do, that they accept your goals, and that they are ready to give you resources.

Managing Change in Your Ecosystem

Work to understand the capacity for change and the reluctance to change across all parts of the organization. This allows you to assess the size of your war, and to identify where initial skirmishes and battles can be won.

As a first step for preparing a well-documented change-management action plan, identify internal stakeholders and external stakeholders within your ecosystem. Your list will vary with your company (as we saw when conducting priority assessment on page 253 in Chapter 12), but it will likely include and hinge upon these functional areas:

- Marketing
- Sales
- Customer Service
- Product/Service Delivery
- Finance/Billing
- Shipping/Delivery
- Channel Partners/Dealers
- IT
- Human Resources
- Top Management
- Manufacturing
- Operations

Map the connection between each of these stakeholders, and their likely place in the early stages of a new customer experience ecosystem. As in the sample on page 283, create a 2x2 grid and map the stakeholders along two dimensions:

1. Along the horizontal x axis, evaluate their attitude toward change, from resistance to acceptance.
2. Along the vertical y axis, evaluate their importance to your strategy, from low to high, unimportant to critical.

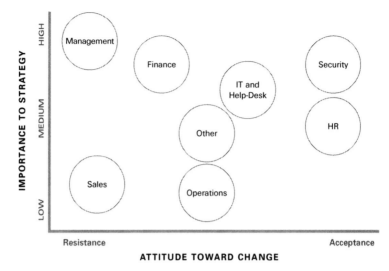

In the example, we have mapped sales as being highly resistant, which is generally true in companies. Sales is often the last silo to accept and support change because of their focus on what they sold last month or last quarter, and on whether they're going to make their commission. Sales departments often respond with an indifferent attitude, basically saying, "That's all very nice, but it's my commission. You must prove to me that it works, and then and only then will I take it to my territory." Yet, in this example, Sales is also unimportant to our strategy.

In the example, management is rated even more resistant than Sales, so that function will warrant perhaps the greatest expenditure of preparation and energy. Moving the needle with them will take work, yet that needle must be moved. Of course, your situation may differ.

This stage of mapping and examining the connection between the different stakeholders allows you not only to begin developing strategies for securing buy-in at the departmental level, but also to establish leverage points for introducing the strategy to the organization as a whole. The map helps you identify who provides the strongest beachhead within the organization—who will buy in early *and* have significant impact on the initiative, vs. who will waste most of your time and energy if you try to overcome their resistance, particularly if they also are unimportant to your success. Now you can identify one or two areas in the company to build the case for the strategy, areas from which you anticipate the quickest wins or the fastest results. As well, identifying the people best suited to support this initiative provides guidance as to who you should work with to get involved, and at what stage.

The Customer Experience Map

Next, map out a profile for each stakeholder important to your strategy, on a table like the one you see on page 283. Initiatives that fail often do so because the designers don't take the time to understand the actual and perceived impact of the initiative on stakeholders. To avoid this problem, use this worksheet to identify and specify:

- **The Stakeholder.** These are the functions and perhaps even the individual people you have mapped on your 2x2 chart of the organization's ecosystem. Remember, the customer experience agenda impacts *every* corporate agenda.

- **The Stakeholder's Internal Agenda.** What are they trying to achieve? How are they measured?

- **The Stakeholder's Resistance Factors.** What will likely motivate their hesitation to consider change, or to fight actively against it? Again, get used to the fact that people might be fighting you even though they don't demonstrate outward evidence of such a fight.

- **The Stakeholder's Cooperation Factors.** What will motivate their willingness to work with you? How can you align the customer experience agenda with the Stakeholder's agenda? What is the value proposition to each stakeholder? To be blunt, why should they care?

- **The best communication strategy for each Stakeholder.** What communication vehicle should you use? What frequency of communication should you apply to each stakeholder?

Two key elements to building and acting from the analysis:

1. Build function-specific financial models. This critical business step is core to your project, as we saw in our discussion of Return on Nothing in Chapter 3. Doing your homework and building the financial models enables you to build the case for shifting from a self-centered product focus to a true customer-centric organization. Without financials relevant to each Stakeholder, you will have no conversation within the organization.

Today, your organization's functions are still being measured by operational numbers, which dictate bonuses, promotions and so on. The functions don't undergo the unifying measurement that we've discussed earlier. You can't ignore this. Simply instructing everyone to "love the customer" won't make the motivation of the numbers disappear.

Armed with numbers specific to each silo, you can begin to connect to individuals within the organization. For example, if HR's agenda includes minimizing employee turnover, you can link that goal to the better numbers that customer experience can deliver. You can demonstrate that building employee experience and empowering customer-facing associates will create a less-stressful working environment, and employee churn will drop.

You must ask and answer these questions to get buy-in, budget and resources. If you do this well, you may find that the budgets already exist in different places within the company. If you can demonstrate how your agenda will accomplish individual department objectives, you can redirect some of their budget into the master plan, and aggregate various budgets to build the resources that you need.

Most of all, frame all conversations in the context of The Number—the money that your organization leaves on the table by not executing customer experience correctly. The Return on Nothing is less than nothing.

2. Present the customer experience strategy as an integral part of the overall corporate agenda. Stress that the customer experience agenda supports existing objectives that each function/touch point is trying to achieve. Often, a customer experience strategy is perceived as just another responsibility on top of what people are chartered to do, resulting in resentment and lack of cooperation. Only when viewed as complementing and accelerating existing agendas in the organization will the customer experience receive a fair chance of success.

The Change-Management Map allows you to answer not only the threats that executives and departments fear from change, but also specific questions about the impact of the changes—to the positive. People will ask, "Why is it good for me? Why should I commit to customer experience? How does it support my objectives? How does it fit with all the other initiatives in the organization? How is it different from what I have done so far?" Your answers, developed from your map, will show specific evidence that customer experience is good for employees' numbers, it's good for their organization, and it's good for their careers. By playing an important part of a significant upgrade in corporate innovation and return on investment, and by coordinating efforts that help them more efficiently achieve their own agenda goals, on which bonuses, advancement and perks are based, employees will further their goals, and refresh their own vocational passion in doing so.

Customer experience is not about personal agendas, but rather about financial results, about money lost and goals unachieved if the strategy is *not* incorporated.

Stakeholder Threats and Opportunities

The specific agendas, threats and goals of Stakeholders will, of course, vary widely, and your analysis must be carefully tailored to your situation. When developing your stakeholder map, however, keep these general insights in mind, and reflect back on the innovative solutions you can bring to these Stakeholders, as we discussed in the " Memories at Every Touch Point" section on page 83.

Information Technology. The IT department's agenda revolves around systems reliability and uptime, and infrastructure consistency. To them, change means taking down the system and risking reliability—and so you must respect that they are measured on uptime. Yet, the biggest threat to IT is being outsourced. Plenty of outsourcers can guarantee uptime. If IT adheres only to providing infrastructure, they are writing off their relevance to the company. Therefore, the CIO is concerned about where and how his function connects to the company's business. A strong connection strengthens IT's position and introduces challenge and variety to their workload. As an example, financial institution HSBC has combined CEM and IT, so that the CIO is now in charge of both functions. Imagine IT being involved not with just infrastructure but also with generating new capabilities and increasing the efficacy of customer interaction.

Besides, IT people have a passion for new technology. Customer experience challenges allow them to exercise that passion and allow them to rise above everyday maintenance, administration and repair tasks.

Finance. The collections and finance functions are all about getting paid, and making the numbers make sense. Here, the world is one big spreadsheet. From you, they want to know where you put it in the pie chart and can you sign your name at the bottom, and nothing more. People and imprecision threaten them. Yet, because numbers speak for themselves, this is one of the groups easiest to prove how your agenda aligns with theirs.

For example, collecting past-due billings from customers avoiding payment because of dissatisfaction or financial hardship is a harrowing job. A customer experience focus makes the job less stressful, and produces better results. Imagine a customer who can pay only two of his past-due bills. Who do you think he will pay first—the company that treats him with dignity and respect, or the one employing obnoxious tactics to frighten him? Customer experience can help increase bottom-line collection and overall cooperation.

Legal. Compliance and Legal are two of the organization's trickiest touch points you'll deal with, because as far as they're concerned, nothing on their agenda is related to the customer. Even worse, they can fall into the trap of seeing all customers as liars and cheaters who must be caught.

It seems that we all work for the legal department. Lawyers manage the whole company to cover the most extreme case that can happen with one customer. The number-one threat they guard against is exposure and liability. Lawyers never see an upside—only what might go wrong.

Conversely, the reason for them to cooperate is exposure and liability. The exposure created when a customer feels mistreated has quantifiable value. Creating happier customers reduces exposure, while keeping the business running. Working with Legal to design unintimidating legal experiences will encourage customer cooperation. Customers who feel that the legal experience is a win-win, focusing on benefits to both sides, are more likely to handle their share of the responsibilities. And less likely to sue.

Communicate that closing all loopholes simply isn't possible. If you create an agreement that absolutely covers everything, you might as well close your business. Business is indeed about managing risks, but if you always manage to the most extreme customer in the most extreme case you can think of, you punish all other customers. Look at this by way of an analogy: In the internet security space, if you want to secure your network completely from hackers, you must shut down the network. Then you're secure. You turn on the network, and no matter how many firewalls you've erected, you have exposure. That's life. If your company is run by lawyers, you basically shut down your capabilities.

Human Resources. There are two types of HR:

- **The administrators**, those who are very good at administration, and are therefore very good at bureaucracy. They wonder why they should change if what they're doing is currently working.

- **The people people.** It's easy to show the advantage to them. They'll be engaged, they'll promote your principles, because they want to bring in the right people.

HR can see threat in the difficulty in finding and recruiting employees who will perform above parity. Depending on this function's metrics, they might see a disadvantage in watching their recruiting success rate drop as placement requirements get more stringent—for instance, finding one person in seven interviewed instead of one in three. Populating the company with those attuned to customer experience changes the way HR works work and significantly increases their workload.

The key to inspiring cooperation from this function lies in the fact that customer experience creates a workplace environment of pride. Employees are eager to work for companies that treat customers with exceptional experiences. They share their pride with friends and create buzz—and broaden the pool of potential hires. Research shows that companies with such a customer experience core enjoy significantly higher levels of employee loyalty and length of employment.

As well, you will find that that today HR is a support mechanism, which allows them to perform more strategically and connect with the overall company agenda, rather than simply existing as "those people who fill positions." Involving them with customer experience involves them with the core of their agenda.

Sales. The agenda governing salespeople boils down to landing the deals and making the numbers. As you approach them with creating deeper levels of interaction with not only existing customers but also potential customers, salespeople are wondering why they should the risk commissions doing something they've never done before.

Here, establish agenda alignment artificially. First, reduce the obstacle of additional preparation and research. Do that work for the salespeople, and deliver to them exactly what to say and how to say it.

Second, let the salespeople themselves establish the alignment within their own ranks. When working with companies, we take a few salespeople aside, educate them about the customer experience program, and then demonstrate that they can increase their sales and commissions. Make a few salespeople heroes, and word will spread quickly to the rest of the sales organization. The other sales people will come to you—and *then* you can roll the initiative out to the rest of the group. Creating a pilot to confirm the worth of investing time and energy and then expanding its each is far more effective than knocking on the VP's door and requesting department-wide training and change.

Lead generation. Finding potential new customers to freshen the sales pipeline is a constant challenge. Customer experience guides how to engage with prospects in ways that add value and target their interest more naturally. Lead generation efforts become less costly while generating more genuine interest.

Marketing. Every company has two types of clients: The ones smiling in the commercials on TV, and the ones on the phone to the call center. The ones on TV are very nice, they never have any problems, and they say "Thank you" at the end of every engagement. The problem is that many in marketing believe they work with the TV clients, not the real ones.

Marketing loves the brand, and seeks the most creative way to communicate the brand. Having the best customer service is of secondary interest, because in old-school marketing, branding showcases, but it doesn't deliver any sort of experience. That's the job of the silo down the hall. To demonstrate that this customer cognitive dissonance does indeed exist, consider, how many times marketing has launched a campaign without informing the call center. You hear call center agents saying, "Just what did you receive, sir? Can you read me the letter?"

Marketers fear the threat of reality—the customers' actual situation and demonstrated interaction with the brand—and by the implied insult that they're not overcoming reality. You must teach marketing that without customer experience, the brand does not exist. The cooperation trigger is this: "We can make your brand come alive." Customer experience creates interactions that fulfill the brand promise and increase the overall brand strength. It also makes the brand authentic through the performance of the employees. If the brand comes alive, showcasing brand creatively and winning awards becomes easier. Innovation that breeds success commands attention.

Service. Reducing costs is ever-important. Customer experience results in more relevant, first-time resolution service that reduces the redundancy of efforts and the number of customer complaints.

Innovation and R&D. Even though it occupies the top of the priority list of R&D organizations, coming up with the next best thing is tough. If you count on solely your ideas, you have access to only a limited pool. If you leverage your customers' experience and insight, you're more likely to come up with relevant innovation that customers will be willing to pay for. To gain access to customer insight, you must create engaging experiences that encourage customer willingness to share with you their creative ideas, dreams, hopes and aspirations

Executives. On upper management's agenda are, of course, numbers. As we've seen in finance, numbers speak for themselves, but you must translate what they communicate. Upper management thinks in terms of revenue and profit, and finds threat in cost and budgets. Stop talking about budget and start talking about revenue that's on the table. Focus on The Number. Start the conversation in such terms as "I have $10 million within reach, and I want to grab it." If you approach it from the other side—"I need half a million dollars to pursue an opportunity," you've launched an entirely different conversation. Lead with RON—Return on Nothing.

You can begin the numbers conversation quite simply. If you can quantify, for instance, an increase in share of wallet and multiply that increase by the number of customers, you've developed a solid starting point. In financial conversations, lost revenue trumps budget every time, as lost revenue represents a pain point that everyone has experienced.

But don't stick only to numbers when assessing the Resistance and Cooperation Factors of senior decision-makers, especially the CEO. For example, consider the ego factor. Someone doesn't work 30 years to become CEO without having a healthy ego. Feed it—make it healthier. Recognition, both corporate and personal, is also on the upper-management agenda.

Also, understand that CEOs in search of smoothly running operations resist interruptions. They don't want the VP of finance fighting with the VP of legal fighting with the VP of marketing and so on. CEOs don't want unproductive noise in their system.

Before you approach the CEO, clear your proposal with the other VPs reporting upstairs. Work with them to establish buy-in. Remove the objections, and therefore remove potential confrontation. And that brings us full circle to the Customer Experience Map, the tool that establishes that cohesive—and noiseless—program plan that will enrich not only customer experience but also the corporate bottom line.

How to Speak "Opportunity"

Ultimately, speak the language of the function you're courting. In these summaries, we've spoken the language of cool to IT, the language of numbers to finance, the language of strategy to HR, the language of efficient success to sales, the language of security to legal, and the language of recognition to marketing.

In this way, you're applying some of the same principles of customer segmentation to internal audiences. Different approaches to different customers, but this time your customer is down the hall.These are general principles. Your corporate ecosystem, with differing procedures, products and personalities, will have many specific agendas and points of resistance to analyze and overcome. Let's examine a more-specific example of how a company might approach this change-management exercise, by considering a hypothetical HR executive change-management scorecard at a higher level of detail:

The **_Agenda_** of HR executives might include such specific objectives as:
- Increase employee morale.
- Effectively manage employees.
- Reduce employee turnover.
- Increase productivity.
- Improve employee satisfaction.
- Reduce "wasted time."

Why might these executives resist? What threats and obstacles compose the **_Resistance Factors_**?
- Potential organizational shock and instability.
- Slow organizational buy-in.
- Fear for job security.

- Not knowing the impact of change management.
- The hassle of changing processes.

Why, on the other hand, should HR executives cooperate? What benefits and agenda alignments lead to **Cooperation Factors**? The HR department will:
- Achieve its goals.
- Look good when employee satisfaction increases.
- Reduce friction between internal silos.
- Reduce complaints.

Given such factors, how might you approach the HR executives, and win their buy-in and cooperation?
- Involve HR from the beginning.
- Clarify HR's own agendas and objectives.
- Align your objectives with HR's priorities.
- Assign clear roles and activities for HR.
- Minimize HR's share of the "burden" of executing change.
- Share recognition for the initiative's success with HR.

Further Tactics

When conducting your assessment and setting the strategy for change management, keep these tactics and approaches in the kit bag for your transformation from the Planet of the Product to the Planet of the Customer:

Don't concentrate only on change. Clarify what will *not* change when any new strategies are deployed. Any endeavor of the significance we're discussing here inevitably straddles the fence between past and future. All organizations have brand values and traits that they want to retain, and others that they want to drop as they look to the future.

Take a positive tone in communications. Explain procedures and policies the organization has executed well and will therefore remain in place. Stress that touch point profiles are not evaluations of what those touch points have done wrong, but are tools to enlighten what can be added and expanded to move performance up a notch or two to secure the revenue opportunities that are before you on the table.

Another practical advantage of detailing what will not change is assuring employees that their entire world is not about to morph into something completely alien. As well, it defines the stable foundations that your new initiatives will launch from.

Leave the word *change* out of the vocabulary. The concept of "change" is emotionally charged from many perspectives, provoking emotions from fear of the unknown to, as we discussed before, pride in previous performance. Concentrate on pointing out the successes the company and its individual departments have achieved. Establish that new initiatives will improve, enhance, refocus, recommit, reemphasize, leverage . . . all words that emphasize growth rather than retrenchment, and all words leading to the concept of "taking the efforts to the next level"—which is in itself a good phrase to use, as well.

Recognize efforts that are already in place. Sometimes people really *are* already doing it. Point out those efforts and celebrate them so that those involved with current initiatives don't feel that their good work is underappreciated and being pushed aside. Recruit those involved, and use their positive results to validate your proposition and inspire cooperation from other touch points.

Fight the war in phases. Although a strategy's execution requires involvement of and adoption by all parts of the organization, a phased approach toward the strategy's execution offers the best chance of success. Begin with those individuals most receptive to change, or at least most likely to embrace change, even if it means defining such receptivity in the negative, by identifying those least reluctant to change. By demonstrating positive results in one part of the organization, a strategy owner can build momentum and accelerate the adoption and implementation across the rest of the organization. We once worked with a company who had a budget of $100,000 to prove the viability of their proposed customer experience program. We targeted only a segment of the customer base, and we collected $1,000,000 in 100 days, above and beyond the revenue generated by the control. When you can demonstrate ROI at even far lesser levels, you'll have no problem securing a budget for the entire project.

Face your most intransigent resistors head on. Identifying those individuals most resistant to change is no less important than identifying those individuals who are likely to embrace change. Approach these individuals directly to persuade them to adopt and embrace the impending strategy and its associated change. Confront and overcome the resistors to change to give the customer-centric strategy its best chances for success.

Identify the saboteurs. Never underestimate the power of resistors to sabotage an otherwise great strategy. Resistors often have the ability to either water down a strategy or ensure that it is scrapped altogether. I can't tell you how many times a champion of a company—Chief Customer Officer, Director of Customer Experience, Vice President of Customer Experience— comes to me and says something on the order of, "A year and a half of analysis and more analysis, and nothing to show for it." In your planning, you'll likely encounter people who seem to be on board but always need further convincing. These people will ask for a report or a complex analysis of something not as ridiculous as buying patterns of people under 30 in Pennsylvania vs. people with six children in Louisiana, but equally useless. And when you deliver that report, they demand another study. After that, they say, it's time to break out the focus groups. And so on. We call these people "Silent Delayers," and they're everywhere. Silent Delayers aren't defeating the strategy per se; they're postponing action, in a sort of analytical filibuster. Be acutely aware that this behavior exists. The fact that some people don't argue with you about the initiative in public doesn't mean that they agree with you.

Identify the true source of resistance. Silent Delayers are often emissaries of vice presidents, tasked with attending every meeting and making sure that nothing happens. The instruction given to the Silent Delayers, whether implied or stated baldly, boils down to this: "Your job is to protect my position. Don't take the stance that the customer isn't important—that's not a very good thing to say. Just make sure that we 'check the business case' in every detail." When you identify the Delayer, discover who is really being threatened—the Delayers themselves, or someone a layer or two above them? Add the true Delayer as a Stakeholder on your Customer Experience Map.

Bring external pressure to bear. Often internal stakeholders are more change-resistant than external stakeholders. When possible, mobilize the external stakeholders to influence internal stakeholders. When working with clients, we sometimes use external stakeholders to create validation or early buy-in, and then build that foothold out to the internal stakeholders. For example, let's say you want to introduce a new service. Select specific customers from the outside, and conduct a test control. This way, you can demonstrate the effectiveness of customer experience, while exposing the concept to customers who not only prove the concept, but also may begin demanding it directly of your company.

Sales is the classic platform for employing external stakeholders to bring pressure on internal stakeholders, and motivate cooperation. When you communicate to customers the availability of new products, procedures or assistance, through PR or marketing, the customers in turn begin making requests of and putting pressure on the salespeople.

The CEO agenda represents another opportunity to leverage external stakeholders to influence internal stakeholders. CEOs listen to outside experts, consultants and even media sources, often more than they do their own people. External contribution not only delivers fresh perspectives and new ideas, but also delivers validation, and gives the CEO additional firepower in dealing with the divisions under him.

Don't bring out the big guns. Yet. In preparing for and managing change, the executive evangelist is not the enforcer, particularly in the early stages of the process. The evangelist is the unifier that supports and energizes change. For example, using the CEO to solve your every problem will not work. You must employ executive power and influence gently. Forcing buy-in won't accomplish what you need to build a vibrant customer-centric environment that occupies your organization's core. You must build companywide buy-in on your own. But when even the best arguments fail to persuade, senior leadership intervention will be required to eliminate any bastions of resistance. But overcoming resistance through persuasion first and upper-management intervention second is crucial.

Establish a support platform for the customer experience evangelist. Provide the tools that the evangelist will use in communicating the customer experience vision, and paving the way for across-the-board adoption of the customer-centric strategy. Customer experience professionals in supporting roles communicate and build awareness and commitment in the organization; build a customer experience theme that links to the organization's overall goals; and provides executives with key messages, measurements and methods to track them, early success stories to evangelize, ongoing examples and communication messages, and tangible successes to discuss and promote.

Begin now. Get underway immediately. Delay can scuttle the implementation of the entire strategy.

Summing Up:
From Resistance to Meaningful Change

Now you've come full circle, and you're ready to take our case to the executive evangelist. You have established a business case, identified obstacles and the changes needed to overcome those obstacles, replaced the threats that change brings to silos with opportunities and benefits for themselves, and have identified not change, but a proud step up to the next level.

You're nearing the point where we're ready to launch the transformational journey to the Planet of the Customer—and what an exotic and wonderful location it is.

CHAPTER 14

Reinvent the Experience:
A Governance Model

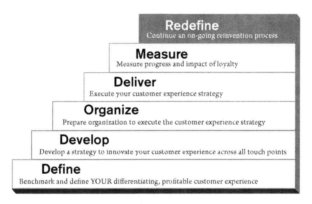

Strategic Steps: Redefine

Hewlett-Packard (HP) makes the most popular printer in the world, boasting such statistics as commanding 80% of the European market share for printers. They reached such heights by relying on a simple but aggressive philosophy: "No one will ever cannibalize our products." Preventing cannibalization requires an equally aggressive, but also equally simple, strategy: Cannibalize yourself before the cannibals can. HP commands the marketplace with a multitude of versions of its printers. The traditional life cycle of an electronic product is three years. HP shortened the life cycle of its products to six months. Old model out, new model in, twice a year like clockwork. HP gave up the revenue related to an additional two and a half years of shelf life and the stability that comes with it, and in doing so leveraged a couple of realities inherent in the business.

HP recognized that the first six months of the electronics life cycle were the most important part, and that soon after that time passed, products would slip in sales, find their way onto discount shelves, and stop generating any excitement about the product's initial innovation. HP knew that stability on the shelf opened the door to competitors copying and cannibalizing the products, drawing them down to parity, and even surpassing the existing product and staying ahead for two-plus years until the next model came out. HP never gave competitors that chance.

Perhaps even more important, HP never gave the customers a chance to become bored with their products. In the electronics industry, after six months, more than sales begin to flag. Customer satisfaction and loyalty begin to flag as well, as customers seek new innovation, and new experience. And typically they'd find both with competitors.

Keep in mind, too, that HP took the non-cannibalization defensive position *before* the internet era introduced simple and easy product-comparison capabilities, meaning that leading in differentiation is even more crucial now.

Experience is not like wine. It doesn't get better on the shelf over time, quietly resting. If you create great customer experience, your competitors will eventually copy and cannibalize you. Customer experience is more like milk; you regularly need a fresh supply. Your customers will become accustomed to the experience, and crave more. Expectations rise. Experience must be managed continuously, taken down from the shelf, reinvented and reintroduced to your customers.

As I've noted many times, customer experience is not a destination but a continuing journey. The innovation process described in Chapter 4 is not simply a stage in designing your customer experience initiative—it is an underlying driver of every stage in the in the initiative, and in keeping customer experience not only alive but also vibrant, compelling and growing. Reinvention is continual, just as constant as breathing, and just as critical to the survival of your customer program.

The changes that force regular examination of the design and execution of customer relationships are many. They include:
- New competitors entering your marketplace.
- Shifts in the branding and marketing positions of your competitors, including new products.
- Change in customer sophistication—and you can be fairly certain that sophistication will only increase as customers gain access to new technologies, new products and services, and new sources of information.
- Change in customer budgets. The amount of money customers can spend fluctuates, generally in accordance with the economy, but a myriad of other factors impact budgets, as well. Assume downward pressure on budgets.
- Change in customer tastes and preferences, which you must monitor assiduously.

- Change in vendor positions. These changes might be economic, or they can be strategic. If the nature, cost or availability of vendor deliverables shifts, your business must shift with it.

- Emerging technologies, potentially affecting how you do business, how your vendors operate, how your customers live their lives—and the very expectations of those customers. The emergence of new channels, for instance, will require updates to your systems and the way you relate to your customers.

- Cultural shifts, which in essence are mass-scale customer shifts in tastes, preferences, and demands of the brands that serve them. Customer focus on corporate involvement with sustainability and ethical behavior in the past few years is a prime example of how cultural shifts demand changes and further rounds of innovation in customer experience relationships.

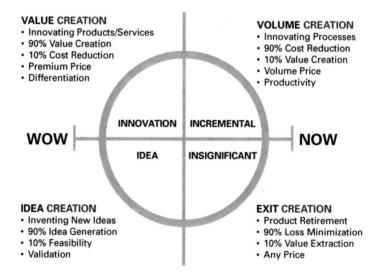

Innovation has a distinct life cycle that, left to its usual progression will crest and then decline, slipping into obsolescence, unprofitability and, *a propos* to customer experience, boredom. This is not a natural cycle. Organizations control its progression from one stage to the next,

As we'll see, within this life cycle resides something of a 90/10 concentration of effort. Control of this 90/10 balance is critical.

The Innovation Cycle

Innovation begins with **Idea Creation**. At this stage, 90% of your effort is invested in generating the idea in the first place, and 10% is invested in testing and proving the idea's feasibility. Your goal: Validate the innovation and its potential contribution.

Eventually, the life cycle moves to **Value Creation**—innovating and improving products, services and experiences. Now, 90% of your effort is invested in extracting additional value from your idea—establishing product variations, expanding and personalizing services, marketing through new channels, and so on. The remaining 10% of your effort is devoted to reducing costs to increase your ROI and, of course, the value of that idea to the organization. Your goal: Differentiate your products, services and brand, increase value to customers so you can charge premium prices, and establish the WOW experience.

The next stage is where more natural evolution, and even deterioration, begins to creep in. Competitors are seeing your success and moving toward you by copying your innovations and developing innovation of their own. As well, the other change factors that I've described are beginning to impact you. The life cycle is moving to **Volume Creation**. Your customer experience is mature, and is now just meeting market expectations instead of beating them. You're losing differentiation. In this stage, 90% of your effort is invested in cost reduction, and the remaining 10% in value creation— a flip-flop of the investments during the Value Creation stage. Innovation at this stage is more incremental. Your goal: Volume pricing and high productivity. You've progressed to NOW versus WOW.

Companies lose control over differentiation and customer delight when they become trapped in the Volume Creation stage, forgetting to move to the next WOW. This isn't to say that you should abandon Volume Creation. In truth, you must balance Value and Volume Creation. You must continue to respond to the incremental innovations requested and expected by your customers, while planning for the next transformation, the next WOW.

Part of the innovation life cycle includes a necessary final stage: **Exit Creation**. This involves winding down and retiring products, services and experiences that no longer return acceptable levels of profit, or will soon reach that point. Exit Creation is integral to innovation, because you must clear out the lagging underbrush, as it were, to make room for fresh growth. In this stage, 90% of your effort is devoted to minimalizing loss, and 10% to extracting value. Your goal: Move out the old for any price.

Critically more important, though, is that return to the Value Creation stage of the innovation life cycle, that return to the WOW. Success is your moment of truth, because when success hits, failure starts.

Often companies get mired in the mindset that current acceptable performance precludes the need for change. Before they reach success, they operate in WOW mode. They're alert, focused and aggressive. They work hard to innovate. They are motivated by internal forces—whether you call them paranoid or realistic—to create something different that will bring success, and are driven by a spirit of newness. When they reach the pinnacle, they slip into operating in NOW mode. When they've conquered Everest, they look down and say, "There's nowhere else to go. Back there—well, going down isn't very interesting." The attitude shifts from paranoia to confidence, from the offensive to the defensive. They become cautious, and exercise a new paranoia—that change will hurt them. They become satisfied with the status quo, and even take a risk-averse stance to protect the status quo, instead of moving immediately to exploring the next level. Often companies that reach success instigate their own demise by becoming too comfortable, expecting the success to last forever. Many technology companies suffered from this syndrome. When was the last time you bought a product from Wang Labs or Digital? They're gone because they became irrelevant.

However, as Intel's CEO once said, "Paranoia is the best strategy." NOW brands initiate change only as a last resort. WOW brands initiate change because they refuse to get complacent.

A great example of refusing to maintain a comfortable position at the apex comes from a group we worked with—U.K.'s Manchester United Football Club. I posed a question to them: "You've been very successful—you've won all the major cups. What motivates you to get up in the morning and continue to work at top level? You've hit the top, and at best, you protect your position at Number-One." The answer, I learned, was found in their mission statement, which had once read "We will be the number-one football club in the world" but was changed to "We will be the pioneer football club in the world." This change is not merely semantic—it is attitudinal. "Number One" implies a final destination, with no other peaks left to climb. "Pioneer" means that new peaks are yet to be created.

Certainly, elements of NOW remain steady through any corporate life cycle. Some elements of operation are purely practical, or aren't considered important in terms of experience by customers, and don't need WOW treatment. Therefore, balancing NOW and WOW must be managed carefully.

Introducing the Customer Council

Because transitions through the innovation life cycle—particularly reverting back to Value Creation—don't fully occur naturally, you must install a formal governance mechanism to keep the company focused on innovation and creation of value, and to reinvent and reinvigorate customer experience on a continuing basis. At the same time, this governance mechanism can work to balance the WOW and the NOW. That mechanism can take the form of what we call a Customer Council, or an Action One committee.

Establish this committee very early in the CEM process—before the program launch, if possible. Empower the committee to act the moment that results from your customer experience initiative are available. Often, an action committee is established only *after* results are available. Such delayed installation of an element critical to governing customer experience erodes an overall sense of urgency. Lack of a sustained sense of urgency leads to failure in achieving results. After all, the Customer Council is like emergency services—ready before you need them, and quick to act as they're required.

Ideally, the Customer Council comprises a group of stakeholders that will, in essence, build new Everests, allowing the company to improving itself and "cannibalize" itself to keep the competition from easily walking the mountain trail that you have worked so hard to blaze. The Council is chartered to examine successes and failures within customer experience—and in fact the Customer Council is able to do what no single touch point can. This team can and must evaluate the voice of the customer in context of the complete journey in order to prioritize efforts and resources. Because their primary focus is managing the complete voice of the customer across different channels, the Customer Council can manage NOW insight from customers while identifying opportunities to satisfy unmet needs that can become the next WOW. The Council can ask what else can change, and what additional innovation is needed to fuel customer loyalty. In other words, "What's next?"

As an organization, you must answer this question yourself. You can't afford to allow the competition to tell you what's next—or, more accurately, to demonstrate to you what's next as they pass you by.

A significant additional benefit of operating from WOW mode is that the pioneer mentality keeps employees on track and on focus. They'll be better prepared to be proactive instead of reactive, because they always have new battles to win. Pioneers have but one competitor, one that's both challenging and exciting. The only competitor facing Pioneers is the future.

The Customer Council is tasked with determining the level of steps to be taken next:

- **Nurture.** Incremental innovation that tweaks and complements what's working within your customer experience.
- **Reinvigorate.** Expanding the customer experience, and possibly redefining it.
- **Reinvent.** Initiating significant change to and perhaps complete rebuilding of elements of the customer experience framework.

Note that this list contains no mention of "Maintain." Even nurturing remains a notch above maintaining—which is the trap you want to avoid.

The Customer Council provides the nexus for assessing the need for innovation and change within your customer experience initiative, and then coordinating and prioritizing the development and execution of such change. The Council might comprise the members of the cross-functional team that first designed the program, but it will be most effectively staffed with executives who have the interests of the entire enterprise at heart. Council members should represent all key touch points, and must have the authority to establish and enforce next steps within their groups—and be granted the power to hold the organization as a whole accountable for executing recommendations based on customer insight.

The job description of the Customer Council includes these directives:

Consolidate all data sources. You've done much of this work already in establishing correlative metrics that apply across functions while developing and selling your customer initiative. You can't have customer service with one data base and sales with another. Consolidate the data and the data sources, moving them to the Council, so that they can aggregate, analyze and recommend actions against customer information. This group is responsible for analyzing information—whether transactional or behavioral, quantitative or qualitative—for developing responses to that information, prioritizing the resulting needed actions, and assigning those actions to appropriate parties within the organization.

Here, once again, establishing meaningful metrics takes critical importance. Just as you have applied the principles of Chapter 12, "Measure What Matters," against your performance when designing the customer experience and benchmarking your current state, you now apply those same principles against the benchmarks and toward your goals.

Assess the voice of the customer. The Customer Council monitors more than just business results. The Council also listens and responds to customer input. The voice of the customer informs you of perceptions, opinions, satisfaction levels, suggested changes and additions, and points of potential behavior shift. The voice of the customer is critical in maintaining organizational alignment with customer needs and expectations. A variety of sources will feed such information to the Council—among them:

- **Customer advisory boards,** which can take such forms of panels or online communities. Choose profitable customers, and formally empanel them, with some sort of payment—perhaps something as simple as free products. Task these customers with improving the overall customer experience. Turning to them in this formal way will both honor and motivate these contributors.

- **Focus groups** are a more traditional and less permanent way to directly solicit customer feedback on the same sort of personal level that advisory boards allow.

- **Surveys**, of course, feed higher-level information back to you.

- **Studying complaints, exceptions and direct customer suggestions**, as has been discussed, reveal patterns to address and actionable guidance.

Effective voice of the customer programs should provide constant feedback to enable organizations to improve the operation. Design frequency into your customer voice efforts as stringently as you design frequency into other measurements so you can see trending and success rates. Those frequencies can be quarterly or annually in the case of surveys. Or they can be trigger-based, such as a just-in-time survey conducted immediately after a transaction, or spurred by complaints or inquiries. The lesson is to be consistent in when and how the listening mechanisms are deployed.

The best utilization of the voice of the customer is in identifying dissatisfiers, defining customer expectations and emotions, prioritizing issues, qualifying new ideas and assessing progress. It is also, as we saw in our discussion of such customer communications platforms as Dell's IdeaStorm.com, a way for delivering new ideas and potential solutions.

Keep in mind, however, that the common practice is to not count on customers to provide the full solutions or innovate the customer experience. Customers do well in articulating problems, but solving them is the role of the organization. Only the organization can effect change that not only solves problems, satisfies complaints and delights customers, but also returns profits and increased customer engagement.

In our Nurture/Reinvigorate/Reinvent triumvirate, you can expect that customers can assist in developing incremental changes in the spirit of nurturing, but can only help you identify areas that need more serious attention. Solutions and innovations of any order of magnitude must come from organizational efforts. There are infrastructural concerns here, but in many ways this point boils down to what I noted earlier: Customers can't tell you how to surprise them, because then it wouldn't be a surprise.

In the area of listening to the voice of the customer, return to Chapter 12, "Measure What Matters," and apply the lessons about customer dialogue found there to the Customer Council's charter to consolidate actionable and consistent data and input.

Confirm the customer voice. The Customer Council should also be tasked with an important element we discussed previously—communicating back to the customers what action will be taken to address their input and suggestions. No, the Council members aren't calling individual customers to thank them and announce study results (though they could). Instead, the Council oversees feedback mechanisms, and sometimes helps design them, to make sure that the customer voice is indeed being confirmed.

Nurture, reinvigorate and reinvent. At this stage, the Customer Council is returning to the principles of innovation outlined in detail in Chapter 4, "Innovation of Customer Experience." Listening to the customer voice will have either confirmed or denied the success of the key component of designing customer experience: The Memory.

What memory did you set as your target? What memories do your consulting customers tell you they retain? If there is a gap, first evaluate whether the target was appropriate in the first place. Perhaps modifying the memory is the appropriate step. If that's not the case, identify points of failure and bridge execution gaps operationally or through whatever means is appropriate.

If target and achieved memory matches, the question about the appropriateness of the memory remains. Did you achieve the right target? Do the numbers show appropriate upticks to justify the approach you developed? If they do, return to your innovation toolkit to develop the next level of WOW.

Also assess the level of additional innovation needed. Again, depending on your analysis of success vs. goals, new innovation can take the form of incremental steps to nurture progress, bolder moves to reinvigorate customer experience, or creating new memories and new opportunities in a more significant effort to reinvent customer experience anew.

Prioritize Value Creation actions. During the Value Creation stage, you must keep the 10% factor in mind—reducing costs. You can't focus on everything. Identify one or two high-impact areas, and direct your focus there. Therefore, prioritization from the Customer Council is critical. For example, IT will of course have a number of items already on its agenda—requests from marketing, from sales, from customer service and on and on. The head of IT needs guidance on which the department must focus. Establish where the customer experience side of the equation fits in. Without such guidance—and without a committee with the authority to back up such decisions—the customer experience efforts will be fighting other company silos for resources.

Can You Afford the Change?

Make certain you have budgeted for governance and continued change. There are certain things in life that you cannot do half way. You cannot be pregnant 50% of the time. You cannot be 50% committed to an organizational cost-reduction initiative. Similarly, you can't launch and sustain a change-oriented customer experience campaign without 100% commitment.

Many organizations confuse launch with sustainability. They don't budget for the wider scope of change required beyond the logo change on signage and corporate stationery. This confusion and an inadequate change budget of both time and financial resources cause resentment in the employee ranks. If resources are reallocated but aren't distributed in a way that executes the requisite change, employees can't live up to the brand promise.

During one client engagement, we encountered a new brand launch that involved the company plastering new brand messages all over New York City. By the end of this exercise, which granted only 24 hours of exposure, no budget remained to educate the employees and explain the implications of the launch to their daily work. The customer experience initiative must include proper budgeting to bring the message to every employee and apply it to the daily customer experience of every employee.

WOW brands budget for the entire journey while NOW brand budget for a launch. Singapore Airlines, another major WOW brand, spends double the industry benchmark on training and retraining their people. This budgetary commitment allows the airline to enjoy a disproportionately positive reputation and garners huge loyalty despite the very small passenger base in Singapore.

Organizations must budget for continuous change and create an environment in which change can and will happen. Processes and procedures must be examined carefully and adapted, if necessary. Information systems may be required to support the new promise. Change will inevitably have implications at every level of the business, everything from redesigning forms to customer-service education. All are necessary to ensure successful launch and execution. All changes must be budgeted for, otherwise you're back to brand promise without brand performance. This sends a strong signal to customers and employees regarding your true commitment (or lack thereof) to the brand.

Before launch, establish the answers to these questions:
- What is the larger scope of change required to adapt to the new brand guidelines?
- How much should such change cost?

- What is the scope of investment required in every touch point?
- What timeframe does your brand implementation budget cover?
- Who will pay once you are past the launch date?

The Value Creation Cycle at Work

For an example of a company that understands experience reinvention and the need to return continually to the Value Creation stage of the innovation life cycle, let's look at Starbucks' reinvention initiatives in response to several business factors. Success was Starbucks' moment of truth; as I've noted, when success hits, failure starts. Achieving the delicate balance between delivering loyalty-driving customer experiences while accommodating the sort of rapid expansion that Starbucks experienced is difficult for any company. During the previous years of rapid expansion, Starbucks compromised on certain elements of its customer experience, including a shift to automated coffee machines and adding breakfast sandwiches to the menu. If that wasn't enough, McDonald's and Dunkin' Donuts had entered Starbucks' market, selling new coffee, undercutting Starbucks on price, and installing coffee baristas.

The Volume Creation compromises, coupled with adding mugs and other paraphernalia to the product list, not only led to reduced product quality, but also eroded customer perception. Consumers increasingly viewed the company as being "corporate." Starbucks was slowly losing its image and unique value—its original coffee soul. During 2007, for instance, store traffic was essentially flat, and Starbucks even witnessed the first quarterly decline in the U.S. since 2004.

But the principles that led to Starbuck's original legendary customer experience remain as vibrant today as they did yesterday. Starbucks' customer-centric DNA energized their commitment to reconnect with customers who were increasingly disenfranchised with the company's experience. Starbucks didn't implement "lipstick-on-a-pig initiatives," the phrase I use to describe strategies and initiatives that mask a systemic problem with lipstick or a façade, often in the form of emotional advertising, press releases, memos and posters, all without any actual follow-through. While these strategies and initiatives might realize immediate but brief gain, they are only likely to aggravate the underlying challenges and alienate the very customers that the companies employing these strategies are trying to attract and retain. Customers are unimpressed with slick advertising campaigns or promotions that over-promise and under-deliver—the typical outcome of lipstick-on-a-pig initiatives

Instead, Starbucks set about identifying, acknowledging and addressing systemic challenges to its customer experience. In the spirit of the IdeaStorm.com website that we discussed in the context of the Voice of the Customer, Starbucks established the MyStarbucksIdea.com portal to build a more intimate relationship with its customers. Through this portal, customers can post, rank and discuss ideas regarding what the coffee vendor should do to offer a more-compelling value proposition and customer experience. Starbucks implemented a number of these suggestions, including free in-store Wi-Fi service and its loyalty card. Such a project invokes voice of the customer with massive impact.

This initiative helped push the company away from the Volume Creation stage of the innovation life cycle back to Value Creation. And Starbucks' efforts within that stage reflect the levels of Value Creation I outlined above:

- **Nurture**. Despite its exponential growth and financial success, the company remains humble and true to its roots of seeking innovative ideas to improve its customer experience. Nothing is ever too small or insignificant for innovation. For example, the company introduced a green splash stick to prevent its customers from spilling coffee through the hole in the coffee cup's cover. While a splash stick won't solve the company's core challenges or generate additional revenue, its introduction illustrates to customers that the company cares about them, listens to their concerns, and acts on their suggestions.

- **Reinvigorate**. By installing flat screens in some stores displaying the names of the songs being played over the in-store sound system, Starbucks aimed to connect and familiarize its customers with the songs its stores play, so that they can become part of the larger Starbucks experience. Though this initiative, Starbucks stores become not only a more familiar and personal place, but also a venue of discovering new tunes. Rejuvenation through coffee and music!

- **Reinvent**. The company (unlike most others) took a courageous step of recognizing that the actual product needed improvement. Following this admission, the company launched Pike Street Roast, which combined a new and rejuvenated taste with a new look and feel to the cups.

- **Retire**. As I noted, sometimes the final stage of the innovation life cycle is essential: Exit Creation. Some ideas, products and services simply don't work, and must be cleared out to make room for new viable ideas. Or, in Starbucks' case, to make room for old viable ideas. The hot breakfast menu was one innovation that diluted the company's customer experience. Preparing bacon sandwiches, it turned out, produced smells that overwhelmed the coffee aroma that was so central to the in-store experience. Despite the financial implications, Starbucks decided to eliminate the hot breakfast menu in order to stay true to its original experience promise.

This decision and many like them took a degree of courage seldom seen in today's corporate environment.

Any company hoping to succeed in its customer redesign efforts must openly and honestly evaluate every aspect of the value proposition and determine which among those aspects necessitates change. Starbucks recognizes that redesigning its customer experience is a continuing process that takes time, effort and resources. The company understands that while it will have successes, there will undoubtedly be failures. Above all, Starbucks recognizes that there is no magic pill or secret formula that will solve its challenges overnight. The Value Creation stage of the innovation life cycle must be active always.

To develop the ability to maintain that activity, establish the answers to these questions:

1. Who manages the experience on an ongoing basis?
2. Who is involved in the experience assessment and adaptation process?
3. What processes do you have in place to gather and consider experience adaptations?
4. How frequently do you assess the experience and its uniqueness?
5. What financial factors do you consider to support the strategy?
6. How do you monitor financial progress?

And just as you're doing with customer experience itself, review these questions regularly to keep the customer experience governance as fresh and meaningful as the experience it governs. You may find that you may need to reinvent some of the questions, or reinvigorate some of the answers.

Summing Up: Retaining the Pinnacle

Keep it WOW. Don't be mesmerized by success, and don't succumb to an even darker trap. We as marketers have an innate advantage: We are customers ourselves. Yet, a certain dark magic seems to transform us when we swipe our security cards and enter our workplace. We become executives, and we forget what customers are all about. We forget what *we* are all about. As businesspeople, if we only return to our selves and relate to customers the way we want to be related to, we will tap into the most natural business aphrodisiac of all.

This attitude will inspire us to remember that the customer is not a nuisance, an annoyance, an interruption, an enemy or a moron. The customer is a person in need. The customer is our spouse. The customer is our mother. The customers are our children. If we can't picture selling our offer to them, no one else will buy it. Or if they have taken our offer, they will abandon us quickly enough.

As we start this journey, we are inherently armed with powerful customer instincts. We consume products. We consume services. We love, we hate. We get annoyed, we get excited. We are human beings. The knowledge is within us. We just aren't applying that knowledge to our business decisions and to our customer-experience designs. Rather, we restrict ourselves with industry or product constraints or inertia fueled by many many years of history, convention or rote execution.

When we as customers work with service providers, we are nagged by simple questions: "Why can't you do it this way? Why don't you do it that way?" We can ask those questions and come up with what-ifs and why-nots because as service recipients we're not restricted by industry limitations or "That's how we always do things." As marketers, we must place ourselves in the customer environment once more.

One of the best examples tapping customer DNA in the business world comes from Sir Richard Branson of Virgin Group. Branson illustriously enters markets of which he has no knowledge whatsoever—thus his company's name: Virgin. He started in the music business and has branched out into airlines and telecommunications and health insurance. He enters these markets as a customer, asking questions like "Why can't we have massages on the planes? I think that would be really cool." The people from British Airways couldn't contemplate that question, because such benefits have never been offered in the airline industry. Branson instead operates from the unrestricted perspective: "I'm the customer, and that's what I want. Why can't I have it?"

Our ability to unleash the why-nots and what-ifs depends on our ability to shed industry limitations and approach our own businesses from a perspective of a customer, the perspective of a human being, an emotional person, not just from the logical what's-always-within-the-box perspective.

Today we're buried under layers of regulations, perceived or real, under layers of procedures and processes and this-is-the-way-we've-always-done-things-in-this-company excuses that have skewed our way of looking at things. Remember the point I made early on in this book: there are no tired businesses—there are only tired executives. When you are in a mature market, or in a tired market, there will be an entrepreneur who will think like a customer and say, "There must be something better than that. There must be a better way." We must master the art of what-ifs and why-nots to avoid being mesmerized by the beautiful view atop Mt. Everest.

Remember that as you're ascending Everest, you are not only establishing new standards and setting new bars, but also redefining parity. Competitors will follow you, if for no other reason than to achieve parity. Worse still, the best of your competitors will realize that they, too, must climb higher than Everest. Some competitors will simply follow you in the trail you blazed. Others will attempt to blaze new trails that make yours obsolete.

Thus the need for vigilant, formalized and authoritative customer experience governance. Such management consolidates all the elements that went into designing the first place—the benchmarking, the innovation, the training, the invigoration, the granting of permissions, the team-building, the change management. But such governance then loads all those elements into a large backpack to be used continually on your ascent of Everest. At the mountain's pinnacle, you deploy a new base camp to further deploy innovation, training, team-building and all the other critical components of executing this new endeavor.

Therefore, treat each summit you achieve as if it is merely parity. To reiterate, when success hits, failure starts. Once upon a time, the only opportunity you had to observe that "There's nowhere to go but up" was after you'd fallen to rock bottom. In customer experience, "There's nowhere to go but up," is no longer a statement of mildly optimistic resignation, not merely a half-hearted rallying cry, but instead an imperative command.

CHAPTER 15

Launching the Strategy

When a New York energy company launched its customer experience program a couple of years back, the executives decided to simultaneously announce the initiative companywide while laying its previous customer approach to rest—literally. Company management placed a coffin labeled with "The Old Ways" in a conference room, invited all the managers into the room, and staged a funeral, complete with eulogies, while praising the ways of the future. The managers then served as pall bearers, closing the casket, carrying it outside, and burying it on organization property.

Laying the "groundwork" for your customer experience initiative won't likely be as literal as this humorous approach, but a good deal of heavy lifting and a strong element of burying the past will indeed be called for.

Launching your customer experience strategy cannot take place until you have installed the framework that we've been discussing in the chapters leading to this one. The framework is held together by numbers—by the demonstrated value of bringing customer experience to the customers. CEOs from major corporations most often come from finance or operations. For many years, these people managed life through spreadsheets. You're not going to change them after they've spent 30 years doing things in a certain way. Thus, the necessity of speaking their language, focusing the strategy on such financially measured objectives as differentiation, customer advantage, additional revenues, customer retention, and customer expansion.

Only when the CEO and his direct reports understand they're losing business daily by not enhancing their customer experience will he listen and eventually sponsor your efforts. Such is the foundation of the framework. It is built upon The Number. In the case of the credit card company I mentioned in Chapter 1, The Number was $3 million lost as a Return on Nothing. In our example of ABC Image In Color Corporation that I outlined in Chapter 3, "The Economics of Customer Experience," The Numbers were $1,568,000 in losses from not providing superior experiences to its customers, representing a 19% decline in annual revenue. Everyone must know The Number, understand The Number, and believe The Number. Everyone must be able to recite The Number.

As we've seen throughout this book, the framework founded upon the burning number that will drive CEM with resolve and urgency is built of these elements:

- **Identifying and eliminating dissatisfiers across all touch points.** If you can't address consistent sources of dissatisfaction, you can't transition to customer experience. This is a foundation of the framework, and you can't build a framework of surprise and delight on a cracked foundation.

- **Redesigning complaint resolution.** Design procedures not just to surprise and delight, but to shock and delight. Know that the customer is watching you, asking if you are seeking a true relationship or just a fling.

- **Building a culture of excellence.** The organization and employees must work toward a common goal of top customer performance at every moment. This culture can't materialize without eliminating dissatisfiers and reinventing complaint resolution. Employees won't commit to a culture of excellence if they see a lack of organizational commitment in addressing the cornerstones of customer satisfaction.

- **Engaging and empowering employees.** Within the culture of excellence, employees are given the tools to create differentiated experiences and the permission to use them. If you do nothing more than tell your employees, "Please smile nicer next time around," you've lost the battle.

- **Visualizing the value.** Excellence has specific benefit. Make sure both the organization and the customer can quantify the value of that benefit.

- **Expanding and reinventing the experience.** Build the memory.

This framework also entails monitoring progress toward The Number, beginning by understanding where the company stands currently. Toward that end, conduct a new benchmark study dedicated to customer experience. This study must be fresh, as the results of old satisfaction studies may simply return you to the disconnected position you started in. Measure and evaluate all touch points, because, as we've seen, every function is either an experience creator or experience enabler. Then share this benchmarking across the organization. Don't allow silos to lead the organization to the next stage in customer experience. The organization's goals as a whole must lead the silos. Provide a view into the complete journey that is customer experience.

Today, companies are organization-centric, centered around finance, around sales, around a number of specifically identifiable silos, but not around customers. Each department has its own issues, strategies, agendas and metrics, so each is pursuing only what they want to pursue or are chartered to pursue. Lacking a track record of these silos working together, and lacking incentives for them to do so, instilling cooperation won't be easy.

Worse yet, each department is working with its own metrics, and in many cases, their own customer surveys. Customer service notes a problem with customer dissatisfaction while those in sales scratch their heads and say, "Our satisfaction numbers look fine."

To break silo-centric thinking, shatter the ownership of knowledge. Such alignment of data will likely require the services of business analysts. Consolidate the data, using the Customer Council described in Chapter 14 as your central lens for focusing information and illuminating actions. Employ the Customer Council to create agreement around the benchmarking work you've done. In doing so, avoid using conflicting data sources. Unify the data used by the various departments, and eliminate conflicting data that allows silo-based metrics to disguise overall problems. One group may be using statistical data; another group, anecdotal data. Surveys may be conducted with one set of procedures here, and another set there. One department may use predictive modeling, while another bases its perceptions on real-time transactional data. You can't justify your strategies and instill cooperation when silos operate from unreconciled data points. Again, this points to the need for universal awareness of The Number, so that silos can connect their work to the overall goal, and become more receptive to aligning toward that goal.

Here's where corporate sponsorship becomes very important. Your executive evangelist may need to step in not only to offer support and reinforcement, but also to resolve conflicts. When you start this process, you will expose pockets of the company—departments and individuals—that aren't performing their jobs. The executive will bring pressure to get the slackers in line. This will require creating incentives for cooperation and penalties for the lack thereof.

When unifying the silos for the customer experience initiative, focus everyone on the customer, not on internal agendas, as we discussed in Chapter 13. Investigate the different stakeholders' isolated strategies, and design the customer experience solution to complement existing efforts and strategies to ensure the customer experience is fully supported. Remember—you need to sell it.

Build mechanisms for cooperation, such as brainstorming workshops that involve as many employees and managers as you can. One such mechanism, and an important one, is a cross-functional team to lead the effort. When assembling such a team, recruit decision-makers. Avoid possible disconnects, delays and misinformation that can result if you settle for a "coordinator" who reports back to the decision-maker. Assign clear responsibilities to each function's representative.

Use these cooperation mechanisms to build a consensus on a reasonable timeline to achieve your objectives, to evaluate possible resistance and prepare for it, and to create a prioritized list of actions based on customer insight. This is the framework upon which your launch will be constructed.

With this groundwork laid, it's time to start digging in.

Different Approaches to Getting Started

Your next step is to determine the scope of your launch. You don't have to "boil the ocean." It's difficult enough to change departments, let alone entire organizations. Consider starting small, learning the process, and then shooting for the stars. This approach may actually be mandatory if you don't yet have backing from senior leadership.

Some companies choose to approach the transformation to customer experience in phases rather than tackling the new strategy all at once. Beginning in phases has several advantages, including proof of concept, or in self-education in the concept's execution. An incremental approach allows space to learn from mistakes, to solidify the principles and design that suits best, and to demonstrate feasibility and profitability. When considering the transition to customer experience, the company will likely exhibit two bits of skepticism: 1) Can this company execute such a strategy?, and 2) Can *you* execute it? You must prove that both are possible. The company may be looking at you and thinking that just because the plan is good doesn't mean that *you* can make it happen. You have no track record in executing such an endeavor. Incremental implementation allows you to build that track record.

With a phased strategy, aim for a point of significant potential impact. Target the area of business that will benefit most from the strategy. Or look for an area where you can demonstrate maximum impact with minimum disruption. Within each isolated target, apply the principles of customer experience, and monitor not only your return on investment but also your development of competencies. Once you have demonstrable return and skills, apply your successes to other parts of the organization. Targeted approaches can include:

- **Start with a single touch point,** such as customer service or the web.

- **Start with a single customer segment,** such as Platinum loyalty program customers, or customers with special needs, before rolling the strategy out to the broader customer base.

- **Start with a single product line.** Design the experience from A-to-Z with a single group of products or services.

- **Start holistically.** Some organizations like to start with a vision, with the end game in mind. They design the target customer memory for the organization as a whole, and then define how various functions will create and own their memories, which in turn roll out to the greater memory. These companies start with a complete top-to-bottom definition, then turn to the stakeholders and say, in essence, "Now that you have the blueprint, the guidelines, values, the commitment and the standards we all share, apply them to your own situations."

Each approach is legitimate in the context of your business model, your relationship with customers, and, your organizational readiness. The approach you select will depend on these factors:

Your leadership commitment. How serious is the CEO? A fully committed CEO can open the door to across-the-board change. A reticent CEO will need convincing, and incremental wins will help make your case. As we established in Chapter 13, "Leadership and Change Management," you can't fight the CEO's agenda. You can work to change it and to develop the CEO's commitment, but running counter to the CEO's mandate will leave you without support, resources and effectiveness.

Your own commitment. Are you simply testing the water to see if customer experience will pay off for you? Without clear conviction, you might want to start incrementally.

Organizational appetite for change. Are you an organization that can handle change very fast, very well? Technology companies are often good examples of organizations with such a culture. Product-centric companies, particularly those who have administered certain product lines for years and decades, usually must incrementally build organizational confidence in their ability to innovate.

Financial drivers. Do you have a burning platform because you're position with customers is in dire shape? If so, you probably want to start with a holistic approach.

If opting for the incremental approach to transformation, consider these strategies:

- Select one of the weakest links in your organization to use as a test case. Position your approach as a micro-strategy to fix a well-known problem. But avoid high-profile people/projects that are most likely to attract resistance. You can't afford high-profile failure right out of the gate. As I've previously cautioned, based on a wide range of personal experience, don't try to fix sales first. Sales is set in their ways, and this department is best approached when most of the organization is on board.

- Develop a balanced list of high-impact and quick-win efforts.

- Focus on experience elements that have the highest gap between customer importance and customer satisfaction.

- Select an area you fully understand or get professional help to avoid rookie mistakes.

- Develop and use clear criteria to avoid internal objections and to ensure maximum impact.

- Work on your customer database and start segmenting your customers. Begin tailoring new offers to each target group. Focus on experience elements that matter to your profitable customers first.

- Conduct feasibility and brainstorming sessions to ensure exploring all possible ways to address the selected issues.

- Bring more people into the project to share the success.

- Identify the next-weakest link or least desired area for the next test case.

- Aggregate your results, and begin taking your case to other organizational stakeholders.

In fact, you can begin with very small points of incrementality, by softening the ground for the overall initiative. Elements of your overall customer experience goals can be put into place immediately—perhaps before even beginning your formal exploration and design of your customer experience initiative. Start delighting your customers right now. As possible within your current structure, provide employees with permission to do what's right for their customers in the ways we've explored in previous chapters. Educate them so they understand customer needs and the financials behind your margins and customer profitability. Then just let them do it—again, employing some of the spirit and tools discussed earlier. Set the tone and the rest follows.

To forge the path using immediate delight, start right here, right now. Don't delay. Consider deploying these customer-centric gestures:

1. Send a customer a personal apology letter with a small compensation when something goes wrong.

2. Assume responsibility when something goes wrong, even if it is not your fault.

3. Respond quickly. Set goals to return calls or emails within 30 minutes, with resolutions or answers at the ready. Because most companies don't do this, you have opportunity to generate a WOW reaction from customers. Fast response also reduces overall engagement resolution times.

4. Give the customer a bit extra beyond what they actually ordered.

5. Call customers before sending invoices to ensure they are ready for what's coming. And triple-check the invoices to make sure they're correct.

6. Ask your B2B customers how their businesses are doing, and what else you can do to help them.

7. Ask your B2C customers about their hobbies–engage them in conversation on the subject.

8. Upgrade your customer to the next level of service, as a measure of appreciation.

9. Let your customer know you noticed and appreciate their increase in business with you.

10. Develop a post-transaction survey with immediate escalation if the survey reveals problems or exceptional satisfaction.

11. Celebrate milestones with something as simple as a mailed card. Milestones can be within your relationship with the customers—anniversaries of the beginning of your business relationship, for instance—or within the personal lives of your customers. For example, send out birthday or wedding anniversary cards.

12. Distribute recordings of customer calls to executives, or require them to personally staff a customer-service desk regularly. Let best customers know that they're speaking that day with someone with top authority.

13. Require customer service leaders to attend marketing meetings.

14. Create a "customer experience" wall in a break room or in a hallway displaying with customer pictures and quotes.

15. Invite employees to take part in the innovation process.

16. Enable non-customer-facing employees to meet customers.

17. Feature employees' commitment and pictures in your advertising.

18. Link to a cause that matters to your employees.

19. Create a "competition" wall in a break room or in a hallway help visualize the challenge and to highlight the need for urgency.

20. Prepare a managers' brief about customer experience needs and successes to incorporate into staff meetings.

The quick-hit ideas listed above are just a start. Facilitate discussion with your employees to generate additional ideas. In all our studies, we identify caring as a major factor in making an impact. It's the difference between the customer as a one-time transaction and the customer as a relationship. Companies that truly believe in customer relationships invest in caring and generous service. They invest in the long-term aspect of their business. Sure, employees would like to delight customers by sending them a birthday card, but they don't have the budget to do it. Of course, they would love to chat more with the customer and try to understand their problems and business issues, but such activity isn't in line with corporate productivity objectives. Grant employees permission to take these steps.

Of course, such quick hits don't replace a comprehensive, enterprise-wide strategy. But they will assist in forming the strategy and softening the ground for it. The moment the organization notices the changes associated with the quick hits, they'll realize that the company is ready and willing to make the leap toward customer-centricity. This realization sets the stage for the larger, more formal launch, by lowering resistance, demonstrating effectiveness, and expediting the work of the cross-functional strategic team.

Deploying the Customer Experience Strategy

Rolling out this brand-new initiative will certainly employ the usual fanfare and pomp of other initiative roll-outs, whether a new product launch, instituting new employee benefit programs, and so on. We'll concede the usual arrival of mugs and posters and T-shirts (and probably not caskets). Awareness and excitement are integral to any major strategy shift or improvement. Quickly move beyond the superficialities and potential stopping points of a cool slogan and a nice new mouse pad to concentrate on communication. Be detailed and transparent in explaining the changes, their impact on the organization and employees and customers, and be relentless in delivering the message. Set the strategy in motion, and keep it in motion with these critical tactics:

Broadcast The Number. It is, after all, the foundation of the initiative itself, and therefore should be at the core of all communications about the strategy.

Explain clearly and completely the mission and its objectives. Detail and document the expectations of each element of your ecosystem—departments, touch points and individuals. Tie each stakeholder's role to the overall mission and specific objectives within the mission. WOW Brands experience a smoother transition to their aspired wow world. They respect the past and have clear answers about change and why it takes place.

Similarly, establish strong linkage of compensation and the measurements that evaluate the success of achieving the mission.

Clarify the sense of urgency. Communicate the reasons behind the burning platform to change to a cross-section of employees. Explain the necessity and timing for change. Openly discuss market trends, financial pressures, customer requirements, competitive dynamics, and legislative issues that are driving the need for timely change. Keep employees updated on the status of the project. Involve them to help overcome challenges that arise along the way.

Launching a major initiative without conducting these types of discussions communicates that the brand remains the sole purview of marketing professionals, not the broader organization. Companies should undertake such initiatives only if it will effectuate change in the organization, not because a so-called marketing guru thinks that "it's time." Ultimately, your employees will ensure the success of the customer experience initiative. If they don't share your urgency for change, the initiative is doomed to fail.

Generate energy through promotional campaigns. In launching a program, you aren't seeking only buy-in. You're seeking excitement. Echo the goals of customer experience and delight in presenting your program internally. You want to convince people that the organization is taking absolutely the right step, and you can drive home that point by increasing the frequency and the volume of your communications.

Incorporate the long view into your presentation. A WOW initiative is more than a launch date. It is a long-term commitment, reflecting a decision to change organizational behavior and performance. NOW brands, on the other hand, lack any substantive, long-term plan, beyond the launch party. Stress the long-term nature of the new program, and the importance of sustaining energy and concentration over the coming years. Present not only the launch plans but also the plans and schedule for organizational follow-up and evaluation. Demonstrate to those you present to that you will come back to them in a week, in a month, in a year—and detail the exact form of that return to set expectations and establish accountability. Document how compensation and evaluations will be structured and deployed.

A detailed long-term action plan will prove crucial to the success of the initiative. In the absence of such a plan, the new project will be dismissed as a branding or marketing ploy, leading to employee and customer disappointment, cynicism and lack of trust.

Document a specific program timetable. When launching your program, detail what will happen when during the first two years of the program's operation. Share that timetable with everyone to reinforce the long-term commitment you have made. A typical overview timetable might look like this:

- **Day 1:** Launch the program, and announce program-related incentives, high-level metrics, annual performance goals, specific bonuses (perhaps quarterly) based on program performance, and targets for years 2 and 3.

- **First 3-6 Months:** Identify and celebrate quick wins, make first rewards for program execution, release regular reports, and institute redesign of processes (which will continue through the life of the program).

- **Year 1:** Distribute and celebrate annual rewards and first-year wins, conduct formal evaluations of the program and the performance within the program, and establish benchmarking upon which future performance will be measured.

- **Year 2:** Continue with Year 1 celebrations and evaluations, continue process redesigns, and establish the first formal benchmarks upon which future performance will be measured.

CUSTOMER EXPERIENCE INSIDE LOOK — CASE STUDY

ProCure Treatment Centers, Inc.

Headquartered in Oklahoma City, Oklahoma, ProCure provides complete services to cancer patients through its proton therapy facility. Proton therapy works much like X-ray therapy (photon therapy), but is less invasive because less healthy tissue is destroyed during treatment. John Cameron, Ph.D. created ProCure, as he says, "to move proton therapy from research hospitals, where it had its development, into the mainstream."

THE CHALLENGE

"ProCure is dedicated to bringing proton therapy to patients using a comprehensive approach which provides state-of-the-art proton therapy in a healing environment," the company notes. Because of the relatively new nature of the treatment, and the fear and difficulty in dealing with cancer for both patients and family, ProCure understood that it had to work to make the customer experience as supportive and empathetic as possible. "Patients are our primary focus," states ProCure's approach to cancer treatment. "Approaches at the centers have been created to support exceptional patient care. Medical teams are committed to ensuring that patients' needs are met, their time respected, and their dignity upheld."

THE STRATEGY

Provide a complete solution for patients undergoing treatment, building a positive, nurturing experience for both physical and emotional needs. A senior leadership team approached the challenge using these tactics, among others:

- **Develop customer-centricity from the very beginning.** ProCure began with a vision as stated in its motto: "Precision Therapy. Passionate Care." As a company moving from research to functioning centers, ProCure took the opportunity to design the customer experience in all elements of the centers execution. In one way, customer experience was built literally from the ground up. The design of the first of several planned centers integrated a customer-welcoming atmosphere.

- **Build the experience across all touchpoints.** ProCure VP of Marketing Melissa Sturno and her team and consultants conducted extensive experience mapping to identify the five areas most important to patients, and then conducted extensive research to identify significant customer-experience touch points within those areas. The team discovered 26 touch points to address within the customer experience context.

- **Engage in continuous employee education in customer experience.** Initial training for frontline employees included stressing the company's values, and instruction on finding and demonstrating appropriate levels of concern and empathy so patients will feel that they are the only ones that matter. Even the doctors themselves were considered frontline (as indeed they are), and received customer experience education. Follow-up training includes quarterly offsite coaching for customer service representatives.

- **Make the patient comfortable at every tur**n. The customer wants that comfortable chair that we've described in crafting innovative experience. In addition to conducting focus groups, ProCure customer experience designers visited cancer patients in their homes. No detail of stress-reduction was overlooked, including instituting appointment-scheduling efficiencies to reduce distractions. ProCure works to answer as many questions in advance with such tools as a robust informational web site and an informational on-site welcome kit that introduces patients to the local area so that they can better feel at hom**e.**

Building Momentum

One of the most frequent fatal mistakes of those embarking on customer experience is creating the sizzle and then allowing the fizzle—failing to follow through on the strategy. Organizations tend to focus on the launch and on the destination, and then expect everything to work on its own from there. You must travel your design and follow through on a long-term quest. And you must bring the rest of the company along on the continuing ride.

When you introduce change, some will doubt its need, as we saw in Chapter 13, "Leadership and Change Management." Building post-launch momentum is an extension of the change management we discussed earlier, geared toward building the confidence of doubters, eroding resistance from those who aggressively fight change, and recruiting the cooperation of those apathetic people who shrug their shoulders, consider your campaign just another T-shirt and mug celebration, and wander back to their offices and do nothing differently because they're seen it all before and they can live without participating.

But don't fall into the trap of one-mug-and-gone—as I said, sizzle followed by fizzle. Dispel any perception that this is the program of the month. Instead, sizzle and then drizzle—be steady. Work to establish and promote momentum and continued awareness. Again, we're dealing with people, and therefore must keep their interest fresh through evolving their experience and the program itself. Vary the incentives and the targets to make them ever more challenging—challenging, yet attainable. Follow up on strategy execution, and identify and publicize early successes. Show that the strategy is working, and that it is benefiting the customer, the organization, and the stakeholders. To achieve and maintain forward velocity for your customer experience strategy:

Repeat repeat repeat repeat repeat. Maximize the communications tools available to you. Utilize all corporate communications assets to announce, explain and build buy-in for the strategy. Consider this a multi-pronged advertising and word-of-mouth campaign directed internally.

Evaluate every aspect of your organization—every bit of "real estate," and determine how you can take over that real estate. Whether counter talkers next to the sink in the bathroom, posters in the break room, napkins in the cafeteria, or a billboard in the parking lot, the more you can ratchet up the volume in announcing your message, the more attention you'll get. When airplane manufacturer Honeywell deployed its customer experience initiatives, the CEO used the outside of his corporate jet to display customer experience messaging. Seeing that, how could employees doubt the importance of the new strategy? What real estate within your organization will communicate the seriousness of your new endeavor when your message occupies it? Paychecks are of course important to employees. Use pay stubs or benefits communications to deliver your message. Every communiqué, every elevator, every door to the stairwell, every log-on to the intranet—all are open territory. In one client engagement, we replaced all employees' pens overnight with pens that stated simply, "Writing a new chapter."

Other important communication media include face-to-face meetings, webcasts, tailored education sessions, internal brochures, signage, giveaways, and dedicated intranet and internal websites.

Your goal: don't let employees escape from the message, or from understanding its scope and its importance. Drive home the point that customer experience is here to stay.

Unleash the pioneers. Focus on early adapters to help you evangelize and disseminate the messages. Recognize and reward early adopters.

Identify pockets of resistance and address them quickly. In Chapter 13, I discussed the importance of identifying the specific threat that each touch point believes it is facing. Now consider your biggest threat: cynicism. Any strategy is susceptible to undermining and to failure if middle management is cynical. A gesture as small as manager making a snide remark or a cynical joke during a coffee break will kill the spirit you're trying to engender. If you sense underlying cynicism, it's time to employ your CEO, your customer experience evangelist. Take the mission statement that you created earlier, and print it and the specific pledge to your customer on a poster. Ask all managers to sign the poster in an official ceremony conducted by the CEO. Print copies of the signed poster for display throughout the company. Now the managers' signoff is real, and their personal signatures are there for all to see. As a truly public step, reprint the poster in newspaper and trade journal advertising so the customers understand the commitment, and will return pressure on the organization and the managers simply by asking that the organization deliver on its public promise. Backing off such public commitment is very difficult.

Address potential pockets of resistance specifically, creatively and publicly. You might even have some fun with it. One of our clients took the concept of asking managers to place their John Hancock on the customer pledge literally. They recreated the poster-sized customer pledge in the style of the Declaration of Independence, and upper management dressed in the period garb of our Founding Fathers to sign it theatrically and publically.

Broadcast progress toward The Number. Measure performance vs. your original benchmarks and publicize improvements as you make progress toward the ultimate goal.

When you spot early successes, celebrate. Look for examples of employees going above and beyond, and reward those employees publicly. Don't just make an announcement in the company newsletter. Don't just hand the performers a check. Throw a party. Especially in the early stages of the initiative, convince any doubters of your seriousness. Broadcast evidence of the strategy's momentum to maintain the momentum, and to convince doubters that they'd better get on board, because there's nothing they can do to stop it.

Especially when successes are particularly dramatic, promote employees based on their adherence to the program and the degree to which they take initiatives. Communicate to the organization that the promotions resulted from such adherence—this is public celebration on a larger scale.

Leverage new employees to solidify momentum. Be realistic: the changes you're instituting will lead to a certain level of attrition. There are those who won't accept the changes, who might consider what you're asking of them to be too much work, and will move on. This is to your advantage, because you are losing anchors to the past whose loss will make way for new energy. Create a coaching program specifically for recruits to assure that they don't learn the old mistakes, and that they take the fresh approach from the very start. Recruits are in danger of learning the past from current employees; make sure you teach them first.

Remember: Steady as she goes. Establish the discipline to review results regularly. Review the objectives and the success of achieving each in regular meetings. Task the Customer Council with maintaining consistent flow of feedback from customers and appropriate data from touch points.

Be steady, but don't be static. Your Customer Council is chartered with refining your plan as you learn about the effectiveness of the plan itself and of its execution. Don't hide their important work. Roll out refinements and reinventions publicly, and include them in the celebration. Identifying a course correction is a win in and of itself. Adapt ideas from stakeholders' ecosystems to give those stakeholders additional ownership, and to leverage the opportunity to further promote the seriousness with which the organization is taking the new program. Your people have the answers right now. They have simply lost hope or the power to make it happen.

Summing Up: The True Question

Whatever your approach to customer experience, whatever level you choose to roll out to the organization and to the customers, it's imperative that you get the process underway, and get the organization on board with the overall program. The question "How do we get started?" is really a question of "How can we reignite the fire in our organization?" If you've finally realized the severity of the issues associated with customer loyalty and profitability, it means the issues are burning. You must get started, here and now, and make it happen. One employee at a time. One customer at a time. One idea at a time.

Final Words

One Thursday, a shopper in a Pennsylvania Wal-Mart reached for her wallet, and found it gone. She had lost it somewhere in the store, she knew, because she had taken something from it earlier in the store visit. The associates scoured the store for her, and found the wallet. Though the wallet still contained the shopper's credit cards, $300 in cash was missing. This, of course, upset her, but there was nothing to be done. The money was gone.

The next Monday, a Wal-Mart manager called her, and said, "We found your money. Please come to the store." When she arrived, the manager gave her $300, in a huge stack of one-dollar bills.

"Where did you get this?" she asked.

"On Thursday, I told my associates about what happened to you," the manager said. "Someone said that we shouldn't allow such a thing to happen in our store, and she suggested a solution. That night, all the associates went home and baked chocolate chip cookies. We sold them at the store all weekend, and we earned you your money back."

So when you think you're doing all you can for your customers, when you think you're exceeding their expectations, ask yourself a very simple question: How many cookies have you made for your customers today? We live in a new world. We are no longer measured by the number of breaths that we take, but rather by the number of breath-taking moments we make for our customers.

End

Lior Arussy

Lior Arussy is the founder and president of Strativity Group, Inc., a global customer experience research and consulting firm specializing in design, innovation and deployment of differentiating, profitable customer experiences. His books include *Excellence Every Day: Make The Daily Choice* (Information Today, May 2008) and *Passionate & Profitable: Why Customer Strategies Fail and 10 Steps to Do Them Right!* (Wiley, 2005) In addition, he has published more than 200 articles in publications around the world, including at *The Harvard Business Review*.

For his thought leadership and contribution to the industry, Mr. Arussy received *CRM Magazine*'s "2003 Influential Leaders" award and served as a juror on *Fast Company*'s Customer First Awards 2005.

Prior to establishing Strativity Group, Mr. Arussy held executive positions at Hewlett-Packard and other companies.

His accomplishments have been recognized by leading press and analysts such as ABC, *The Wall Street Journal, Financial Times, The Times of London* and Gartner.

Strativity Group

At Strativity Group, we do more than customer experience research and strategic planning. We take a strong, multi-disciplinary approach to customer experience strategy design and implementation. Through proprietary research tools, strategic analysis, customer experience innovation design and education programs we help our clients operationalize profitable customer experience strategies.

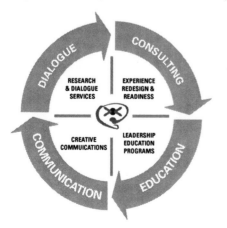

We measure our success by a single method: execution.

Throughout the years we had the privilege of serving some of the world's leading organizations including: Avaya, Capital One, Cargill, CATIC, Circle K, CA, E.ON UK, FedEx, Herbalife, Honeywell, Lockheed Martin, Microsoft, Nokia, Nordea, Ricoh, Sage, SAP, Seagate, Thomson Reuters, Siemens, Telus, University of Pennsylvania, Wyeth.

Index

Personal Portfolio Manager 233, 130

Persona Portfolio Management 128, 130

personas 120, 123, 124, 126, 127, 128, 130, 131, 132, 174, 191,
    210, 225, 228, 229, 243

Pew Research Center 140

Plaxo 108

podcasts 89, 103

portfolio manager 128, 130

ProCure Treatment Centers 320

PunkYourChucks 99

Q
Qatar Airways 157

R
Random Acts of Generosity 241

Regent Seven Seas Cruises 101, 102, 107

Reichheld, Fred 6, 250

relationship banking 130

reluctant employees 150

Resistance Factors 284, 290

Return on Nothing Loyalty Model 21, 53, 54, 56, 61, 103, 116

Formula 53

Ritz-Carlton 2, 33, 133, 177, 183, 185, 189, 190, 250, 268

RON. *See* Return on Nothing Loyalty Model; *See* Return on Nothing Loyalty Model;
    See Return on Nothing Loyalty Model

Ryanair 79

S
Sahara airline 157

sales force automation (SFA) 215

SAP CRM 209

Schwarz, Jonathan 106

Second Life 106

segmentation differentiation 119

self-responsibility 184

Self-Service 1.0 94, 95, 97

Self-Service 2.0 90, 96, 97, 99, 109, 222, 237